Life after Tragedy

Figure 1: Geoffrey Anketell Studdert Kennedy

Life after Tragedy

Essays on Faith and the First World War
Evoked by Geoffrey Studdert Kennedy

Edited by
Michael W. Brierley
and Georgina A. Byrne

Foreword by
Andrew G. Studdert-Kennedy

CASCADE *Books* · Eugene, Oregon

LIFE AFTER TRAGEDY
Essays on Faith and the First World War Evoked by Geoffrey Studdert Kennedy

Cascade Books
An Imprint of Wipf and Stock Publishers
199 W. 8th Ave., Suite 3
Eugene, OR 97401

www.wipfandstock.com

PAPERBACK ISBN: 978-1-5326-0226-9
HARDCOVER ISBN: 978-1-5326-0228-3
EBOOK ISBN: 978-1-5326-0227-6

Cataloguing-in-Publication data:

Names: Brierley, Michael W., 1973– | Byrne, Georgina A. | Studdert-Kennedy, Andrew
G.

Title: Life after tragedy : essays on faith and the First World war evoked by Geoffrey
Studdert Kennedy / edited by Michael W. Brierley and Georgina A. Byrne, with a
foreword by Andrew G. Studdert-Kennedy.

Description: Eugene, OR: Cascade Books, 2017 | Includes bibliographical references and
index.

Identifiers: ISBN 978-1-5326-0226-9 (paperback) | ISBN 978-1-5326-0228-3 (hardcover)
| ISBN 978-1-5326-0227-6 (ebook)

Subjects: LCSH: World war, 1914–1918—Religious aspects—Christianity. | World war,
1914–1918—Religious aspects | Studdert Kennedy, Geoffrey Anketell, 1883–1929 |
World War, 1914–1918—Poetry

Classification: D639.R4 B742 2017 (paperback) | D639.R4 (ebook)

Manufactured in the U.S.A.   07/05/17

Contents

Part III: Conclusion

Illustrations

Contributors

Peter Atkinson is the dean of Worcester. His publications include *Friendship and the Body of Christ* (SPCK, 2004) and *The Lion Encyclopedia of the Bible* (Lion, 2011).

Michael Brierley is the canon precentor of Worcester. He is the editor of *Public Life and the Place of the Church* (Ashgate, 2006) and the author of a dozen articles on the history of twentieth-century theology.

David Bryer is a lay canon of Worcester. He holds a doctorate in Middle Eastern studies from the University of Oxford, and was director of Oxfam from 1992 to 2001 and chair of Oxfam International from 2003 to 2008.

Georgina Byrne is a residentiary canon of Worcester and a chaplain to Her Majesty the Queen. She is the author of *Modern Spiritualism and the Church of England, 1850–1939* (Boydell, 2010).

Mark Chapman is the vice-principal of Ripon College Cuddesdon, professor of the history of modern theology at the University of Oxford, and canon theologian of Truro. His books include *Anglican Theology* (T. & T. Clark, 2012), *Theology and Society in Three Cities* (James Clarke, 2014), and, most recently, *Theology at War and Peace* (Routledge, 2017), on theology during the First World War.

Mark Dorsett has been the chaplain of the King's School, Worcester and a minor canon of Worcester since 1996. He was awarded a doctorate by the University of Birmingham for his thesis "The Church of England, the State, and Politics 1945–1983," and has published articles on the Church of England and twentieth-century public life.

John Inge is the bishop of Worcester, and lord high almoner to the Queen. He chairs the council for the archbishop of Canterbury's examination in theology, and his books include *A Christian Theology of Place* (Ashgate, 2003).

Robert Jones is the archdeacon of Worcester, and an honorary canon of Worcester. He studied German at Durham University, and is a member of the Meissen Commission, which is responsible for the relationship between the Church of England and the Evangelical Church in Germany.

Ilse Junkermann has been the bishop of the Evangelical Church in Central Germany (EKM) since 2009 and is the deputy lead bishop of the United Evangelical Lutheran Church of Germany (VELKD). She is an editor of the journal *Göttinger Predigtmeditationen* (Vandenhoeck and Ruprecht) which provides theological resources for preaching.

Alvyn Pettersen is the canon theologian of Worcester. He is the author of *Athanasius and the Human Body* (Bristol Press, 1990) and *Athanasius* (Geoffrey Chapman, 1995).

Michael Snape is the inaugural Michael Ramsey professor of Anglican studies at Durham University, and a lay canon of Durham. The secretary of the Church of England Record Society, and the official historian of the Royal Army Chaplains' Department, he is the author of *God and the British Soldier* (Routledge, 2005) and co-editor of *The Clergy in Khaki* (Ashgate, 2013).

Andrew Studdert-Kennedy is the team rector and rural dean of Marlborough, an honorary canon of Salisbury, and the grandson of Geoffrey Studdert Kennedy.

Foreword

Andrew G. Studdert-Kennedy

I cannot read this writing of the years . . .
I can but hand it in, and hope
That Thy great mind, which reads
The writings of so many lives,
Will understand this scrawl
And what it strives
To say—but leaves unsaid.
I cannot write it over,
The stars are coming out,
My body needs its bed.
I have no strength for more,
So it must stand or fall—Dear Lord—
    That's all.[1]

IN THE FINAL DECADE of his comparatively short life, in the poem "It Is Not Finished," my grandfather wrote not just of his sense of failure, but also of the incompleteness of his ministry to which he had given himself so unsparingly. Nearly ninety years later, this remarkably wide-ranging collection of essays can be seen as endeavouring to carry on the work that he himself began.

A charismatic and intriguing character, the story of his life and ministry is simultaneously impressive and impossible: impressive, because he clearly practised what he preached, impossible because the circumstances

---

1. From "It Is Not Finished," in Studdert Kennedy, *Sorrows*, 121–22.

in which he did so were so different from those of today. As a fellow-priest, let alone as a grandchild, I wish to emulate him and yet know that I cannot.

His life presents us with a tension because we want to learn from it and yet we are not sure which parts of it can or even should guide us today. The different contributors to this book recognise both the challenge and the opportunity that his ministry presents. While some specifically focus on Studdert Kennedy himself, the book as a whole uses his ministry as a peg on which to hang wider-ranging thoughts and reflections that apply to contemporary Christian life. Each of the essays invites some sort of a response from the reader and is thus an invitation for all of us to learn from the events of the First World War.

The death of both my father, Christopher Studdert-Kennedy, aged ninety-four, in September 2016, and my uncle, Michael Studdert-Kennedy, aged eighty-nine, in January 2017, makes this publication all the more poignant: my grandfather's life, although now even more removed from the current generation, still seems able to feed it. Such distance, however, also provides clarity, and it is striking that the contributions in this book, while appreciative, are not in the least bit hagiographical—a feature of which my grandfather himself would surely have approved.

Accordingly, the family as a whole are greatly indebted to the chapter of Worcester Cathedral for the genesis of this project and we are pleased that it should emanate from Worcester itself—the place that my grandfather regarded as home and where for thirty-five years after his death in 1929, my grandmother Emily (an invisible element of the story) continued to live.

Marlborough
19 February 2017

Preface

Michael W. Brierley and Georgina A. Byrne

It was a common enough scene in those days, an advanced col-
lecting post for wounded in the Ypres Salient, on the evening
of June 15, 1917. Twenty men all smashed up and crammed
together in a little concrete shelter which would have been full
with ten in it. Outside the German barrage banging down all
round us. The one guttering candle on the edge of a broken
wire-bed going out every five minutes when a salvo of 5.9's from
Pilkom Ridge shook the place to its foundations. A boy with a
badly shattered thigh in a corner moaning and yelling by turns
for "Somefing to stop the pain." So it had been for an hour or
more. Between this Black Hole of Calcutta and Battalion H. Q.
Death and Hell to go through. Hell inside and hell out, and the
moaning of the boy in the corner like the moaning of a damned
soul. "The pain—the pain—my Gawd—the pain. For Gawd's
sake gimme somefing to stop the pain."

There was no morphia. That was the horror. Some one must
go for it. I went. I went because the hell outside was less awful
than the hell in. I didn't go to do an heroic deed or perform a
Christian service; I went because I couldn't bear that moaning
any longer. I ran, and as I ran, and cowered down in shell-holes
waiting for a chance to run again, I thought—thought like lightning—whole trains of thought came tearing through my mind
like non-stop expresses to God knows where. I thought: Poor
devil, I couldn't have stood that a minute longer. I wasn't doing
any good either. If I get through and bring the morphia back, it
will be like bringing back heaven to him. That is the only heaven
he wants just now, dead-drunk sleep. If I bring it back, I will
be to him a saviour from hell. I'd like that. It's worth while. I'm

glad I thought of that. I can't pretend that it was that I came for.
It wasn't. Still I'm glad. He wants to forget, to forget and sleep.
Poor old chap. Heaven in a morphia pill.[2]

So runs the account by Geoffrey Studdert Kennedy of the episode during the First World War for which he was awarded the Military Cross. The
official citation in August 1917 spoke of his "attending to the wounded under heavy fire," his searching "shell holes for our own, and enemy wounded,
assisting them to the Dressing Station," "his cheerfulness and endurance,"
and his "constantly visiting" the frontline trenches.[3] It was arguably the pin-
nacle of Studdert Kennedy's work as a chaplain to the British troops in the
war, for which he was justly famous, and for which he acquired the nickname "Woodbine Willie."

In the summer of 2014, the air was thick with the centenary of the First
World War. The war had featured as a theme in the Three Choirs Festival
hosted by Worcester Cathedral, and the cathedral, like many other churches,
was holding a service at the beginning of August to mark the outbreak of
the war. Two neighbours on the cathedral green, both residentiary canons
of the cathedral, both with interests in twentieth-century church history—
Georgina Byrne had studied the period 1850–1939, and Michael Brierley,
the twentieth century as a whole—viewed the centenary from a theological
perspective. They were familiar with recent revisionist history of the church
and the First World War offered by a number of scholars, such as Michael
Snape and Adrian Gregory;[4] but were not aware of any volume of essays that
addressed the First World War from a theological angle. Indeed, they came
to the conviction that a theological treatment of the war could be of considerable interest and help to those churches and other faith communities who
would be preparing to mark in November 2018 the hundredth anniversary
of the armistice. All it took was a bibulous Sunday lunch between the two
neighbours at the end of the Three Choirs Festival in 2014 for the idea of a
book of theological essays on the First World War to be conceived and set
in motion.

2. Studdert Kennedy, *Lies!* 198–99.

3. Carey, "War Padre," 143.

4. For example, a great deal of work has been done in the last decade on British
Army chaplaincy in the First World War: see Snape, *God and the British Soldier*, 83–116;
Snape, *Royal Army Chaplains' Department*, 175–260; Parker, *Whole Armour*; Madigan,
Faith under Fire; Snape, "Church of England Army Chaplains"; Howson, *Muddling
Through*; and Snape and Madigan, eds., *Clergy in Khaki*. For the post-war activity of
Anglican army chaplains, see Parker, "'Shell-shocked Prophets'" and *Shellshocked
Prophets*.

Worcester Cathedral was particularly well-placed to produce such a volume, for all three of its residentiary canons held theologically-related doctorates.[5] To our credit, we were not so taken with this distinction as to investigate whether, apart from Christ Church, Oxford, this was unique among English cathedrals. On the other hand, it seemed sufficiently unusual to consider whether our theological propensities might be worth putting to some use. There were further members of the cathedral community with academic inclinations who could be involved in such a project, including the dean, Peter Atkinson, and the bishop, John Inge, who both had theological books to their names;[6] Mark Dorsett, one of the cathedral minor canons (and chaplain of the King's School), who had a PhD on the church and politics; and David Bryer, a lay canon of the cathedral chapter who had a doctorate in medieval Middle Eastern theology.

Worcester was also well-placed to produce a book of essays on faith and the First World War, on account of Studdert Kennedy, who, as well as being one of the best-known chaplains of the war, was one of Worcester's adopted sons: he was the vicar of St. Paul's parish in the city when he volunteered as an army chaplain in 1915; indeed, a commemorative "blue plaque" was erected on the outside wall of St. Paul's Church in 2014. Studdert Kennedy provided the natural starting-point for a series of studies of faith and the First World War. Taking their impetus from his example, the essays would be of relevance not only to historians and churchpeople with a general interest in the First World War, but also to local people. A book of such essays would be a highly fitting tribute for the centenary of his Military Cross, and the return of the Three Choirs Festival to Worcester in the summer of 2017 presented the ideal occasion at which the anniversary could be publicly observed.

A memoir about Studdert Kennedy, *G. A. Studdert Kennedy: By His Friends*, had been published by Hodder and Stoughton in 1929, within six months of Studdert Kennedy's death;[7] and thus far, two further biographies had been written about him. The first was published in 1962 by William Purcell, himself a residentiary canon of Worcester, a clerical biographer

---

5. Alvyn Pettersen had been awarded a PhD from the University of Durham in 1981 for a thesis on Athanasius; Georgina Byrne received one from King's College London, in 2007, for a thesis on spiritualism and the Church of England; and Michael Brierley one in the same year from the University of Birmingham on the rise of panentheism in British theology.

6. Atkinson, *Friendship*; Inge, *Christian Theology of Place*, drawing on his PhD thesis of the same title from Durham University.

7. Other early reflections include Matthews, "Studdert Kennedy," and (Hugh) Studdert Kennedy, *Arise Shine*, 107–14.

and a former producer of religious programmes.[8] The second was written in 2013 by Bob Holman from the perspective of community action against poverty in Glasgow.[9] In addition, local newspaper material was mined in 1997 by Michael Grundy, a life-long journalist with the *Worcester News* and a member of the congregation at the cathedral, to produce a booklet, *A Fiery Glow in the Darkness*.[10] The biographies tip towards the hagiographical; they cannot be described as critical; and they are the product of single voices. There was room for a collection of theological essays that benefited from different voices and that was also academically rigorous. It is telling that while the hagiographical treatments of Studdert Kennedy followed history that suggested that the church performed poorly in the First World War, as though the church wished to narrate a "good story" about itself, the more nuanced assessment of Studdert Kennedy in this book follows the more balanced treatment of the church's role in the First World War provided by the recent revisionist school. During the course of work on this book, we became aware that a new biography of Studdert Kennedy was in progress, by Linda Parker, whose doctoral work on the contributions to the church by former British army chaplains after the First World War had been supervised by Snape and added to the output of the revisionist school, and which she followed up with a biography of another well-known First World War chaplain, Tubby Clayton.[11] We have shared ideas with Parker as much as publication schedules have allowed, and we look forward to her completed volume.

A book of essays on faith and the First World War, evoked by the life of Studdert Kennedy, would not only have local appeal and engage those with an interest in the war, but would also have theological implications for how God and suffering might be associated more broadly still. That is to say, if it is possible to speak of God in the context of the horrors of the First World War, then it might be possible, in other tragic situations, to speak of God in related ways. Hence the title of this book, *Life after Tragedy*: it conjoins two

---

8. Purcell, *Woodbine Willie*. Purcell (1909–99) was a residentiary canon of Worcester from 1966 to 1976. See further, the obituaries by Richard Holloway in the *Guardian*, 30 September 1999 (http://www.theguardian.com/news/1999/sep/30/guardianobituaries2), and by Richard Harries in the *Church Times*, 8 October 1999, 20.

9. Holman, *Woodbine Willie*. It was reviewed by Mark Chapman in the *Journal of Anglican Studies* 12 (2014) 237–38, and (among other books) by Michael Brierley in *Modern Believing* 55 (2014) 305–11. For Holman (1936–2016), see the obituary in the *Guardian*, 16 June 2016 (http://www.theguardian.com/society/2016/jun/15/bob-holman-obituary).

10. See also Walters, "Introduction."

11. Parker, *Shellshocked Prophets*, and *Fool for Thy Feast*, reviewed by Michael Brierley in *Modern Believing* 57 (2016) 457–59.

subjects that are often regarded as remote from each other; indeed, the fact or "problem" of suffering is often cited as the most significant reason for rejection of belief in God. This volume is not "theodicy," in the sense that it does not set out to justify the existence of God in the face of suffering. Rather, it asks the question of how God, or "Life" (to use the Johannine term intimately associated with the divine), might be spoken of in the midst and wake of tragedy. It represents a recognition that both the language of "faith" and the language of "suffering" need to be taken seriously. Such a recognition refuses to let the former prematurely dissipate the pain of the latter, or the latter obliterate the possibility of the former. "Anything less than this sells short both human suffering and God."[12] There is no easy path between tragedy and life, between suffering and glory. To use an ecclesiastical analogy, it is like wearing black or purple vestments in liturgical contexts of death, rather than the alternative of white: black or purple vestments do not deny hope of resurrection, but allow full expression to the emotion of bereavement; and only by attending fully to the situation of suffering does Christian hope carry any sort of weight or traction. "Perhaps . . . a way forward is to be found only once the full extent of what is happening has been confronted and expressed, so that the prayer of protest becomes a small but vital part of that process of facing the reality of the present."[13] Or as a recent volume on the relation of Christian theology to the dramatic representation of tragedy has put it, "An attentiveness to tragedy is vital to a properly disciplined Christian theology and . . . by the same token, Christian theology can be a way of vouchsafing the true significance of tragedy. With the breakdown of . . . caricatures of Christianity and tragedy, new possibilities for conversation are opened up."[14]

This is ultimately because Christianity has an experience of tragedy at its heart—the torture and execution of an innocent human being. "The theological interest in tragedy has its source in the proximity of the genre to theological questions."[15] As the early sixth-century philosopher Boethius said, the incarnation is a "tremendous tragedy."[16] A number of theologians, in debt to (if not following the refinements of) Han Urs von Balthasar, characterise the fundamental Christian condition in terms of "Holy Saturday": living in the wake of tragedy, and awaiting its redemption.[17] For the last two

12. Walters, "Introduction," 2.

13. Mursell, *Out of the Deep*, 156.

14. Taylor and Waller, "Introduction," 1.

15. Hedley, "Sacrifice," 208.

16. Taylor and Waller, "Introduction," 7.

17. Cf. ibid., 9.

thousand years, Christianity has been speaking of God in the light of the crucifixion and its aftermath, and it would therefore be odd if Christianity had nothing to say to contemporary situations of suffering.[18] Yet it needs to do so in ways that do not diminish the integrity of the experience of suffering or explain it away. The life of Easter can only be understood in the context of the passion of Good Friday. To focus too much on joy and hope is to negate the significance of Christ's suffering; to speak too comfortably of "life" is to deny the experience of many of the world's citizens. It is a difficult balance to learn what to say and what not to say in the context of tragedy—Rowan Williams has referred to "the holding of tension, not a resolving into false simplicities."[19] It is often pastorally appropriate, initially, to say nothing at all, perhaps for a long time.[20] Williams has recently shown, however, how speaking of tragic situations, recounting the narrative of tragedy, can be part of ensuring that it does not have the last word.

> Speaking about and showing the risk of disaster and the cost of different sorts of loss, in a language that is not just individual but allows listening and sharing of perception and emotion—this liturgical [and, we might add, theological] activity is [a] way of affirming our recognition of one another as participants in a continuing labour. And it signifies that we—as a community and as individuals within it—are not exhausted by either the experience or the memory of loss.[21]

That is to say, the danger of not speaking theologically about tragedy is an expansion of the sphere of terror, "an expanded place for action that arises from ignorance and anxiety":

> To *avoid* confronting the worst atrocity is to make the self and the city less secure; to be silent about extremes of suffering is, by a stark paradox, to invite a more serious risk of being "silenced" as an active self or a civic community, because what we do not name or confront, what we refuse to know, becomes the greater danger.[22]

---

18. Indeed, British theology has distinctively maintained the importance of the category of tragedy in the work of Donald MacKinnon and those who have been influenced by him: see Waller, "Freedom, Fate and Sin," and cf. Quash, "Four Biblical Characters," 21.

19. Williams, *Tragic Imagination*, 14.

20. Cf. the silence of Job's friends for an entire week on their arrival after the disasters that had afflicted him (Job 2:13).

21. Williams, *Tragic Imagination*, 16.

22. Ibid., 17, Williams's emphasis.

The naming of loss is itself a refusal to settle for passivity, resignation, or despair. The narration of trauma has the capacity to generate "unexpected new readings," an open-endedness that can "move us towards truthful and just action."[23] While it may show us that the dangers, too, are open-ended, in the sense of indicating what human beings are capable of, they "can be shown in a way that changes the world we inhabit"; re-telling the story of tragedy can be "a showing of the sacred, that excess of unearned, unexpected life."[24] As Ben Quash has written,

> Christianity (at its best, which is to say its most responsible) does not evade the actual challenges to interpretation presented to it by the experiences we habitually call tragic. It does not round off their jagged edges into some reassuring shape that will comfort us. On the contrary, it looks all the harder at them, in all their angularity and discomfiting resistance to assimilation. It does so in the hopeful expectation that there is more, not less, to them than meets the eye.[25]

Allowing tragedy to be re-told has the potential to contribute to its redemption. This is not to idealise the First World War as a type of tragedy to which all others must conform or through which they must be viewed; it is to see what possibilities of meaning might be discernible in that enormous tragedy, in order to offer hope that meaning might be discernible in other tragedies as well.

The core of this book thus consists of seven essays, all by ministers of Worcester Cathedral, who use the work of Geoffrey Studdert Kennedy as a springboard for surveying how different aspects of faith impinged on, and were impacted by, the tragedy of the First World War, and how the re-shaping of faith during the First World War applies to the possibilities of faith amid the tragedies of today. In the first of these seven essays (chapter 3), John Inge points to Studdert Kennedy's ability as a pastor to integrate experiences of suffering with experiences of God. Inge establishes a parallel between the doctrine of God for which Studdert Kennedy became known, a God who is "at home" with suffering, and Studdert Kennedy's integration of suffering and faith in the places where he carried out his pastoral work. In a development of his own Christian theology of "place," Inge identifies "home" as the place of integration of negative and positive experiences, and examines some of the implications of this for the nation state as the "home" of its citizens, and indeed, for Europe as a continental "home."

23. Ibid., 141 and 27.
24. Ibid., 7 and 27.
25. Quash, "Four Biblical Characters," 33; cf. 16.

In chapter 4, Peter Atkinson looks at Studdert Kennedy as a poet, and tells "a tale of two Geoffreys," comparing Studdert Kennedy with the last poet to survive the First World War, Geoffrey Dearmer. Atkinson shows how Studdert Kennedy has been treated unfairly in twentieth-century literary criticism, and in challenging readers to consider afresh what makes poetry "good," demonstrates the role of poets' contexts in determining what they are able to say and how they are received.

In chapter 5, Michael Brierley analyses Studdert Kennedy as a passibilist, that is to say, one who subscribes to the idea that God suffers, indicating how this element of Studdert Kennedy's legacy was a particularly powerful and popular expression of a doctrine that had already been articulated in British theology before the war. In parallel to the idea in Inge's essay of God and suffering humanity being "at home" with each other, Brierley shows how Studdert Kennedy's doctrine of God "being with" people in their suffering was an outworking of, and further spur to, Studdert Kennedy's own principle of associating as closely as possible with those in his pastoral charge. Having acknowledged Studdert Kennedy's deconstruction of the image of a divine throne, Brierley develops the hints of doctrinal reconstruction within Studdert Kennedy's work, towards the metaphor of God as an eternal stretcher-bearer, who is forever roaming through No Man's Land to locate, retrieve, and heal creatures in their injury, distress, and brokenness.

In chapter 6, Georgina Byrne places Studdert Kennedy as a preacher alongside Arthur Winnington-Ingram and Maude Royden, and traces how their approaches to sermons changed (or not, as the case may be) during the course of the war, from its outbreak, through its central years, to its end. These voices represent a bishop who essentially echoed back the populist sentiments of his listeners, a powerful speaker who was limited by his vision of social reform, and a laywoman who exercised a forthright and radical critique of the status quo. Byrne makes connections with prominent preachers who have spoken in more recent contexts of conflict, and invites us to respect the diversity of genuine, honest attempts to grapple with complex issues from the standpoint of faith.

Mark Dorsett, in chapter 7, picks up on Studdert Kennedy's role as a prophet, and is less sympathetic in his assessment. Like Byrne, Dorsett compares Studdert Kennedy to two others, in this case the then bishop of Lincoln and R. H. Tawney, and uncovers the deficiencies of Studdert Kennedy's social vision, urging the church in our own day to be actively involved in the particularities of reform, in partnership with other bodies that care about human flourishing in contemporary pluralist society.

Chapter 8 alludes to Studdert Kennedy as a pacifist, or at least as a person who developed leanings in that direction, the First World War having effected significant changes in his attitude to war. David Bryer seeks to reveal how the war acted as a critical point in the history of humanitarian concerns, enlarging humanitarian sympathies in general. The scale of the war meant that emerging humanitarian needs were unprecedented and unexpected. Churches were very rarely at the vanguard of concern and activity; and the development of humanitarianism is a story of individuals on the fringes of faith, well-networked and affluent, who used their influence to alleviate suffering, and initiate movements that have had profound effects on the contemporary humanitarian scene and the ways in which conflict is conducted today.

Finally, in chapter 9, Alvyn Pettersen examines Studdert Kennedy's public addresses as a parish priest in Worcester in the immediate aftermath of the war, when memorials were being established to those who had been killed. Pettersen draws on the longstanding link between the cathedral of Worcester and the cathedral of Magdeburg in Germany,[26] in order to compare the First World War memorial of the former with that of the latter, and he uses the life of Antony of Egypt to critique the conceptions of glory and sacrifice implicit in English memorialisation. This raises significant questions about the employment of theological motifs in the context of war, in ways that are healthy, wholesome, and constructive.

Pastor, poet, passibilist, preacher, prophet, pacifist, and parish priest: in this way, the seven central essays of this volume each take a different dimension of Studdert Kennedy's work as a gateway to exploring various fields of faith and the First World War. Not all of these aspects of Studdert Kennedy's work were equally important to his ministry; neither have they received equal treatment here, some essays being focused exclusively on Studdert Kennedy, others utilising him in passing, the volume pressing Studdert Kennedy into service precisely insofar as he illuminates the broader aspects of faith and the First World War that the authors wish to study.

Taken together, these seven central essays represent a significant contribution to the subject of faith in the First World War; they cast light on the person of Studdert Kennedy; and they indicate the capacity of twenty-first-century cathedrals to be places of theological fertility and enterprise. In recent years, collections of essays have appeared, edited by Stephen Platten, about the distinctive contributions that cathedrals can make to contemporary church life;[27] indeed, Leslie Francis has inaugurated a "science of

26. The diocese of Worcester has had a partnership with the Protestant church in central Germany, now the Evangelical Church in Central Germany, since 1992.

27. Platten and Lewis, eds., *Flagships*; Platten and Lewis, eds., *Dreaming Spires?*; and Platten, ed., *Holy Ground*. For a slightly older collection, see *Cathedrals Now*, edited by Iain MacKenzie, a residentiary canon of Worcester from 1989 to 2001.

cathedral studies."[28] These works suggest that cathedrals have much to offer the contemporary church, and our own experience, conviction, and hope is that collaborative theological endeavour can and should feature among such goods.[29]

That is not to say that cathedrals should operate within their own bubble, and as editors, we have been delighted at the interest in this volume taken by such prominent academics as Michael Snape and Mark Chapman, and their keenness to contribute to it. Michael Snape, ideally positioned to provide an overview of recent themes and relevant literature on the subject of faith and the First World War, sets the scene for the seven central essays with an introduction to the subject (while Michael Brierley introduces the life of Studdert Kennedy). Mark Chapman provides the other "book-end" to the essays, distilling, from his expertise in theology of the period, how the war impacted on theology in the immediate aftermath of the war, into the 1920s. The collective relevance of the essays to issues of faith in the longer term is ignited by a concluding editorial piece by the editors, which stemmed from discussion with their cathedral colleagues. In this way, this volume of historical theology functions and has value as practical theology: all theology should make a difference to the way in which life is lived, and the best theology indeed makes such a difference.

Theology is always a matter of dialogue: no group holds a monopoly on truth. And it has therefore been our special pleasure as editors to have these essays topped and tailed by different voices again: Andrew Studdert-Kennedy has, more than any of the writers, lived with the legacy of Geoffrey, his grandfather, and kindly provides the foreword. And the last word is given to Ilse Junkermann, the bishop of Magdeburg. John Inge in his essay writes about the importance and power of integrating memories and perspectives of different kinds, mentioning the German contribution to the service in Worcester Cathedral in July 2016 that commemorated the battle of the Somme, and Bishop Ilse's contribution to this volume is particularly valued and welcome.

Producing a book alongside the day-jobs of residentiary canons has been an enjoyable challenge, dependent on the goodwill and help of a great number and variety of people. In addition to thanking the contributors to this volume, the editors would like to express their sincerest thanks to Dr. David Morrison and his volunteers in the cathedral library; Dr. Adrian Gregson, the collections manager (and diocesan archivist) at the Worcester

---

28. Francis, ed., *Anglican Cathedrals*.

29. Six of the contributors, for example, reviewed books in a recent issue of *Modern Believing*: see *Modern Believing* 57 (2016) 449–54, 457–61, 464–66, and 481–82.

Archive and Archaeology Service, whose own specialism lies in the First World War;[30] Canon Paul Tongue, for furnishing us with local copies of Studdert Kennedy's books; Chris Guy, the cathedral archaeologist, and James Atkinson, the diocesan digital media adviser, for providing us with images for this volume, along with Michael Sussmann, the retired master of fabric at Magdeburg Cathedral, Arthur Moore of St. Mildred's Church, Whippingham, Jack Deighton, Tudor House Museum, Worcester, and the Imperial War Museum; Worcester Cathedral Enterprises and the Friends of Worcester Cathedral for support with costs related to the volume; Susie Arnold, the cathedral chapter secretary, who has kindly given administrative assistance; Robert Beattie, cathedral verger, for his compilation of the index as well as his willingness to follow up odd leads and tie up loose ends; and Dr. Robin Parry of Wipf and Stock, who has been a wise, generous, and patient publisher, as well as an exceptionally stimulating theological colleague.

All proceeds from the sale of this book are being split between the cathedral, which nurtured Studdert Kennedy and which continues to nurture its current clergy, not least through its congregations; and St. Paul's Hostel, a charity for the homeless in Worcester. The latter not only reflects Studdert Kennedy's concern for the poor; it was founded by local churches in 1977 in the derelict vicarage attached to St. Paul's church, in which Studdert Kennedy himself once lived, and from which he left to embark on those periods of service as a chaplain in the First World War which were to prove so formative.

Worcester
8 March 2017

---

30. Gregson, "1/7th Battalion King's Liverpool Regiment."

Abbreviation

ODNB *Oxford Dictionary of National Biography*

PART I

Introduction

1

Reconsidering British Religion and the First World War

Michael F. Snape

From that moment all my religion died, after that journey all my teaching and belief in God had left me—never to return.[1]

THE CENTENARY IN NOVEMBER 2016 of the conclusion of the battle of the Somme, the bloodiest battle in British history and the most sanguinary of that worldwide conflict, produced the usual slew of media commentary on the First World War. The words above are those of Charles Bartram, a Yorkshire colliery worker speaking of his experiences on 1 July 1916, a day on which nearly 20,000 British soldiers died while trying to breach German defences in the rolling country of the department of the Somme. Prefacing a BBC Education report posted by Sean Coughlan on 17 November 2016, Bartram's words encapsulate what many think *ought* to have happened to religious belief on the Somme, and in the larger cauldron of the war. Although he failed to develop Bartram's story, or pursue the subject of faith in the trenches, Coughlan explained that Bartram's striking testimony formed part of a huge collection of interviews conducted by Martin Middlebrook, a pioneering oral historian of the First World War, whose Somme material

1. Coughlan, "Graphic Eyewitness Somme Accounts."

3

had now found its way into the archives of the Imperial War Museum. Middlebrook's Somme collection, Coughlan went on, amounted to "more than 500 remarkable first-hand accounts of the World War One battle . . . , the 'vast majority' of which have never been seen before."[2] However, this is clearly not a claim that could be made for Bartram's testimony, for it stood among eleven survivors' statements that concluded Middlebrook's classic account of 1 July 1916, *The First Day on the Somme*, which was published in 1971, and appeared as a Penguin paperback in 1984.[3]

The compelling allure of the theme of war-induced, protest atheism was even more apparent in an article that was published in the Episcopalian magazine the *Living Church* the day before Coughlan's story was posted. Here, under the title "The Great War's Damage to the English Soul and Church," Richard Kew, an Episcopalian priest and adoptive American, deplored a litany of woes that had been visited on "English" faith and society by the implicitly avoidable, self-inflicted calamity of the First World War: "That horrific war scarred the character, personality, and beliefs of the British people," Kew claimed. "My assessment coming back to what is now home in the United States is that the English church, like the rest of the nation, is still wrestling with the consequences of a terrible demographic, psychic, spiritual, cultural, and philosophical catastrophe."[4] Significantly, even First World War veterans proved susceptible to the suggestive power of this myth. Ninety years after being wounded near Ypres, Harry Patch, the last surviving British veteran of the trenches, declared: "I left the army with my faith in the Church of England shattered. When I came home, I joined Combe Down church choir to try to get the faith back, but in the end I went because I enjoyed the music and had friends there, but the belief? It didn't come. Armistice Day parade—no. Cassock and surplice—no."[5] However, this is hard to reconcile with Patch's account (in the same volume) of an experience on the battlefield which Patch interpreted as his having been "allowed" to glimpse, for a moment, "the next world," and which convinced him "from that day . . . that death is not the end."[6]

However satisfying such narratives might be, and however compelling a dramatic trope, stories of universal loss of faith speak more of the sensibilities of later generations than they do of the direct, contemporary

---

2. Ibid.

3. Middlebrook, *First Day on the Somme*, 316.

4. Kew, "Great War's Damage."

5. Patch with van Emden, *Last Fighting Tommy*, 137; cf. 195.

6. Ibid., 94. See also the apparent continuing importance for Patch of devotional experiences at Combe Down (148–49) and Talbot House (200).

experience of those who witnessed the war at first-hand. Impressive though Middlebrook's endeavours certainly were, like Harry Patch his numerous interviewees spoke with the benefit (even handicap) of considerable hindsight, and even fifty years later, their views on the war often diverged, a fact illustrated by the nine other British survivors of the Somme quoted by Middlebrook at the end of his landmark book. And what an eventful and sobering experience that half-century had been: the Great Depression, the rise of Hitler, the Second World War, the advent of the atomic bomb, the Cold War, the Korean War, wars of decolonisation in Kenya, Malaya, and elsewhere, Suez, the Cuban Missile Crisis, and (more recently) the shocking spectacle of the first televised war unfolding in Vietnam. Well might one of Middlebrook's British survivors have said: "One's revulsion to the ghastly horrors of war was submerged in the belief that this war was to end all wars and Utopia would arise. What an illusion!"[7]

But no less illusory are the popular and academic myths that have clustered around the First World War and those who waged it. As "Tubby" Clayton protested in response to the avalanche of semi-fictionalised and sensationalised "war books" that appeared in the late 1920s, "fact and fiction do not after all mix easily. . . . Abolish the rules of the game; and enterprise, unchecked by the referee, will never cease to score."[8] Despite this warning, the interwar reaction to the carnage of 1914–18, of which the popularity of these "war books" was but a symptom, was rediscovered and enthusiastically amplified in the Cold War era—aided by the passing of a generation that would have taken understandable exception to the general portrayal of their lost sons and husbands as unthinking dupes and hapless cannonfodder. What has resulted is a British national myth of 1914–18 that is often wildly at variance with demonstrable fact. Hence, for example, we have the 300 or so quasi-martyrs (a number that is oddly redolent of the total of Protestant martyrs burned by Mary Tudor) who were "shot at dawn" for military offences—clearly, it is assumed, the victims of a callous and remorseless process of military justice. In fact, these represented but one in ten of those who were actually sentenced to death by court martial, the remaining 90 percent never being executed, a statistic that indicates a prevailing culture of official clemency when it came to applying the harsh sanctions of military law.[9] Allied to these tragic figures (and, in the confused mythology of

---

7. Middlebrook, *First Day on the Somme*, 315.

8. "A Memorandum on the Book 'Retreat' by Instructor-Lieutenant-Commander C. R. Benstead MC, RN, Prepared by the Chaplain-General to the Forces for the Permanent Under-Secretary of State for War" (Museum of Army Chaplaincy, Amport House, Hampshire).

9. War Office, *Statistics*, 649.

the war, sometimes co-opted into their ranks)[10] is that of the conscientious objector—usually envisaged as a Quaker, or a Primitive Methodist—cruelly hounded by the authorities for his principled and prophetic stand against a terrible and futile war. Once again, however, this conjuration disregards the fact that, among the First World War's European belligerents, legal recognition of conscientious objection to combatant service was all but unique to Great Britain,[11] and that such was the popular basis of support for the war that even the Society of Friends had to grapple with the problem of hundreds of its young men who conscientiously chose to fight. Last, but by no means least, we have the overarching impression of "a lost generation" of British males wiped out on the Western Front, and of a whole generation of British females who were widowed or consigned to spinsterhood by the cruel vagaries of war. However, the figures tell a different and even uncomfortable story: one-third of eligible British males remained civilians, and nearly 90 percent of those who joined the army actually *survived* the war.[12]

And so it goes with the churches, and with British religion in general. If partly redeemed in national folklore by the poetry, prose, theology, and showmanship of Geoffrey Studdert Kennedy, the famous "Woodbine Willie" (introduced in the next chapter and featuring in the chapters that follow); by the fabled haven of rest that was Talbot House ("Every Man's Club") in Poperinghe;[13] and by the vaunted sacramental ministry of Roman Catholic priests in the trenches, this was otherwise a story of clerical hypocrisy, ecclesiastical inadequacy, and wholesale loss of religious faith. Very much part of the larger, black legend of the war, and understood as a major cause of the decline of British church life over subsequent decades, eventually it became an article of faith that the experience of the First World War had been a major causal factor—even *the* causal factor—in the decline of British Christianity over the twentieth century. Against the backdrop of a deepening Cold War and the misadventure of the Suez Crisis, in an early example of such reasoning, the famous Anglican worker-priest E. R. Wickham claimed in *Church and People in an Industrial City*:

> The war had its own devastating effects on the religious life of
> the nation. For the few, the more serious-minded, it increased
> scepticism at the same time that it fostered more serious occu-
> pation with the foundations of faith. And for these, as for the

10. Much to its credit, this is a myth that even the Peace Pledge Union is anxious to dispel: see http://www.ppu.org.uk/coproject/guide.html.

11. Robbins, "British Experience," 693.

12. Todman, *Great War*, 44; Middlebrook, *Your Country*, 134.

13. See further, Snape, ed., *Back Parts of War*, 161, 184–86, and 246.

many, a reaction set in against "organized religion." . . . There
is much evidence that the easy degeneration of the Almighty
into the God of Battles and the British cause, though a reflection of the national struggle and in keeping with the national
mood during the war, proved a further stone of stumbling and
a further occasion for contempt, once the passions of war had
cooled.[14]

For nearly sixty years, this verdict has been asserted and reasserted
by historians, becoming a monocausal explanation for the decline of British Christianity that gained from rhetoric and repetition what it lacked in
substance. In 1965, for example, A. J. P. Taylor declared in *English History
1914–1945* that: "the sight of priests and bishops blessing guns or tanks during the Great War was not a good advertisement for the gospel of the Prince
of Peace," especially when intellectual and material progress had rendered
society much "less concerned with pie in the sky."[15] A decade later, in his
study of nonconformity and British politics, Stephen Koss pronounced that:
"However much a commonplace, it is no exaggeration to say that war, when
it came unexpectedly in August 1914, dealt a shattering blow to organised
religion. The churches never recovered from the ordeal, either in terms of
communicants or self-possession. Thereafter, men looked elsewhere, if any-
where, for their moral certainties."[16] As late as 2008, and with reference to
falling church attendance in the inter-war years, Martin Pugh asserted the
old truism that "The churches never really recovered from the role they had
played as agents of official propaganda during the Great War."[17] So ingrained
has this mythology of a popular reaction against the churches become that,
in a recent study of global religion and the Great War, Philip Jenkins has
aptly remarked that the war to end war has been didactically transformed
into "a war to end faith."[18]

In demonstrating the decisive contribution of the First World War
to the self-evident, long-term failure of the British churches, during the
1970s scholars increasingly turned to what they perceived as the salutary
example of the Church of England. As the established church of the prime
component of Great Britain, with its historic ties to the social, political, and
military elite, and with the monarch as its supreme governor, the Church
of England was easily cast as the chief culprit in the egregious ecclesiastical

14. Wickham, *Church and People*, 206.
15. Taylor, *English History*, 168–69.
16. Koss, *Nonconformity*, 125.
17. Pugh, *"We Danced All Night,"* 7.
18. Jenkins, *Great and Holy War*, 191.

blunder that was the churches' support for the First World War. Nevertheless, it should be stressed that this view had not prevailed up to that point. In 1952, for example, Stephens Spinks, editor of the *Hibbert Journal*, said in *Religion in Britain since 1900* that, during the First World War, "the bishops as a whole showed a sense of Christian restraint which was often, and sometimes violently, criticised by those whose passions under the stress of war overwhelmed their more compassionate feelings."[19] More than a decade later, Canon Roger Lloyd could still claim that England's national church had emerged with credit from the conflict, arguing that: "The impression which any fair-minded student of the evidence will get is that during the First World War the church was blessed with genuinely Christian and unusually wise episcopal leadership, and that hardly ever in history has Lambeth Palace played a more noble part than it did in those dreadful years."[20] In fact, as late as 1973, in an Open University textbook entitled *War, Peace and Religion*, Francis Clark maintained that, throughout the era of the two world wars, "the Church of England showed its perennial ability to survive and to adapt itself to changed circumstances. However unfavourably critics might speak of it, the national Church showed its vitality in many ways during the period we are considering." Significantly, Clark even saw its 1916 National Mission of Repentance and Hope ("a courageous failure or a misguided effort," according to Spinks)[21] as symptomatic of this "vitality," despite its obvious failure to induce a major religious revival among the nation at large.[22] Finally, the Church of England was in no sense exempted from Clark's assessment that "the clergy and members of the Churches were by no means the pious jingoists and ecclesiastical Colonel Blimps that some suppose."[23]

Nonetheless, a different tone prevailed by the late 1970s, for in the intervening years, a new generation of scholars, such as Albert Marrin, Alan Wilkinson, and Stuart Mews (in his widely read, if still unpublished, Cambridge doctoral thesis), had come forward to sift, weigh, and judge the statements and positions of Anglican leaders and thereby present an aggregate picture of uncertainty and failure.[24] In his book *The Last Crusade: The Church of England in the First World War* (1974), Albert Marrin argued that the war had "had a chastening influence upon church and nation," and

19. Spinks, *Religion in Britain*, 67.

20. Lloyd, *Church of England*, 222.

21. Spinks, *Religion in Britain*, 69.

22. Ferguson and Clark, *War, Peace and Religion*, 98.

23. Ibid., 114.

24. Lloyd, *Church of England*, 219 and 238.

that "the realization in later years that they had been taken in by propaganda as well as by their own predispositions induced a sense of shame and disappointment."[25] Although Marrin was roundly criticised by Owen Chadwick, one of the greatest church historians of his day, for indulging in "many adverse judgments against people or utterances," and for his presumption "that an authentic Christianity will be pacifist,"[26] Alan Wilkinson published a similar study four years later entitled *The Church of England and the First World War*. Now the best-known study of British religion in this era, Wilkinson reassured his readers that he had long "learnt to be critical of conventional patriotism," dismissing Lloyd's earlier verdict on the Church of England's wartime record as "over sanguine."[27] Though not as trenchant as Marrin, Wilkinson was strongly influenced by his literary and theological sources, and maintained that posterity had "the right and the duty to be critical" of the Church of England during the First World War, claiming that its failures were akin to those of the Cold War Church of England in its refusal to take a firm stand against nuclear weapons.[28] For his part, Mews adopted a somewhat broader perspective in his thesis, "Religion and English Society in the First World War," covering the English Free Churches as well as the Church of England, but his conclusions very much corresponded with those of Marrin and Wilkinson, arguing that "the First World War was a revelation of the extent to which the churches had lost their hold on society and it accelerated the process."[29] In subsequent years, this consensus was complemented and reinforced by David Thompson's research into the origins of the Church of England's 1916 National Mission of Repentance and Hope, whose very conception he found to be vague and confused,[30] and by Arlie Hoover's comparative study of the heady wartime preaching of British and German churchmen, boldly entitled *God, Germany, and Britain in the Great War: A Study in Clerical Nationalism* (1989). This strong current of highly judgmental pessimism also coloured a 2002 article by Shannon Ty Bontrager who, insouciantly billing the Church of England "the state church of an imperial nation," went on to extrapolate from a study of only two church periodicals that it ultimately failed in its craven and self-interested wartime bid "to gain status and power after a long period of losing them."[31] Even

---

25. Marrin, *Last Crusade*, 253.
26. Chadwick, review of *The Last Crusade*, 648.
27. Wilkinson, *Church of England*, xi and 1.
28. Ibid., 3–4.
29. Mews, "Religion and English Society," 339.
30. Thompson, "War, the Nation, and the Kingdom of God."
31. Bontrager, "Imagined Crusade," 774.

in 2016, and despite the growth of a strongly revisionist literature in the intervening years, this stream of criticism had by no means ceased, with the contents of wartime sermons still providing rich pickings for sharp critics of the Church of England's wartime record.[32]

Whether or not one shares the moral indignation that drives much of this scholarship, there are some serious methodological problems with its heavy and selective reliance on published sources and on the opinions and activities of the Church of England's clerical and lay elites. First, in focusing exclusively on the opinions and reactions of the church's leading figures, its exponents simply ignored popular religious attitudes and behaviour. Albert Marrin, for example, freely conceded that he had "had to rely heavily on printed sources," especially published sermons and on the national church press. In fact, he confessed to having little patience with manuscript sources—which, he bizarrely claimed, were "unfortunately less full and less available than in other areas of English history"—and frankly disdained diocesan and parish publications, which were simply "dull and packed with local small talk."[33] Although Alan Wilkinson's *The Church of England and the First World War* also drew heavily on published sources, it did not ignore the humble parish magazine entirely, surveying the experience of a single Cheshire parish in a book of more than 300 pages.[34] Secondly, this heavy reliance on published sources (national church periodicals, printed sermons, and more heavyweight religious commentary) led to some misleading conclusions, as some critically important published texts had important agendas that remained ignored. For example, the findings of *The Army and Religion* report of 1919 were largely taken at face value by Marrin and Wilkinson, rather than understood more critically as a highly selective body of evidence in favour of a particular agenda for post-war church reform— as Mews correctly deduced from his more extensive study of manuscript sources.[35] In addition, some of these works happily rehearsed the notorious story of the bishop of London, Arthur Foley Winnington-Ingram, who purportedly urged his listeners to slaughter Germans in what Adrian Gregory has described as "the most infamous sermon in Anglican history."[36] Significantly, recent research by Stuart Bell into the transmission of this tale has shown that the accepted construction of this sermon appears to have been

32. Barbeau, "Christian Empire."

33. Marrin, *Last Crusade*, ix.

34. Wilkinson, *Church of England*, 58–62, 191–92, and 297.

35. Ferguson and Clark, *War, Peace and Religion*, 95; Marrin, *Last Crusade*, 203–5; Wilkinson, *Church of England*, 160–65; Mews, "Religion and English Society," 174.

36. Gregory, *Last Great War*, 168.

the work of a secularist propagandist, George Bedborough, who sought to ride the pacifist tide of the mid-1930s by publishing a doctored compilation of clerical declarations on the First World War, under the incriminating title *Arms and the Clergy*. Moreover, and in a remarkable gesture of academic magnanimity, the populariser of this story, Roland Bainton, repudiated his original account of Winnington-Ingram's sermon in an issue of the journal *Theology*.[37]

If the conduct and reputation of the Church of England has been unduly savaged by historians, studies of other Christian traditions have usually followed the same lines. While focusing on specific denominations, or denominational families, they have shared the emphasis on church leadership that has characterised the historiography of the Church of England, while also stressing the supposedly toxic effects of war on organised religion. As Edwardian England's second largest church constituency, interest has naturally focused on the English Free Churches, an evolving body of Protestant denominations that had customarily defined themselves against the state and the established Church of England. These "nonconformist" churches also included the Society of Friends, England's historic citadel of Christian pacifism. In the context of the 1970s narrative, the hallowed traditions of the nonconformist churches were compromised by the Free Churches' general and close alignment with the national war effort between 1914 and 1918, their decline throughout most of the decades that followed the First World War being assured by this tragic and catastrophic lapse. According to Mews's scathing perspective on one significant "milestone" in the history of English nonconformity: "On 16 November, King George V and Queen Mary attended a Free Church thanksgiving service to mark the end of the war. . . . Free Churchmen could only comfort themselves with the crumbs of royal patronage which marked their acceptance or toleration by an establishment which no longer had reason to fear them."[38] In 1986, Alan Wilkinson surveyed the impact of both world wars on English Christianity in *Dissent or Conform? War, Peace and the English Churches 1900–1945*. Characteristically viewing his subjects through the prism of literature, theology, and history, Wilkinson endorsed the view that nonconformity's support for the First World War had been a damning experience, concluding that "the close identification of Nonconformity with the war effort was contrary to some of its deepest instincts. . . . This identification therefore led to a destructive confusion in its own mind and that of others as to what it

37. Bell, "Malign or Maligned?" 127–29; Bainton, Letter to the Editor.

38. Mews, "Religion and English Society," 334.

really stood for now."[39] Twenty years later, Alan Ruston captured the enduring scholarly consensus as to the impact of the First World War on the English Free Churches: "The Great, or First World War, saw the Nonconformist
churches become more a part of the establishment than they had ever been
before, particularly in attitude. They became an integral element within the
political machine in almost the same terms as the established church [of
England]. But flying into the sun in this way burnt their wings and like
Icarus they fell to the sea. They did not drown like Icarus but the weakness
engendered by the war remained with them for the rest of the century."[40]

Again, studies of Scottish Presbyterianism (whether established or
non-established) and Scottish and Welsh nonconformity have usually
reflected the dominant emphasis on leading personalities and institutional
affairs.[41] And they have also largely echoed the judgments that have prevailed
elsewhere. For example, in a seminal study in 1994 of the established
Church of Scotland and the United Free Church in the First World War,
Stewart Brown lamented the effects of the conflict, asserting that "the wartime expressions of Presbyterian ministers and academics, concerning the
elevating effects of the war as religious crusade or the promise of a new,
more just social order, would haunt the Church with a sense of loss and
shame during the troubled years that followed."[42] Likewise, and surveying
the impact of war on predominantly nonconformist Wales, Densil
Morgan found that this was, at best, "ambiguous." While they willingly
cast aside what Spinks termed "their puritan-pacifist traditions,"[43] Welsh
nonconformists were distinctly disappointed in their hopes for a religious
revival, and even before the war had run its course had realised that "post-
war Wales would be a new, strange Wales, where the old values would be
put aside and Christianity be increasingly regarded as an anachronism."[44]
Furthermore, Robert Pope has stressed that the political strains of war, and
especially the introduction of conscription by a Liberal-led government in
1916, overriding the qualms and even opposition of Welsh nonconformists,
signalled the end of the "nonconformist conscience" as a political force in
the principality and elsewhere in Britain.[45]

39. Wilkinson, *Dissent or Conform?* 54.

40. Ruston, "Protestant Nonconformist Attitudes," 240.

41. Brown, "Piety, Gender and War"; Hendry, "Scottish Baptists"; MacLeod,
"'Mighty Hand of God'" and "'Own Little Share of Service'"; Matheson, "Scottish War
Sermons"; Morgan, *Span of the Cross*, 41–77.

42. Brown, "'Solemn Purification,'" 102.

43. Spinks, *Religion in Britain*, 68.

44. Morgan, *Span of the Cross*, 76.

45. Pope, "Christ and Caesar?"

Nevertheless, and despite its currency, there are two major problems with the scholarly consensus that identified religious decline with the baleful consequences of the First World War. First, the case of Roman Catholicism in mainland Britain clearly defied the dominant trope of calamitous misjudgment and inevitable redundancy. In Marrin's opinion, the Roman Catholic Church was "universally recognized as doing splendid work" during the war,[46] and Mews has concurred that the First World War was a "good" war for British Catholicism.[47] However, the Catholic hierarchies of England and Scotland were no less zealous in their support for the war than were the leaders of the principal Protestant churches (Quakers excepted), a stand that was patently at odds with the neutrality of Pope Benedict XV.[48] As Keith Robbins has rightly emphasised, the singular demographics of English, Scottish, and Welsh Catholicism—and not least the fact that "the Roman Catholic Church included more non-native born in its ranks than any other church"[49]—fed strong, ultra-patriotic instincts among leading Catholics, feelings that were born of centuries of marginalisation and a firm determination to become part of the national mainstream. Moreover, despite its wartime record of yielding to no one in patriotic fervour, the Catholic Church grew in the 1920s and 1930s, due to natural increase, conversions, and immigration from Ireland. These factors effectively forestalled attempts to condemn its wartime leadership along the lines of their Protestant counterparts and underlined the fact that far more was at work in influencing the fortunes of the churches in the inter-war period than reactions and recriminations over the war itself.

The consensus formed in the 1970s was, secondly, undermined by the emergence of a new chronology of the secularisation (or "dechristianisation") of British society, one that has cast its underlying assumptions into question. Through a greater use of qualitative rather than quantitative evidence, and based on the revolutionary premise that "what made Britain Christian was not levels of churchgoing but the way in which Christianity infused public culture and was adopted by individuals, whether churchgoers or not, in forming their own identities,"[50] a new chronology has argued that the secularisation of British society was not a consequence of industrialisation and urbanisation ("the long, inevitable religious decline of the conventional secularisation story," as Callum Brown put it) but "a remarkably

46. Marrin, *Last Crusade*, 203.
47. Mews, "Religious Life," 452.
48. Snape, "British Catholicism."
49. Robbins, *England, Ireland, Scotland, Wales*, 115.
50. Brown, *Death of Christian Britain*, 8.

sudden and culturally violent event" triggered by the cultural upheavals of the "long" 1960s.[51] Consequently, and with reference to the First World War, Brown has contended that "much of what British churchmen at the time characterised as loss of faith was actually loss of Edwardian reverence for social authority, for obedience to the clergy. The class system was changing, but popular Christian faith still retained resilience."[52] Significantly, Keith Robbins has also come to the conclusion that the war caused no significant changes to the religious landscape of Great Britain, and certainly did not cause any seismic shifts that led to its collapse. As Robbins has put it, the truth was much more prosaic: "the war had brought neither a general revival of religion nor a mass alienation from it."[53] More recently, and through the interrogation of masses of statistical data, Clive Field has demonstrated the survival of a robust and resilient religious culture in Great Britain throughout the first half of the twentieth century. Although subscribing to a gradualist rather than a revolutionary model of religious change, Field has shown that during and after the First World War, the British churches were more affected by the simple disruption of peacetime norms and routines than they were by any mass rejection of Christianity and the churches.[54] Moreover, Field has concluded that the decline in church membership and public religious practice in the inter-war years should be understood as a function of gradual and longstanding social change, especially the ever-increasing availability of Sunday leisure opportunities, than of "any great 'crisis of faith'" occasioned by the war.[55] In other words, the humdrum attractions of the wireless, the cinema, and the charabanc in inter-war Britain proved a much deadlier cocktail for the churches than the aggregate effects of Gallipoli, the Somme, and Passchendaele. Significantly, in 2011, Simon Green expressed a justified scepticism over the much-vaunted religious impact of the First World War, whether proclaimed by "engaged professionals" or "detached historians," concluding that:

> Surviving organisational statistics point to no sharp break in the pattern of associational membership, worshipful attendance, financial contributions or even popular adherence to the sanctity of the rites of passage, after 1918. . . . Similarly, there was no sign, at least no visible sign, to suggest that all of a sudden "the people" ceased to believe in God, the devil, the after-life and the ultimate

51. Ibid., 175–76 and 188.
52. Brown, *Religion and Society*, 112.
53. Robbins, *England, Ireland, Scotland, Wales*, 157.
54. Field, "Keeping the Spiritual Home Fires Burning."
55. Field, "Gradualist or Revolutionary Secularization?" 91–93.

> triumph of good over evil. . . . Some, hyper-sophisticated minds
> no doubt did have their confidence in a transcendental order
> of justice shattered by the events of the Great War. But most, it
> would seem, did not.[56]

Green's verdict reflects that of a body of scholarship that has been growing over the past decade, one that illustrates that a great deal needs to be re-thought. As with so much of the revisionist scholarship on the First World War, this began with the study of the British army. Through more systematic use of manuscript sources, and especially personal materials held in repositories such as the Department of Documents at the Imperial War Museum and the Liddle Collection at the University of Leeds, the religious experience of the British soldier in the First World War was dramatically reappraised.[57] This process of reassessment had the effect of revealing the resilience—even the vitality—of the religious culture (or cultures) from which Britain's soldiers were drawn. Naturally enough, the reality of a highly pluralistic religious culture, to say nothing of the sheer size and diversity of the army, was reflected in a spectrum of individual religious reactions to the war. These responses could evolve over decades rather than years and they inevitably melded with experiences in civilian life. Significantly, the voice of protest atheism was that of a remarkably small minority.[58] The missionary vigour of the churches, which was so much a characteristic of Victorian religion, was likewise reflected in the army throughout the First World War. More than five thousand British clergymen served as commissioned chaplains during the conflict, representing a system of chaplaincy provision whose scale was unmatched by any other army.[59] Far from being the malingering milksops of popular lore, the Anglican chaplains among them were the pick of the Anglican clergy, winning hundreds of awards for courage in the front line, including three Victoria Crosses.[60] A hidden story that has also emerged from this new body of research is that of the many hundreds of clergymen from the Protestant churches who volunteered to serve as ordinary officers and soldiers, as combatants and non-combatants.[61] Unjustly forgotten by the churches they represented, they included a fourth (Anglican) recipient of the Victoria Cross, namely Bernard William Vann,

56. Green, *Passing of Protestant England,* 61–62.

57. Schweitzer, "Cross and the Trenches" and *Cross and the Trenches*; Snape, *God and the British Soldier.*

58. Snape, *Revisiting Religion.*

59. War Office, *Statistics,* 235; Snape and Madigan, eds., *Clergy in Khaki.*

60. Snape, "Church of England Army Chaplains"; Madigan, *Faith under Fire.*

61. Madigan, "'Their Cross to Bear.'"

who, until his death barely a month before the armistice, combined his functions as an infantry officer with those of a chaplain.[62]

But these reappraisals do not end with the compelling figure of the British soldier, for the war produced a massive boom in Christian philanthropy that was expressed in a huge variety of ways. Reflected at local level in parish or congregational support for the Red Cross, Belgian refugees, or those being cared for by a priest or minister in khaki, these powerful currents of philanthropy converged at a national level in the endeavours of (among others) the Church Army, the Salvation Army, and the Catholic Women's League. Most impressive, however, was the multi-faceted war work of the Young Men's Christian Association, an enterprise that channelled the efforts of hundreds of civilian clergy, many thousands of lay volunteers, and millions of individual benefactors into what was one of the greatest philanthropic endeavours in British history.[63] If the impressive efforts of the non-denominational YMCA have remained, until recently, strikingly neglected, the denominational orientation of most of the literature on religion and the First World War has also served to obscure the efforts of non-denominational Bible agencies, whose colossal wartime distributions underlined the abiding importance of the Bible, whether as text or artefact, in contemporary British society.[64] As Spinks remarked from the relatively unclouded perspective of the early 1950s, and despite the predictable hand-wringing over the religious state of the British soldier (basically, the British working man in arms): "Letters from men serving in the Middle East testified to the effect which Palestine had upon men who had given up religion when they left Sunday School. The Bible, particularly the New Testament, came to life; here was Bethlehem, the Sea of Galilee, the Holy City, the Garden and the Tomb, and if much of what they saw was unhistorical, yet the total impression was profound. Their letters showed how much the life of the British people was rooted in the Authorized Version."[65]

While the nature of civilian philanthropy demonstrates the close elision, rather than separateness, of the home and fighting fronts, scholarly scrutiny of the religious effects of the First World War on British civilians has begun to generate the kind of national and local studies that have so illuminated our understanding of religious continuity and change in other pivotal periods of Britain's religious history.[66] Though in its early stages,

---

62. Beresford, *Christian Soldier*.

63. Snape, ed., *Back Parts of War*.

64. Snape, "Bible, the British and the First World War."

65. Spinks, *Religion in Britain*, 69.

66. Gregory, *Last Great War*, 152–86; Gregory and Becker, "Religious Sites"; Beaken,

this ongoing audit once again seems favourable, with little being unearthed to demonstrate a clear and conscious falling away from the churches, and much being adduced that illustrates their abiding significance, dynamism, and adaptability. In the latter respect, the rapid assimilation of prayers for the dead in the Church of England—and even in nonconformist and Scottish Presbyterian circles—underlines the pastoral and theological responsiveness of large swathes of British Christianity, and throws into question an older contention that the Protestant churches stood impotent and forlorn amidst mass mortality and a surging tide of popular spiritualism (which, as Georgina Byrne has pointed out, was more closely related to traditional Christianity than many historians have actually realised).[67] This new and more favourable image of British religion and the First World War goes a long way towards explaining an otherwise glaring evidential anomaly. If the religious and moral capital of organised Christianity, and of the established churches in particular, had been so egregiously squandered during the First World War, how could orthodox Christianity have exerted such a powerful, immediate, and defining influence on the new, post-war culture of remembrance? From the tomb of the "unknown warrior" in Westminster Abbey (the brainchild of Anglican chaplain David Railton), to the architectural motifs of Britain's war cemeteries and the personal epitaphs marking hundreds of thousands of soldiers' graves, the relevance and resilience of Christianity in the post-war years was, quite literally, set in stone.[68]

Accompanied by these ongoing developments in the historiography of the war and British religion, the centenary of the First World War provides an ideal context for a collection of essays such as this. It is, of course, entirely fitting that this should emanate from the cathedral at Worcester, given Worcester's close association with the perennially fascinating figure of Geoffrey Studdert Kennedy, and that an afterword should be offered by Ilse Junkermann, bishop of a German diocese and city that has been proverbially associated with the horror and brutality of war since it was sacked in 1631, at the height of the Thirty Years' War. Furthermore, its contributors have brought fresh perspectives to bear on familiar figures and themes while opening new fields of enquiry and reflection, ranging from the legacy of the war for Anglican social thought to its influence on the evolution of

---

Church of England; Austin, *"Like a Swift Hurricane"*; Bell, "Church and the First World War," "'Soldiers of Christ Arise,'" and "Faith in Conflict."

67. Cannadine, "War and Death"; Wilkinson, "Changing English Attitudes"; Snape, "Civilians, Soldiers and Perceptions"; Byrne, *Modern Spiritualism*.

68. Snape, *Revisiting Religion*, 31–32. For a thoughtful and wide-ranging exposition of the Christian iconography of memorialisation, see Hammond, "British Great War Remembrance."

humanitarianism. Scholars and interested readers in many fields will find its essays enriching and illuminating, while the range of its authors' perspectives on the war itself speaks candidly of the variety of responses that the conflict evokes in Britain today. Although too often forgotten or ignored in the past, the religious experience of this conflict was inevitably diverse and multi-faceted, and this volume is a testimony to that complex but critical reality.

2

Geoffrey Studdert Kennedy

A Brief Life

Michael W. Brierley

GEOFFREY ANKETELL STUDDERT KENNEDY was born on 27 June 1883, in the vicarage of St. Mary's Church, Quarry Hill, Leeds.[1] His father, William Studdert Kennedy, the son of an Irish dean, had been a curate and incumbent in Ireland, and an incumbent in Lancashire, before becoming vicar of Quarry Hill in 1879,[2] where he remained for thirty-five years until his death at the age of eighty-eight.[3] He had five children from a first marriage, and after the death of his wife, married another Irishwoman, over twenty years his junior, Jeanette Anketell (known as Joan), with whom he had a further nine children, of whom Geoffrey was the seventh.[4]

After tuition at a small private school in Leeds from the age of nine, Geoffrey enrolled at Trinity College, Dublin, in 1897. Within a year, he was back in Leeds studying at the Grammar School.[5] His biographies note this

1. He was baptised on 22 July. The vicarage was demolished by 1962 (Purcell, *Woodbine Willie*, 25), the church in 1979.

2. Not 1876, as given in ibid., 26.

3. For an account of William Studdert Kennedy's (not straightforward) chaplaincy to the cemetery in the same road as the vicarage, Beckett Street, see Barnard, *To Prove I'm Not Forgot*, 70–71.

4. The children of the second marriage were Rachel, Kathleen, Robert, William, Hugh, Maurice, Geoffrey, Cecil, and Gerald. All the boys except Maurice were ordained.

5. See Davies, *High Ideal*, 170–75.

oddity and explain that it was possible to study for examinations at Trinity College without being resident;[6] they do not record, however, that Geoffrey's eldest brother Robert, who was ordained in 1897 to a curacy at Sefton, Liverpool, took his own life on 22 February (Shrove Tuesday) 1898, at the age of twenty-four, and this may have been a factor in Geoffrey's being recalled home.[7]

At Leeds Grammar School, Studdert Kennedy encountered a number of people who were to feature in his subsequent life. His greatest friend was fellow-pupil Kenneth Mozley,[8] with whom he often talked and holidayed,[9] who officiated at both his marriage and his burial, and who disagreed with him about the suffering of God.[10] Charles Matthews, the son of the headmaster, had already left the school, but was asked back by Mozley to help him advocate a motion at the school debating society that "arbitration should be substituted for war," which Studdert Kennedy had been due to propose until ironically switching sides the day before (Mozley and Matthews won).[11] Studdert Kennedy was also friends with Alfred Thompson, who went on to train for ordination at Ripon Clergy College (1906–7).[12]

---

6. Mozley, "Home Life," 16–17 (cf. 21); Purcell, *Woodbine Willie*, 27; Holman, *Woodbine Willie*, 14.

7. Robert was found dead in a Manchester hotel with a bullet-wound to the head. The coroner gave a verdict of suicide while temporarily insane (*Evening Express*, 25 February 1898, 2).

8. John Kenneth Mozley (1883–1946) was fellow of Pembroke College, Cambridge (1907–19 and dean from 1909), principal of Leeds Clergy School (1920–25), warden of St. Augustine's House, Reading (1926–30), and residentiary canon of St. Paul's (1930–41). See further, the obituary in the *Church Times*, 29 November 1946, 728; the entry by the then dean of St. Paul's, W. R. Matthews, in the *ODNB*; Selwyn, "Preface"; and Smoot, "Does God Suffer?" 120–32.

9. See Mozley, "Home Life." Studdert Kennedy dedicated to Mozley his *Food for the Fed-up*, "in gratitude for many years of firm friendship, and many lessons learned" (v).

10. Mozley defended impassibility in a work that began as a memorandum for the Doctrine Commission set up by the archbishops of York and Canterbury in 1922, was in due course submitted for a DD at Cambridge, and was published in 1926 as *Impassibility of God*; see Mozley, *Some Tendencies*, 51–52.

11. Matthews, "Studdert Kennedy," 300. Charles Henry Selfe Matthews (1873–1961) was rector of Catsfield (1908–14), vicar of St. Peter's, Thanet (1914–30), chaplain of Marlborough (1930–38), vicar of Kenilworth (1938–42), and rector of Fenny Compton (1942–47). See his entry in the *Australian Dictionary of Biography* (http://adb.anu.edu.au/biography/matthews-charles-henry-selfe-7523). Matthews, like Studdert Kennedy, served as a chaplain to the forces in the First World War, and, in the 1920s, hosted Studdert Kennedy on parish missions.

12. Thompson (1883–1973) became vicar of Holy Trinity, Wimbledon (1919–37) and St. Andrew's, Earlsfield (1937–53). See Mozley, "Home Life," 20–25.

Studdert Kennedy, having completed his studies at Leeds in December 1901, obtained a degree from Trinity College, Dublin (1902–4), and for two-and-a-half years taught at Calday Grange Grammar School, West Kirby, on the Wirral (1905–7), where he himself resolved on ordination. Thompson persuaded Studdert Kennedy to consider training at Ripon. Studdert Kennedy had already received the offer of a title at Rugby from Albert Baillie, the training incumbent of his brother Hugh (1902–4).[13] He considered attending Lichfield Theological College, but Lichfield only took students for ordination in that diocese[14]—Rugby was then in the diocese of Worcester. After lunch with Thompson and the vice-principal at Ripon, Henry Major,[15] and financial negotiations with the principal of Ripon, John Battersby Harford,[16] Studdert Kennedy began at Ripon in October 1907.[17] A report on his progress by Battersby Harford, for Harold Greig, examining chaplain to the bishop of Worcester, early in 1908, suggested that Studdert Kennedy "shows great promise as a preacher."[18] His mother died during the course of his training;[19] while overall, Studdert Kennedy regarded his time in Ripon as "very happy."[20]

13. Albert Victor Baillie (1864–1955) was rector of Rugby (1898–1912), sub-dean of St. Michael's, Coventry (1912–17), and dean of Windsor (1917–44). See the entry on Baillie in the *ODNB*, and, for his recollections of (Geoffrey) Studdert Kennedy, *First Eighty Years*, 142–43.

14. Geoffrey Studdert Kennedy to John Battersby Harford, 31 January 1907, archives of Ripon Hall, held at Ripon College Cuddesdon (hereafter RHA), Mo/3.

15. Henry Dewsbury Alves Major (1871–1961) was vice-principal of Ripon Clergy College from 1906 to 1919, and principal from 1919 to 1948. For the college, see Brierley, "Ripon Hall" and "'Ambassadors in Bonds.'" For Major, see also Pearson et al., *Scholarship*, and Brierley, "Panentheist Revolution," 118–51.

16. John Harford-Battersby (1857–1937), an authority on the Old Testament, was vicar of Pembury (1889–98), vice-principal of Ridley Hall, Cambridge (1898–1900), principal of Midlands Clergy College (1901–2), principal of Ripon Clergy College (1902–12 and 1915), and residentiary canon of Ripon (1911–37). For scraps of biographical material, see Brierley, "Panentheist Revolution," 124, n. 238. On 6 May 1902, he changed his name to John Battersby Harford, "for some reason best known to himself" (Stephenson, "Theology in the Theological College," 98).

17. Major to Battersby Harford, 16 January 1907, and Studdert Kennedy to Battersby Harford, 31 January 1907 (both RHA Mo/3).

18. Battersby Harford to Greig, 4 December (sic) 1908; cf. Greig's reply, 6 January 1908 (both RHA Mo/3).

19. Studdert Kennedy was summoned home by a telegram, and present at her death. See Studdert Kennedy to Battersby Harford, 22 March 1908 (RHA Mo/3). Purcell was misled by her memorial in St. Mary's, Quarry Hill (*Woodbine Willie*, 25–26) into stating (76) that she died in 1913.

20. Studdert Kennedy to Battersby Harford, 21 June 1909 (RHA Mo/3).

Studdert Kennedy was ordained in Worcester Cathedral on Trinity
Sunday (14 June) 1908, the same year as his brother Cecil in the diocese of
Carlisle. The bishop of Worcester, Huyshe Yeatman-Biggs, officiated,[21] and
the precentor, Herbert Hall Woodward, gave the sermon.[22] Studdert Ken-
nedy's fellow-curates at Rugby included Percy Herbert, the first bishop of
Blackburn and then bishop of Norwich, and Julian Bickersteth, who, like
Studdert Kennedy, was awarded the Military Cross for conduct while a
chaplain in the First World War, and became archdeacon of Maidstone.

Studdert Kennedy had a difficult diaconate: his siblings began to convert to Christian Science. "Thus did the family . . . disintegrate with the
years."[23] Five of the surviving eight children from his father's second marriage made the transition, including two who accordingly resigned their
orders,[24] and Geoffrey himself felt the movement's attraction.[25] In a heady
letter written by Geoffrey from his curacy, to Battersby Harford in November 1908, enclosing a periodic loan repayment for his training at the college,
he questioned the purpose of his continuing studies and the usefulness of
academic theology in general ("I am puzzled to death by Books like Gores
[sic] Body of Christ. It is very fascinating but why write it?"), and went on
to remark, "I have not yet found the Pernicious Heresy in Xian Science and
it has cured my sister. Why are the Bishops so hard on it? . . . If a belief cures
a person of a long standing complaint, and makes them ready to thank God
every five minutes, is there not a reasonable presumption that it is true?"[26]
He signed off, trying to reassure Battersby Harford that "I really am quite
sane and comparatively orthodox." But a letter the following June was more
subdued: "Dear Principal, I am not going to be Ordained Priest until Advent. I have had a stormy Diaconate from an intellectual and Spiritual point

21. Huyshe Yeatman-Biggs was born at Manston House, Dorset, in 1845. Ordained
in 1869 to a curacy in Salisbury, after a brief incumbency in west Dorset he was vicar
of St. Bartholomew's, Sydenham (1879–91), before becoming the only bishop of South-
wark while it was a suffragan see of Rochester. He was translated to Worcester in 1905,
and in 1918 became the first bishop of the newly-created diocese of Coventry, until his
death in 1922.

22. He died the following year. Born in 1847, Woodward had been precentor of
Worcester Cathedral since 1890, and a minor canon since 1881. See the fulsome obituary in the Church Times, 11 June 1909, 787.

23. Purcell, Woodbine Willie, 35–36 at 36.

24. Cecil in 1912, and Hugh in 1914: both crossed the Atlantic.

25. Mozley, "Home Life," 57.

26. Studdert Kennedy to Battersby Harford, 20 November 1908 (RHA Mo/3).
Battersby Harford, not Major (Pearson et al., Scholarship, 159) was the correspondent
for this and associated letters.

of view and I want to be more certain before I take Priest's Orders."[27] Battersby Harford clearly took the opportunity, in sending season's greetings at the end of 1909, to enquire both if he had been priested, and if there were any sign of his final loan repayment, for Studdert Kennedy wrote just before Christmas,

> I was not Ordained Priest—the Rector thought I had better wait until Trinity. Our Parochial Mission came on at the same time as the exam—and besides I am not a bit comfortable about things really—and have but little time for thinking. . . . Since the Parochial Mission we have got together a very nice Congregation of the very poorest people in the place—about 250 of them—and they form a Mission of which I am in charge. In fact I have all the poor people now and nothing else—The Workhouse—The Common Lodging Houses—The Public Houses—and the Gaol—are my district—with the poorest streets and courts. . . . I will send you the rest of my debt the first week in February. . . . Give my Love to the Vice—God grant you a real happy Christmas. Yours sincerely [etc.] P. S. My name is Geoffrey not George.[28]

Studdert Kennedy's predilection for ministry to the poor in Rugby concurs with the testimony of Albert Baillie: "We had one small district that was practically a slum, and [Studdert Kennedy] . . . gravitated there, getting me to buy a derelict Nonconformist chapel as the centre for his work. His work was very useful."[29] Studdert Kennedy was indeed ordained priest on the first Sunday after Trinity, 29 May 1910, at St. Michael's Church, Coventry, again by Yeatman-Biggs.[30]

That same year, Cecil Studdert Kennedy returned to St. Mary's, Quarry Hill, to assist his father, by then in his mid-eighties; but within two years had resigned for Christian Science. Geoffrey, having now been a curate in Rugby for four years, was in some ways an obvious replacement assistant, but at the same time this possibility was a sensitive one, given Geoffrey's own brush with that philosophy. Thomas Drury, the incoming bishop of Ripon, resolved the question after interviewing Geoffrey and deciding to

27. Studdert Kennedy to Battersby Harford, 1 June 1909 (RHA Mo/3).

28. Studdert Kennedy to Battersby Harford, 23 December 1909 (RHA Mo/3).

29. Baillie, *First Eighty Years*, 143. For further reflection, see Blagden, *Well Remembered*, 170, and Purcell, *Woodbine Willie*, 61.

30. The preacher was Sydney Rhodes James, headmaster of Malvern College (1897–1914), who became a residentiary canon of Worcester in 1916 and the first archdeacon of Dudley in 1921. He was the older brother of Montague Rhodes James, the translator of the New Testament Apocrypha and author of ghost stories.

appoint a supervisor for his work at Quarry Hill, from outside the parish. He wrote from Cambridge to his recently-retired predecessor, William Boyd Carpenter:

> [Cecil] Kennedy is resigning. His brother at Rugby is willing to take his place. I know about his leanings in the same direction. But I have interviewed him, and have had testimonies from my Exam.[ining] Chap.[lain] Mozely [sic] Dean of Pembroke (a very old friend of K's), who saw him here and is his oldest friend, also from his Vicar. He seems to have quite settled in his mind that Xn Sc. is wrong, except in the common segment which it has with Christianity—and in the strangely difficult case before us, I think it best to let him come, and place him under the eye of some wise friend near. Can you name one when next you have to write.[31]

Neither Drury nor Boyd Carpenter had to think very hard. The patron of the living at Quarry Hill was the vicar of Leeds, at the time Samuel Bickersteth, the father of Julian, one of Geoffrey's fellow-curates at Rugby; he was already responsible for curates of his own at Leeds parish church. Indeed, Samuel Bickersteth's account of Geoffrey's move gives the impression that he, Bickersteth, was responsible for suggesting the supervisory arrangement to Drury.[32] So Studdert Kennedy moved back to Quarry Hill in 1912 to assist his father, under the supervision of Bickersteth. The most significant aspect of Studdert Kennedy's ministry at Quarry Hill, as far as his future ministry was concerned, was a decision by the Leeds clergy chapter to start outdoor preaching in Victoria Square, to which Studdert Kennedy contributed. Bickersteth commented, "Whenever I sent for him to speak, probably nothing gave him greater pleasure, as he and a crowd were born to react on each other. . . . Undoubtedly the experience there gained revealed both to him and to us Geoffrey's gift for open-air work."[33]

---

31. Drury to Boyd Carpenter, 31 January 1912 (RHA RCC 4/245). For Drury and Boyd Carpenter, see Brierley, "Ripon Hall," 118, n. 186, and 92, n. 15, respectively. Studdert Kennedy attended Boyd Carpenter's lectures on preaching while at Ripon Clergy College.

32. Mozley, "Home Life," 69–72. Samuel Bickersteth (1857–1937) was vicar of Leeds (1905–16), and residentiary canon of Canterbury (1916–36). He came from a vast clerical family: his father had been the bishop of Exeter, his brother the bishop of South Tokyo, and his nephew became the vicar of Tavistock, not to mention his own clergy children; see Bickersteth, *Bickersteth Diaries.*

33. Mozley, "Home Life," 72–75 at 74–75. Cf. Moore Ede, "His Life in Worcester," 90: "Soon after his arrival at St. Paul's [Worcester] he organized outside services and preached in the streets."

1914 was "the real year of transition in Geoffrey's life."[34] His personal and professional circumstances changed dramatically, all within five months, before national and international circumstances changed drastically with the outbreak of war. On 19 February, his father died, which raised the question of Geoffrey's own future.[35] One possibility was that he might succeed his father as vicar of the parish, but Bickersteth, as patron, was, on balance, against the idea. Word of Studdert Kennedy's availability evidently spread: for a friend of Bickersteth's, Greig, who as examining chaplain to the bishop of Worcester had known Studdert Kennedy as an ordinand and curate, was now archdeacon of Worcester,[36] and had a vacancy to fill at St. Paul's, Worcester,[37] a parish of between three and four thousand souls outside the city wall.[38] He offered the living to Studdert Kennedy.[39] Studdert Kennedy took the evening service at St. Paul's on Sunday 29 March, perhaps by way of visiting and viewing the living before accepting it.[40] He was primarily attracted to St. Paul's because of its poverty.[41] A few weeks later, on 25 April 1914, back at St. Mary's, Quarry Hill, Studdert Kennedy married Emily Catlow, whom he had met in Leeds through her brother John, who was training to be a solici-tor. The move to St. Paul's took place on 27 May, Studdert Kennedy taking evening prayer that day,

Figure 2: Geoffrey and Emily Studdert Kennedy on their wedding day, 25 April 1914

---

34. Mozley, "Home Life," 82.

35. This was not *after* Studdert Kennedy's wedding, as stated in Holman, *Woodbine Willie*, 24, but before.

36. John Harold Greig (1865–1938) had been curate to Yeatman-Biggs when the latter was vicar of Sydenham, and moved to Hartlebury (the historic residence of the bishop of Worcester) within a year of Yeatman-Biggs's translation there. He became bishop of Gibraltar in 1921, and from 1927 to 1934 was the first bishop of Guildford.

37. The incumbent, T. F. Stewart, had been appointed to the Coventry College of Clergy, and left the parish on 2 May 1914 (soon becoming a temporary navy chaplain); within two years, he had been killed in a motorcycle accident (*Birmingham Daily Gazette*, 16 March 1916, 5).

38. Moore Ede gave a figure of "some 3,000" in his preface to Studdert Kennedy, *Hardest Part* (vii), and a figure of "nearly 4,000" in "His Life in Worcester" (88).

39. Perhaps Greig and the bishop of Worcester came up with the offer between them: see Moore Ede, "His Life in Worcester," 88.

40. Register of services at St. Paul's Church, 1912–14 (Worcestershire Archive and Archaeology Service, 850 BA8486/6). The outgoing incumbent, T. F. Stewart, preached.

41. Moore Ede, "His Life in Worcester," 88.

officiating thereafter, and on 31 May dedicating a new red cope that was presented to him by the parish catechetical group.[42] Greig inducted him into the living at an evening service on 9 June.[43] On 4 August, Britain declared war on Germany.

The new vicar came to the attention of William Moore Ede, dean of Worcester Cathedral.[44] "By degrees we in Worcester perceived that this new, strange-looking vicar was something more than an ordinary parson."[45] Moore Ede invited him to preach in the cathedral at matins on 13 September, and it was perhaps his experience of Studdert Kennedy on that occasion that caused Moore Ede to ask him to return on 15 November for the parade service, an additional morning service begun the previous month for troops who were training at nearby Norton Barracks. The service on 15 November was remarked on in the local press as the largest parade service thus far.[46] Studdert Kennedy "spoke to those two thousand men and held them spellbound—not a cough, no shuffling of feet,"[47] and he was back to preach at parade services on 20 January and 20 June 1915.[48] It

Figure 3: Geoffrey Studdert Kennedy in the cope presented to him by St. Paul's Church, Worcester

may have been these experiences that confirmed his wish to serve as a chaplain to the forces. Events at the end of 1915 were as concentrated for Studdert Kennedy as they had been in early 1914: having applied for a position

42. Register of services at St. Paul's Church, 1912–14 (Worcestershire Archive and Archaeology Service, 850 BA8486/6).

43. Accounts of the service can be found in the *Worcester Herald*, 13 June 1914, 2, and *Berrow's Worcester Journal*, 13 June 1914, 4.

44. William Moore Ede (1849–1935) was dean of Worcester from 1908 to 1934. See further, Neville, "William Moore Ede." A vice-president of both the Peace Society and the Church of England Peace League, he was in Konstanz, Germany, ironically attending a peace conference, on 4 August 1914: see Neville, "William Moore Ede," 16–17, Barrett, *Subversive Peacemakers*, 28–31, and Chapman, *Theology at War*, 25–26.

45. Moore Ede, "His Life in Worcester," 91.

46. *Worcester Daily Times*, 16 November 1914, 2; *Berrow's Worcester Journal*, 21 November 1914, 2; and *Worcester Herald*, 21 November 1914, 6.

47. Moore Ede, "His Life in Worcester," 100.

48. He also spoke at four other services in the cathedral between December 1914 and December 1915.

as temporary chaplain in November,[49] he was interviewed on 9 December,[50] appointed on 21 December, and by Christmas Day was presiding at a eucharist for troops in a barn in France. He wrote movingly about the occasion to the parishioners of St. Paul's: "It was wonderful: no lights, no ritual, nothing to help but the rain and the far-off roll of guns, and Christ was born in a cattle shed on Christmas Day."[51]

Studdert Kennedy reported for duty at Rouen to a seasoned army chaplain, Douglas Carey.[52] On learning of Studdert Kennedy's experience in public speaking, Carey sent him to the canteen at the siding at Rive Gauche, where, for four months, he mixed with the troops passing through from Le Havre, singing songs to them, giving addresses, offering to write home for them, and passing down their departure trains distributing New Testaments and packets of Woodbine cigarettes—the sort of ministry that earned him the nickname "Woodbine Willie."[53] This, however, was insufficient to occupy him, so it was arranged that he would speak to troops at the town hall on Sunday evenings in Lent, and the talks formed the core of his first book, *Rough Talks by a Padre*, published in 1918.[54]

After a period of leave, Studdert Kennedy went up to the Front in June 1916 with the 137th Brigade of the Forty-sixth Division, the first of three short periods that he spent in the line during the course of the war;[55] so he was on the Somme the night before, and during, the worst day in British military history, 1 July. His experiences on the Somme framed his written *oeuvre*, for they provided the opening chapter for *Rough Talks*,[56] as well

49. See Studdert Kennedy to Bickersteth, 20 November 1915, and the reply of 22 November, in Mozley, "Home Life," 76–77.

50. For his interview card, see http://www.chaplains-museum.co.uk/archive/record-cards/224739.

51. Carey, "War Padre," 116–17 at 117; cf. the letter to parishioners preserved in a press cutting in Worcester Cathedral Library, Muniments Add. Mss. 480.

52. Douglas Carey (1874–1947) was ordained in 1900, an army chaplain from 1902, and, after the war, dean of Guernsey (1922–31).

53. Carey, "War Padre," 117–20; cf. the "second" letter to parishioners preserved in a press cutting in Worcester Cathedral Library, Muniments Add. Mss. 480. See also Matthews, "Studdert Kennedy," 304–6: "I well remember Lady Mabelle [Egerton] telling me of the extraordinary influence Studdert Kennedy exercised in that place" (305). For the nickname "Woodbine Willie," see Studdert Kennedy, *Sorrows*, 1.

54. Carey, "War Padre," 122–24. Studdert Kennedy seems to have used these talks, with an additional one at either end, for his preaching on the National Mission: see *Rough Talks*, 11.

55. Carey, "War Padre," 125–26. Studdert Kennedy preached at Worcester Cathedral on 28 May 1916 (Worcester Cathedral Library, Muniments A405 (3), 22).

56. Studdert Kennedy, *Rough Talks*, 17–33.

as a reflection that eventually spun out into the last book that he himself published.[57]

Early in November 1916, at the end of a period of sick leave,[58] Studdert Kennedy was appointed by Llewellyn Gwynne, the deputy chaplain general,[59] to preach to the British army for the National Mission of Repentance and Hope.[60] Within two weeks he had another attack of asthma, which hospitalised him over Christmas,[61] but after eighteen days' convalescence in the new year on the south coast of France, he continued with the mission across France in 1917.[62] It was on account of the mission that his writing developed. He was preaching in Boulogne in February 1917 with Frederick Macnutt,[63] and quoted to Macnutt some verses about Napoleon that he had written before the war.[64] Macnutt suggested that Studdert Kennedy write a poem in soldier-dialect that Studdert Kennedy could use in his addresses, and Studdert Kennedy stayed up into the night, composing "Sinner and Saint."[65] The two men learnt it by heart the following morning and used it in addresses that day, and found that it received very favourable reception.

57. See Studdert Kennedy, *Warrior*, 17–21. A further book (*The New Man in Christ*) was published posthumously: a collection of retreat addresses and other pieces, some in note form, selected from Studdert Kennedy's papers, and edited by Moore Ede (5–6).

58. Studdert Kennedy was in Worcester for a week at the end of October and beginning of November 1916, when he took services and baptised his son Patrick (register of baptisms at St. Paul's Church, 1913–22, Worcestershire Archive and Archaeology Service, 850 BA8486/3b [iii] 16). See the press report of a meeting with parishioners during the visit, in Worcester Cathedral Library, Muniments Add. Mss. 480.

59. Llewellyn Gwynne (1863–1957) went to the Sudan as a missionary in 1899, and became archdeacon of the region in 1905, and bishop of Khartoum in 1908. He served as deputy chaplain general in France from 1914 to 1919, and then as bishop of Egypt and the Sudan from 1920 to 1946. See further, the entry by Peter Howson in the *ODNB*, and the forthcoming biography by Neville Benyon (Helion).

60. For the National Mission, see Wilkinson, *Church of England*, 70–90, and Thompson, "War, the Nation, and the Kingdom of God."

61. See his letter to parishioners of 5 February 1917, printed in the *Worcester Daily Times*, 13 February 1917, 2.

62. See the press report of a talk given by Studdert Kennedy in 1917 at the Boys' School in Worcester, in Worcester Cathedral Library, Muniments Add. Mss. 480.

63. Frederick Brodie Macnutt (1873–1949) was vicar of St. John's, Cheltenham (1903–7), St. Matthew's, Surbiton (1907–18), and St. Martin's, Leicester (1918–27). When Leicester became a diocese in 1927 and St. Martin's became a cathedral, he became its first provost (1927–38). In retirement, he was a residentiary canon of Canterbury (1938–45).

64. On one occasion in Rugby he had preached a sermon in verse: see Blagden, *Well Remembered*, 170.

65. Studdert Kennedy, *Rough Rhymes*, 25–27.

That evening, Studdert Kennedy wrote another, "Thy Will Be Done,"[66] and this was followed by "The Sorrow of God."[67] Macnutt read the poems to Gwynne, who was sufficiently impressed to have them printed by SPCK for circulation at the Front;[68] and in due course, Studdert Kennedy sent a collection of poems to a friend in Worcester (possibly Moore Ede himself) who arranged with Hodder and Stoughton for their publication in 1918 as *Rough Rhymes of a Padre*.[69] This was followed the next year by *More Rough Rhymes of a Padre*,[70] and in 1920 by *Peace Rhymes of a Padre*.[71]

The encounter with Macnutt also led to Studdert Kennedy's prose writing, for Macnutt was editing a book of essays by chaplains, entitled *The Church in the Furnace*, and invited Studdert Kennedy to contribute. Studdert Kennedy's essay, "The Religious Difficulties of the Private Soldier," was his first theological publication, and it "attracted a great deal of attention. From what he afterwards told [Macnutt], it was the writing of that essay that, for the first time, gave him confidence in his literary powers, and made him feel that he had a vocation to write what he was thinking."[72] Hence, when he was back at the Front in June 1917 with the Seventeenth Brigade of the Twenty-fourth Division, in lulls between active operations,[73] he wrote reflections on his experiences. And, in the later part of 1917, when he was at the Fourth Army Infantry School in Flixecourt, he turned these into a book,[74] which he dedicated to his wife, to which in May 1918 Moore Ede

---

66. Ibid., 31–35.

67. Ibid., 17–24.

68. Carey, "War Padre," 131–35; cf. Gwynne's foreword to Studdert Kennedy, *Rough Rhymes*, 6, written in January 1918.

69. Moore Ede, "His Life in Worcester," 103; cf. Purcell, *Woodbine Willie*, 139.

70. *Rough Rhymes* was dedicated (5) to the officers and men of the Forty-sixth and Twenty-fourth divisions, to whom he had ministered in 1916 and 1917 respectively, and *More Rough Rhymes* was dedicated to the officers and men of the Forty-second division, with whom Studdert Kennedy spent the "wonderful days" of the "great advance of 1918" (5).

71. Studdert Kennedy, *Sorrows*, was a compilation of these three volumes of verse, omitting a handful of poems from each of them, and adding half a dozen hitherto unpublished. Studdert Kennedy went on to publish further collections of poetry in *Songs of Faith and Doubt* (1922) and *Lighten Our Darkness* (1925), about half of which were combined with the contents of *Sorrows* to produce the classic edition of his poetry, *The Unutterable Beauty* (1927).

72. Carey, "War Padre," 136.

73. Studdert Kennedy, *Hardest Part*, xvii.

74. Purcell, *Woodbine Willie*, 143. The introduction to Studdert Kennedy, *Hardest Part*, is signed off from the Army Infantry School (xvii); the foreword to his *Rough Talks* is signed off from the "HQ Physical and Bayonet Training" (13). For an account of Studdert Kennedy's time at the Army Infantry School, see Carey, "War Padre," 127–29;

added a preface, and which was published later that year as *The Hardest Part*. It is arguably his finest work.

It was during his time on the Front in 1917 that Studdert Kennedy was awarded the Military Cross. He was in a dressing station in the Ypres salient on the evening of 15 June, after the attack on Messines Ridge, and, under heavy shellfire, went to obtain morphia for a wounded boy;[75] he then volunteered to fetch in three wounded men, one of whom was blown to pieces. "After that . . . I was rung up on the telephone, and was told that I had ten days leave, and the Military Cross."[76] The break was well-timed: in the meantime, his servant Roy Fergusson had been killed in a blast which Studdert Kennedy himself was lucky to survive;[77] following his leave for the Military Cross, he had a further two months' sick leave.

Studdert Kennedy's spell with the Fourth Army Infantry School saw him into 1918, and in the final months of the war, he was with battalions of the Manchester Regiment in the advance of the Forty-second Division on the Hindenburg Line. In the course of this, in October 1918, he suffered gas poisoning and was given sick leave, so that he was, in fact, in Worcester on the day of the armistice.[78] The following day, at St. Martin-in-the-Fields, he met the vicar, Dick Sheppard, for the first time, who apparently straight-away offered him a job on his staff.[79] Studdert Kennedy had to complete his service in France, and was demobilised at Folkestone on 21 March 1919.[80]

By now, Studdert Kennedy was a household name. He published *Lies!* at the end of 1919, its quirky preface full of disillusion.[81] He was increasingly in demand as a speaker and preacher, and it became evident that his vocation was for a "larger stage" than St. Paul's, Worcester. In May 1920, he

---

cf. Snape, *God and the British Soldier*, 107–8.

75. For the account, see above, xiii–xiv.

76. Carey, "War Padre," 143, where the official citation is given, from the *London Gazette*, 16 August 1917.

77. Studdert Kennedy, *Hardest Part*, 161–88.

78. He took the early morning service at St. Paul's (register of services at St. Paul's Church, 1916–21, Worcestershire Archive and Archaeology Service, 850 BA8486/6).

79. Sheppard, "Friend," 195–96. Hugh Richard Lawrie Sheppard (1880–1937) was vicar of St. Martin-in-the-Fields (1914–26), dean of Canterbury (1929–31) and residentiary canon of St. Paul's (1934–37). See further, Roberts, *H. R. L. Sheppard*; Matthews, *Dick Sheppard*; Scott, *Dick Sheppard*; and the *ODNB* entry by Alan Wilkinson (the old *DNB* entry was by Claude Jenkins). On the similarity of Sheppard and Studdert Kennedy, see Davies, *Varieties*, 97–101 (cf. Davies, *Worship and Theology*, 237–44), and Holman, *Woodbine Willie*, 162–63. Studdert Kennedy dedicated to Sheppard his *Songs of Faith and Doubt* "in gratitude for his constant inspiration and unfailing help" (4).

80. Purcell, *Woodbine Willie*, 151.

81. Studdert Kennedy, *Lies!* ix–x.

accepted the honorary position of chaplain to King George V (his portrait in the Guildhall, Worcester, depicts him in his chaplain's cassock).[82] The newly-founded Industrial Christian Fellowship (ICF) endeavoured to secure his services full-time:[83] encouraged by George Bell, chaplain to the archbishop of Canterbury, it offered him the post of "messenger" in 1920;[84] but the arrangement fell through over housing.[85] Moore Ede encouraged Dick Sheppard to find Studdert Kennedy a post, and correspondence in October 1920 between Dick Sheppard and Lord Stamfordham, private secretary to George V, suggests that Studdert Kennedy declined a parish in London.[86] In 1921, negotiations with the ICF recommenced, and Studdert Kennedy, who that year published both *Democracy and the Dog-Collar* and *Food for the Fed-up*, placed his availability in its hands. He resigned from St. Paul's, Worcester, set up a family home in that city,

Figure 4: The Rev. Geoffrey Anketell Studdert Kennedy (1883–1929) by John Johansen (portrait in the Guildhall, Worcester)

82. A poorer version of the same portrait is kept at Worcester Cathedral. There is also a portrait of Studdert Kennedy in the parish office of St. Martin-in-the-Fields, by Olivia Bryden; and another, which used to hang in the vestry of St. Edmund's, Lombard Street (Purcell, *Woodbine Willie*, 192), now hangs in the vestry of St. Mary's, Woolnoth.

83. The Industrial Christian Fellowship was founded in 1919. For its history, see Studdert-Kennedy, *Dog-Collar Democracy*, and Studdert-Kennedy, "'Woodbine Willie.'" For Studdert Kennedy's involvement, see also Kirk, "I. C. F. Crusader."

84. George Bell (1883–1958) was archbishop's chaplain (1914–24), dean of Canterbury before Dick Sheppard (1924–29), and bishop of Chichester (1929–58). The papers of the ICF show that its executive committee had received a letter from Bell in January 1920, and agreed to offer Studdert Kennedy a position on 13 February: minutes of the ICF executive committee 1918–26 (Lambeth Palace Library, Ms. 4009), 64 and 67.

85. Studdert Kennedy accepted the offer on 6 March, the ICF on 21 May turned down his request for housing, and by 11 June, he had withdrawn his acceptance: ibid., 70, 91–92, and 95.

86. Lambeth Palace Library, Ms. 3746, folios 213–14 and 217–18. See also Dick Sheppard's tribute in *St. Martin's Review* (May 1929), 256–58 at 257.

and, for a parish base, joined Dick Sheppard's staff at St. Martin-in-the-Fields from October 1921 until April 1922,[87] when the archbishop of Canterbury appointed him to the living of St. Edmund the King, Lombard Street—a parish in the city of London with little resident population, thus providing him with an income while allowing him to exercise an itinerant preaching ministry for the ICF.[88] He continued to write books—*The Wicket Gate* (1923), *The Word and the Work* (1925),[89] and *The Warrior, the Woman and the Christ* (1928)—as well as a steady stream of articles for the ICF magazine, the *Torch*.

Studdert Kennedy pushed himself unsparingly—he had a month's leave after Easter 1928 when his doctor declared him to be in danger of a nervous breakdown[90]—and a decade of relentless post-war overwork, combined with his asthma, eventually caught up with him. He had been due to give addresses in Liverpool in March 1929, and was suffering from influenza, but kept the appointment.[91] While there, he developed pneumonia. His wife Emily was called to his bedside in St. Catherine's vicarage, Abercromby Square, and then two of their children fell ill in Worcester, so she returned home to tend to them. Studdert Kennedy's condition deteriorated, and Emily was summoned back to Liverpool, driven through the night by the family doctor (the dean of Worcester's son). Studdert Kennedy died in the early hours of Friday 8 March, and Emily arrived two hours later.

His body was taken to St. Paul's, Worcester, on 10 March, and kept there until 12 March, when it was processed through the city for a funeral

87. The parish magazine for October 1921 (*St. Martin-in-the-Fields Review* 368) includes him in the list of parish clergy, and comments (473), "The Rev. G. A. Studdert Kennedy is now officially on the Staff though we have not the slightest idea where he is or where he is living."

88. Studdert Kennedy dedicated his *Wicket Gate* to "P. T. R. Kirk . . . with all my comrades and colleagues in that great work [of the ICF]" (5). Paul Thomas Radford-Rowe Kirk (1878–1962), like Studdert Kennedy of Irish descent and a graduate of Trinity College, Dublin, was vicar of St. Mary Magdalene's, Peckham (1909–15), chaplain to the forces (1915–18), founder and general director of the ICF (1918–54), and vicar of Christ Church, Westminster (1922–53). See the obituary in the *Church Times*, 21 September 1962, 16.

89. This book appears to have been written for Lent (1 and 84), and commissioned by Arthur Winnington-Ingram, the bishop of London (see iii and v of *Religion in Life*, in which the fifth chapter of *Word and the Work* is reprinted).

90. Minutes of the ICF executive committee 1926–35 (Lambeth Palace Library, Ms. 4010), 69.

91. See the account given by John Brierley, vicar of St. Faith's, Great Crosby, where Studdert Kennedy last spoke before being overtaken by illness, in a letter to Emily Studdert Kennedy, 21 March 1929 (Worcester Cathedral Library, Muniments Add. Mss. 480).

at the cathedral. He was buried in St. John's cemetery, Worcester, and memorial services were held the same afternoon at St. Martin-in-the-Fields, and in Bristol, Liverpool, and Manchester.[92] Emily, with whom he had three sons, Patrick, Christopher, and Michael, died in 1964.[93]

Among the obituaries was one by Russell Barry:[94]

> The early death of Geoffrey Anketell Studdert-Kennedy [sic] has come as a shock to people the world over. He, with Tubby Clayton and Dick Sheppard, are probably almost the only parsons of whom the man in the street has ever heard, or for whose opinion he much cares. There is no one in our whole ministry who had a further reaching influence or who has done more—if nearly so much—for the evangelization of English people both at home and throughout the world. . . . He was one of a group of men of his generation who were first "discovered" in the war, and it was in the war that his Gospel found him. . . . [H]is insistence on a suffering God . . . gave a tortured world what it longed for. . . . All the "war padres" proclaimed it. . . . But Studdert-Kennedy more than any one man called the English world of his generation back from a vague remote "One above" to see God shining in the face of Christ. . . . His sermons to the troops were a revelation: their fiery conviction and irresistible realism and the vernacular of their phraseology made him almost a legend in the army. . . . For his message came upon him as on a prophet . . . and it exhausted him. . . . All his friends feared for the effect of these volcanic fires on his system. . . . God knows how ill the Church can spare him: and England has lost one of its too few prophets. Essentially, we may say, he was a voice; a voice proclaiming the way of the Coming Kingdom with such power,

92. The sermon at the service in Liverpool was given by the vice-dean, Frederick Dwelly, and in London by John Maud, the bishop of Kensington.

93. Grundy, *Fiery Glow*, 86. She died at 5a College Yard, Worcester (*Berrow's Worcester Journal*, 29 May 2014, 16). Patrick was born on 25 August 1916, in due course was ordained, and died in 1988. Christopher, born on 5 January 1922, was also ordained, and died in September 2016. Michael, born on 15 April 1927, became an academic psychologist in the United States, and died in January 2017. See Holman, *Woodbine Willie*, 159–61.

94. Obituaries appeared in the *Times*, 9 March 1929, 14, and (by Dick Sheppard) 15 March 1929, 23; by Kirk among others in the *Church Times*, 15 March 1929, 331; by Kirk, Moore Ede, Sheppard and Maud in the *Torch* 7 (1929), i–vi and viii; by William Temple, Winnington-Ingram, Sheppard, and Kirk in the April parish magazine of St. Paul's, Worcester; and in *St. Martin's Review*, April 1929, 169–70 (by Pat McCormick), and May 1929, 256–58 (Sheppard again). An obituary by Mozley is preserved in the *Leodiensian* 48 (1929) 81–82; Mozley, "Epilogue," is the sermon from a requiem held at the Grosvenor Chapel on 19 April 1929.

directness and conviction as we are not likely to hear for many
years. It will go on ringing though he no longer speaks it. May
God still give him His work to do.[95]

---

95. Press cutting in Worcester Cathedral Library, Muniments Add. Mss. 480. Russell Barry (1890–1976) was fellow of Oriel College, Oxford (1913–19) as well as an
army chaplain with Studdert Kennedy, principal of Knutsford Ordination Test School
(1919–23), professor of New Testament at King's College, London (1923–27), vicar
of the University Church, Oxford (1927–33), canon of Westminster (1933–41), and
bishop of Southwell (1941–63). See further, Barry, *Period*, West, *"FRB"*, and his entry
in the *ODNB*.

PART II

Essays from Worcester Cathedral

3

The First World War, Place, and "Home"

John G. Inge

I've spent hundreds of pages, even whole novels, trying to explain what home
means to me. Sometimes I think that it is the only thing I ever write about.
Home is place, geography and psyche; it's a matter of survival and safety, a
condition of attachment and self-definition.[1]

THE EVENTS THAT SHAPE our lives happen in material, physical places. Our
very existence as embodied beings means that at any given moment, we
will be in one particular place. Place is as necessary to us as food and air.
Nothing that we do or are, nothing that happens to us, is unplaced. Place,
as opposed to undifferentiated "space," is "space which has historical mean-
ings, where some things have happened which are now remembered and
which provide continuity and identity across generations. Place is space in
which important words have been spoken which have established identity,
defined vocation and envisioned destiny."[2]

"Home" is a particular type of place. In the quotation at the head of
this essay, the novelist Barbara Kingsolver alights on what perhaps most
writers "ever write about"—the place of their formative experiences and

---

1. Kingsolver, *Small Wonder*, 178.
2. Brueggemann, *Land*, 5. See further, Inge, *Christian Theology of Place*.

relationships, "a condition of attachment and self-definition," their *axis mundi*, the place where they are rooted.[3] In the context of the Second World War, and not long before she died in August 1943, the French mystic Simone Weil wrote: "To be rooted is perhaps the most important and least recognised need of the human soul. It is one of the hardest to define. A human being has roots by virtue of his real, active and natural participation in the life of a community which preserves in living shape certain particular treasures of the past and certain particular expectations for the future."[4] Weil went on to say that the participation is a natural one, brought about by "place, conditions of birth, profession and social surroundings."[5]

The word "home" comes to the English language from the German *heim*, itself derived from an Indo-European root, which has a basic meaning of "place of settlement." Both aspects of this meaning—*place*, that is to say, geography/topography, and *settlement*, that is to say, the ordering of human society—are important, and each aspect is formative of the other. A "place" becomes "home" when people settle there, with all that settlement involves; and that settlement in turn affects the place. There is, indeed, a sense in which the home, when it operates properly, is our first experience of church, in that, like church, home should be a school of love. The family table is its "eucharistic gathering." As Timothy Gorringe observes: "the Church is always first and foremost a local community, globally networked. What are or were called in Latin America 'base communities' are the building blocks of the Church. True community begins in the face to face, but looks outward to the entire *oikumene*, the whole inhabited earth. In this respect Church is sacramental for human community at large."[6]

This chapter reflects on the meaning of "home." It is an essay in what might be called "psychogeography"—a term that has been used since at least 1955, at that time by Guy Debord, to refer to the effects of the geographical environment, consciously organised or not, on the emotions and behaviour of individuals.[7] I wish to examine the notion of home through the lens of the most un-settled, dis-ordered expression of human interaction—war— in particular, the First World War, the "war to end all wars," in which the contrast between home and war could hardly have been greater. I wish to reflect on the nature of place and home with reference to Geoffrey Studdert

---

3. Eliade, *Sacred and the Profane*, 58.

4. Weil, *Need for Roots*, 41.

5. Ibid., 42.

6. Gorringe, *Theology of the Built Environment*, 185.

7. Its most prominent proponent today is Will Self, who writes popular articles in the genre and has published a collection of them: Self, *Psychogeography*.

Kennedy, a renowned personality of the war and, as "Woodbine Willie," one of its best-known army chaplains. Examination of Studdert Kennedy's experience will suggest that "home" is a place in which we learn to integrate our best and worst experiences, an idea that I will apply to nation states, and then to continents, with special reference to Europe.

Home, the First World War, and Geoffrey Studdert Kennedy

The First World War was, if nothing else, a conflict about place. The question of what caused the war is long, complex, and virtually an academic discipline in its own right, yet no account can afford to ignore the prominence of territorial dispute in the years before the war broke out.[8] The event that detonated the violence—the assassination of the Archduke Franz Ferdinand in Sarajevo on 28 June 1914—was preceded by a generation of increasing rivalry between the Great Powers, which manifested itself in a drastic increase in militarism, nationalism and a thirst for the conquest of territory. Precipitated by the decline of the Ottoman Empire, this rivalry between the Great Powers had resulted in smaller wars of conquest. A chain of opportunistic assaults on Ottoman territories across the Balkans included the annexation of Bosnia and Herzegovina by Austria-Hungary in 1908, and led to the Balkan wars. These wars, like so many other violent human disagreements, involved disputes over territory, over particular places.

In the agrarian age, territory meant food, and lack of it sometimes spelt hunger and starvation. Long after this ceased to be the case, territory still meant wealth and power. When nations increase the territory over which they hold sway, they increase their power and self-esteem. Robert Ardrey's seminal enquiry of 1966 into the "animal origins of property and nations" argued that the "territorial imperative" is a human instinct determined by evolution: "Man is as much a territorial animal as a mockingbird singing in the clear California night. . . . [I]f we defend the title to our land or the sovereignty of our country, we do it for reasons no different, no less innate, no less ineradicable, than do lower animals."[9] Even if there is more to be said than this, there is, at the least, a connection between territoriality and human meta-phenomena such as property ownership, nation-building, and war.

If the First World War arose as a result of nation states wanting to flex their muscles by taking over other nations, or parts of them, the association

8. See recently, for example, Clark, *Sleepwalkers.*

9. Ardrey, *Territorial Imperative*, 5.

of that war with territory and place continued in an all-too-tragic manner as it progressed. Famously, the trench warfare of the battle of the Somme, which lasted 141 days, claimed over one million dead and wounded on both sides. It was a brutal battle of attrition on a fifteen-mile front. "Success" in this battle meant the conquering of a mile or two—or maybe only yards of territory—at the cost of enormous casualties. It was one enormous tragedy comprised of a string of smaller ones. At the battle of Flers Courcelette, for example, on 15 September 1916, British artillery unleashed hundreds of thousands of shells, and twelve divisions of men advanced, aided by their new weapon, forty-eight Mark I tanks. Many broke down: fewer than half of them made it to the front line. The British sustained tens of thousands of casualties to advance only one-and-a-half miles.[10] The irony is bitter indeed, that in a struggle for territory, hardly any territory was gained.

"Place" is commodified by war, and thereby becomes "un-settled." The dis-orientation of troops from their homes can be seen at three levels. First, and most obviously, soldiers in the trenches were far from their geographical place of origin. The area between the opposing sides was "no man's land," a place in which no human could settle: that is to say, the territory in which the war took place was home to no-one. Some sought to convey the desolation of this homelessness in visual form. The artist Paul Nash, for instance, in his landscape painting *The Menin Road*, used the most meagre palette of browns and greys, colours of rust, decay and death: trees are shattered and stripped; water, the source of life, is held stagnant in muddy shell-holes; shafts of cold sunlight resemble gun barrels; two lines of tree trunks stretch away to infinity (will this never end?); four human figures are at the centre, but they are hard to discern—so small, so discoloured by the colourlessness around them. When this no man's landscape is put alongside a painting of English countryside by Constable, say, or of French by Pissarro, the distance from home becomes an aching void. It is therefore not surprising that the attraction of "home" featured prominently in the minds of those who fought in the First World War. The troops of the First World War not only sang militaristic songs which had predominated before the war; they also sang songs of longing about home. Fondness for home (among other sentiments) is expressed, for example, in the popular chorus "It's a Long Way to Tipperary."[11]

10. See Keegan, *First World War*, 320–21.

11. Cf. "Keep the Home Fires Burning" by Ivor Novello, sung to a tune by Gustav Holst.

Figure 5: *The Menin Road* by Paul Nash

Secondly, and more powerfully still, troops were disconnected from their psychological home. Soldiers formed strong relationships with those who fought alongside them. In many cases, especially in the so-called "Pals' battalions" in the early stages of the war, they enlisted together with friends, or with others from similar backgrounds, towns, or communities.[12] Joanna Bourke has shown how, while the practices of writing home and concern for home continued, camaraderie and friendship at the Front became a substitute for the domestic ideal.[13] However, death, injury, and trauma quickly broke up not only the settled nature of home relationships, but also the new, closely-knit bonds formed at the Front. They were shattered by shells. For many survivors, the experience of trench warfare became literally unspeakable; when they returned home, they could not and would not talk of the experience at all: it was just too terrible. Many suffered lasting psychological disturbance as a result.

Thirdly, troops experienced an alienation from their spiritual home. Geoffrey Studdert Kennedy recounted an occasion soon after his arrival at the Front, when he was in a trench with soldiers who were under attack.

> The man immediately in front of me had lost his nerve and was crying, and pleading with God for mercy. The man behind me was better, he was swearing steadily at the Germans, and kicking me and saying between his oaths—

12. Ferguson, *Pity of War*, 205–6.
13. Bourke, *Dismembering the Male*, 22.

"Go on! Go on!"

"I can't go on," I shouted back; "the chap in front of me has got the hump or the blue jibbers or something."

A tremendous kick was the reply, and then in tones of puzzled fury—

"Who the hell's that?"

The situation was getting comic.

"This is the Church," I roared back.

Then came the great question.

"And what the —————— is the Church doing here?"[14]

The fact that the church put increasing resources into reproducing at the Front familiar forms of institutional religion is testimony to the spiritual dislocation that the Front itself involved.[15]

Studdert Kennedy, seeking to be as close to the action as he could be, experienced this sense of dislocation at first-hand, and wrote of it with distilled passion:[16]

> Waste of Blood, and waste of Tears,
> Waste of youth's most precious years,
> Waste of ways the saints have trod,
> Waste of Glory, Waste of God,
>   War![17]

And yet his literary output demonstrates his ability, amid war, to find a spiritual place of "settlement," a "condition of attachment and self-definition." This was the notion of a suffering God, arrived at through consideration of the problem of evil. "His participation in The Great War hurtled him with dynamite-force straight into [the problem of evil]. For Studdert Kennedy, war *was* the problem of evil in 'acute form,' the test case for determining if Christianity can cope with evil."[18] As he struggled with "how to believe in

---

14. Studdert Kennedy, *Rough Talks*, 22. It is said—I suspect apocryphally, but quite plausibly—that Studdert Kennedy's answer to "the great question" was "Its job."

15. Cf. the "Vicarage" sign that was placed outside Studdert Kennedy's hut (Purcell, *Woodbine Willie*, 111). For the history of British army chaplaincy provision in the First World War, see Howson, *Muddling Through*.

16. For the question of how close to the front line Anglican chaplains were allowed to get, see Howson, *Muddling Through*, 123–41; Madigan, *Faith under Fire*, 119–25; and the varying evidence presented in Snape and Madigan, eds., *Clergy in Khaki*.

17. From "Waste," in Studdert Kennedy, *More Rough Rhymes*, 80.

18. Walters, "Introduction," 21, Walters's emphasis.

and love God in spite of [evil]; and how to get rid of it,"[19] Studdert Kennedy set down a stark and bold theology of suffering: "At a popular but deeply felt level . . . he explored the central themes for theology, ethics, and spirituality. Is God beyond or involved in the suffering of the world? . . . Does the Cross make sense of suffering?"[20] The idea of the suffering God, to which the war led him, became his lasting legacy. It was not original to Studdert Kennedy, but his writings on the theme were highly accessible, and had an authority borne of his searing experience:

> How can it be that God can reign in glory,
> Calmly content with what His Love has done,
> Reading unmoved the piteous shameful story,
> All the vile deeds men do beneath the sun?
>
> Are there no tears in the heart of the Eternal?
> Is there no pain to pierce the soul of God?
> Then must He be a fiend of Hell infernal,
> Beating the earth to pieces with His rod.[21]

Studdert Kennedy was finding a "home" amid the unsettledness of war by describing a God who is "at home" in the midst of suffering and pain. The idea was taken up in the course of the twentieth century by more sophisticated theologians, such as Jürgen Moltmann in *The Crucified God*, W. H. Vanstone in *Love's Endeavour, Love's Expense*, and John Austin Baker in *The Foolishness of God*.[22] In the latter, for example, Baker took the proposition that God is Love and went on to observe that "if we take our definition of love seriously, then the implications of this are remarkable. For one thing, it means that, though all owe to God their nature and existence, yet he has granted them an absolute right to exist, to be themselves. In this most fundamental of senses, God is the pattern of all parenthood, and creation itself is an act of love, a sacrifice. For another thing, it means that God bares himself to suffering."[23] In reaching the same conclusion as Studdert Kennedy, Baker acknowledged that "reason cannot prove that there is a God, and that

19. Temple, "Man," 219.

20. Wilkinson, *Church of England*, 244.

21. From "The Suffering God," in Studdert Kennedy, *Rough Rhymes*, 58–63 at 59–60. The poem was written on an upturned biscuit tin in Havrincourt Wood, southwest of Cambrai (Studdert-Kennedy, *Dog-Collar Democracy*, 114). Cf. the second verse of the hymn "God is Love: let heav'n adore him" by Timothy Rees, another First World War army chaplain.

22. The work of Studdert Kennedy itself had a considerable effect on Moltmann, as Moltmann himself acknowledges (Moltmann, *Trinity*, 34–36).

23. Baker, *Foolishness*, 133.

he is good. What it does tell us is this. If there is a God who is responsible for these things, this is the only kind of God he can be."[24]

Studdert Kennedy's spiritual "settlement," his ability, through the doctrine of the suffering God, to become spiritually "at home" in the war, is related to his physical home of Worcester, with which he maintained connections throughout the war, and where he had already been accustomed to integrating negative social circumstances with the positive resonances of Christian faith. He had been instituted to his living in Worcester in June 1914, less than two months before the outbreak of the First World War, and spent eighteen months there before he was appointed as a temporary chaplain. He returned to Worcester after five months in France, at the end of May and the beginning of June 1916, and again in October 1916, prior to the call to a new duty as a "wandering preacher" for the National Mission for Repentance and Hope; and the registers of St. Paul's Church show him returning regularly to Worcester during the remainder of the war.[25] If the Somme and Flanders were formative places for Studdert Kennedy, Worcester was the place to which he returned to process what had happened to him in those fields of action. When he moved from the incumbency of St. Paul's in 1921, having become a national figure, Worcester remained his home: he established a family house in the west of the city. Worcester was also the place of his funeral, attended by thousands, and the site of his burial. His book, *The Hardest Part*, written in France, was made possible by wrestling that had taken place in his adopted home of Worcester. After all, Studdert Kennedy's living in Worcester was a slum parish in which the poverty was acute. He had grown up in the very midst of the poor in his father's parish in Leeds, been drawn as a curate to the destitute parts of Rugby, returned to the family home in Leeds to assist his ageing father, and on moving post after the death of his father, had been drawn to St. Paul's, Worcester, precisely on account of its deprivation. The war intensified these experiences of suffering and his reflections on how God was related to them. It was above all at Worcester that Studdert Kennedy integrated these negative experiences into a constructive whole, and began to use them for greater good. Worcester, as the place to which he constantly returned, developed for Studdert Kennedy the attributes of "home."

---

24. Ibid., 134.

25. Studdert Kennedy attended services at St. Paul's in May/June and October/November 1916; July 1917; February, May, June, and November 1918; and every Sunday in March 1919, except 16 March (register of services at St. Paul's Church, 1916–21, and the banns book for St. Paul's Church, 1915–24, Worcestershire Archive and Archaeology Service, 850 BA8486/6 and 850 BA8486/5).

The nation state and "home"

The integration of positive and negative experiences within the home requires openness to elements that are challenging, a comfortability with difference. Such openness enables a depth of rootedness, which simultaneously mitigates against insecurity. These dynamics operate not just at the level of personal life, but also at the level of the nation. The nation state is a healthy "home" insofar as it is open to difference, diversity, and challenge.

The rise of the nation state was associated with philosophical and political developments following the Enlightenment that were designed to create people incapable of killing each other in the name of God. "Ironically," Stanley Hauerwas writes, "since the Enlightenment's triumph, people no longer kill one another in the name of God but in the name of nation states."[26] Similarly, the philosopher Alasdair MacIntyre describes the modern nation state, in whatever guise, as "a dangerous and unmanageable institution, presenting itself on the one hand as a bureaucratic supplier of goods and services, which is always about to, and never does, give its clients value for money, and on the other as a repository of sacred values, which from time to time invites one to lay down one's life on its behalf. As I have remarked elsewhere, . . . it is like being asked to die for the telephone company."[27]

MacIntyre here alludes to the possibility of nation states attributing absolute worth to their wealth, power, and prestige, as did the pre-war Great Powers in their territorial imperative. If nation states regard their values as ultimate, they cease to be open, and degenerate into corruption. Defining one's nation over and against others on ethnic lines, for example, has taken a heavy toll in Europe even after two world wars, as the terrible wars in the former Yugoslavia graphically demonstrated during the 1990s. Similarly, members of nation states can develop idolatrous attitudes towards their country. Some, for instance, complain that the first allegiance of British Muslims is to their faith rather than their country, to which my reaction is "So is mine." Herein lies the difficulty of the hymn "I vow to thee my country," which bids us give our country a "love which asks no question." A proper love *does* ask questions, difficult questions. The author of the hymn, Cecil Spring-Rice, in fact wrote the words shortly after having been summarily relieved of his post as British ambassador in Washington (and not long before his sudden death), when he was struggling to see his unceremonious dismissal in the

---

26. Hauerwas, *Against the Nations*, 129.

27. MacIntyre, "Partial Response," 303. On the complexity of national identity, see Kwame Appiah's Reith lectures, *Mistaken Identities* (2016), especially the one on "country": http://www.bbc.co.uk/programmes/b07zz5mf.

light of "a love which shared something of the same quality as that sacrifice shown on the cross."[28] Keith Clements comments:

> While the spirit of self-sacrifice is certainly one that stirs the soul to deepest respect, a "love that asks no questions" is—iron-ically—a very questionable kind of love. For, if the claim of one's country is so absolute, it means that there is no moral frame out-side the nation itself. . . . To believe "he can do no wrong" does the loved one no real service at all. In other words, true love of a human person cannot simply be a wondering adoration and submission, which identifies the beloved with goodness itself. It requires seeing the beloved in the light of a goodness which transcends him or her. There is One, and One alone, who is truly good, and who can be worshipped as goodness itself.[29]

If a country is to be a place of settlement, therefore, it needs a "home guard" to keep watch against the promotion of primal instincts and rivalries. Then, maintained as a healthy community, the nation state can be sacramental for humanity more widely. Trevor Huddleston, that great scourge of apartheid, once remarked to me that he had learned the value of human community at his school. From there, his vision extended outwards.

This means that a proper love of our nation involves openness to the rest of the world. Psychologists tell us that the thirst after power and influ-ence is generally fuelled by insecurity. If the inhabitants of a country were able to find true security in their "home," they would be less likely to be aggressive towards others. Graham Cray, a former principal of Ridley Hall, a theological college in Cambridge, coined the expression "roots down, walls down," an expression that the college still seeks to uphold as part of its ethos.[30] He believed that it is only when people are deeply and securely rooted in their own faith that they are able to approach in a constructive manner those whose understanding of faith is very different. Insecurity breeds hostility to difference.

It is important to be so "at home" in our country that we are able to embrace difference within it as well as outside. In *The Home We Build To-gether*, Jonathan Sacks writes:

> The story of the future tells how Britain, where wars were once fought between Protestants and Catholics, became a pioneer of tolerance in the twenty-first century by finding ways of bringing together the diverse histories of its inhabitants while

28. Clements, *Patriotism*, 39.

29. Ibid., 40.

30. http://www.ridley.cam.ac.uk/about/ethos/identity/walls-down.

maintaining its strongly individual character. It became the place where minorities who fought each other elsewhere became friends. Without ceasing to be a Christian country it embraced Hindus and Sikhs and Muslims, as it had embraced Catholics and Dissenters and Jews. It respected others; it learned from them; it incorporated their distinctive gifts into national life. It established informal ground rules—there are certain things you do and don't do if you want to be part of a society that values diversity. Civility matters. So does service to others. So do neutral spaces in which people of all kinds meet.[31]

He articulates something of what this might mean in terms of diversity:

Belonging means giving. It involves a responsibility-based culture of respect, not a rights-based culture of complaint. The majority culture must exercise provocative acts and utterances. Minorities have a responsibility to show that they respect Britain and its traditions. We each have a part to play in the national endeavour. That means orchestrated diversity, integration without assimilation. It cannot be done by Governments alone; it cannot be done by us alone. We need to work out a new relationship between civil society and the state, and that will take time.[32]

One key "site" for the integration of difference, the integration of that which is other with that which is familiar, is that of memory. In her novel *Home*, Marilynne Robinson writes of the Boughton family and how important the place of their home was for evoking memory: "[The] Boughtons, who kept everything, had kept their land, their empty barn, their useless woodshed, their unpruned orchard and horseless pasture. There on the immutable train of their childhood her brothers and sisters could and did remember these years in great detail, their own memories, but more often the pooled memory they saw no special need to portion out among them. They looked at photographs and went over old times and laughed, and their father was well pleased."[33] Homes are places of shared memory, and the healthiest "pooled memory" is that which includes difficult memories as well as those that are happy. Again, this applies to the national level as well as that of the family. If the worldly approach to remembrance is characterised as "forgive and forget," the Christian conception of remembrance can be characterised as "remember and forgive." At the heart of Christian worship, the eucharist involves *anamnesis*, or "re-membering," bringing into the

31. Sacks, *Home We Build*, 240.
32. Ibid.
33. Robinson, *Home*, 8.

present the horrific events of the crucifixion. The contrast to re-membering
is dis-membering. Dismembering is a feature of war, remembering a feature
of home. Both the good and the bad of the past have to be brought to mind
for wholesome relation to the future. At the commemoration of the battle
of the Somme at Worcester Cathedral in July 2016, for example, the lesson
was read by a representative from Magdeburg in Germany with which the
diocese of Worcester is linked, and the anthem was sung by a choir from
Hanover. The involvement of Germans in the service, with their own painful memories, was very powerful.

The Boughtons' home also makes clear that memories are tied up with
material things. Just as material things in the home are vehicles for the integration of painful elements of the past, so particular places can enable national integration of the tragic past with more hopeful aspects of the present
and future. Thus, cemeteries, in the very places where people died fighting
for territory, can, when well kept, help to integrate those tragic losses within
an ongoing, overall context of beauty, and the significant number of people
who visit them and are moved by them is a testimony to the possibility of
such integration. In a not dissimilar way, the Siegestor or Victory Gate in
Munich has diluted its triumphalist origin with a reminder of the more recent, painful past within a single, integrated memorial. Commemorating
the valour of Bavarian troops in the Revolutionary and Napoleonic wars, it
was badly damaged in the Second World War, and now, following restoration, includes the inscription: "Dem Sieg geweiht, vom Krieg zerstört, dem
Frieden mahnend"—"Dedicated to victory, destroyed by war, urging peace."
Neil MacGregor contrasts the memorial with Paris's Arc de Triomphe and
London's Wellington Memorial at Hyde Park Corner: "Where the London
and Paris arches look back only to moments of high success, presenting
a comfortable, if selective, narrative of national triumph, the Munich arch
speaks both of the glorious cause of its making and the circumstances of its
later destruction. Unlike the other two, its original celebratory purpose is
undercut by a very uncomfortable reminder of failure and guilt. It proclaims
a moral message: that the past offers lessons which must be used to shape
the future."[34]

Europe and "home"

The capacity of particular places or "homes" to integrate the painful past
with a hopeful future has special applicability to the continent of Europe. At
the time of writing, the future of Europe is very uncertain, Britain having

34. MacGregor, *Germany*, xxvii.

voted in June 2016 to leave the European Union. The referendum showed Britain to be very fissured: young people voted differently to older people, London differently from the provinces, the educated differently from the less educated, England and Wales differently from Scotland and Northern Ireland.

The challenge in this, as in any national and continental context, is to integrate difference in a way that is open, at the same time as being rooted. Places that are able to integrate negative experience with positive experience have a particular role to play in this task. Since the second half of the twentieth century, and certainly from the perspective of the twenty-first century, one place above all others seems to stand for that integration: Auschwitz, the location of one of the Nazi extermination camps in the Second World War. Samuel Wells has written about its possible role in a renewed Europe:

> A renewed Europe must have a heart. For me, there's only one place that has a claim to be the heart of the new Europe: and that's Auschwitz. Auschwitz is a place that teaches humility to all European pretensions, honesty to all memories, warning to all language of purity and power. A Europe centred on Auschwitz won't give in to nostalgia or content itself with pragmatics, it will be alert to the outsider and wise to malign ideology. Its Christianity will never forget that it comes from the Jews and its rhetoric will never forget that becoming Babel is no idle fear.[35]

There are different ways of redeeming such places. The Anglican cathedral in Zanzibar, for instance, was deliberately built over the site of the slave market and the high altar placed where the whipping-post had been. As such, it is a powerful symbol *precisely because* the evil past of the place remains very much part of its story. Its redemption points to the fact that all places will be redeemed in Christ. The particularity of Auschwitz is different: some years ago, Jewish opinion was very much against the presence of nuns who lived just outside the barbed wire perimeter at Auschwitz, in a convent converted from a two-storey building used by the Nazis as a storehouse for the deadly Zyklon B gas. Many Jews viewed the convent as an affront to Jewish sensibilities. In 1993, just before the fiftieth anniversary of the Warsaw ghetto uprising, Pope John Paul II ordered the nuns to move. The camp is now preserved in all its starkness and horror as a reminder to the peoples of Europe of the depths to which they have stooped and can stoop. Redemption is not cheap and maybe the heart of the new Europe must bleed still.

---

35. Wells, *How Then Shall We Live?* 48.

In similar vein, the late Gillian Rose suggested that, in recent generations, European society has consisted of what might be termed "Athens," the city of relational politics, of democracy, and what might be termed "the New Jerusalem," the city embodying the Christian ideal of love. She went on to propose that society has also been characterised by a third city, in which reality has been replaced by a siren fantasy, the illusion of individuality and imagined community:

> Athens, the city of rational politics, has been abandoned: she is said to have proven that enlightenment is domination. Her former inhabitants have set off on a pilgrimage to the New Jerusalem, the imaginary community, where they seek to dedicate themselves to difference, to otherness, to love—to a new ethics, which overcomes the fusion of knowledge and power in the old Athens. What if the pilgrims, unbeknownst to themselves, carry along in their souls the third city—the city of capitalist private property and modern legal status? The city that separates each individual into a private, autonomous, competitive person, a bounded ego, and a phantasy life of community, a life of unbounded mutuality, a life without separation and its inevitable anxieties?[36]

Rose spoke of Auschwitz as embodying this third city, a city in which we are confronted by the mess of humanity "arising out of, and falling back into, the ambitions and the tensions, the utopianism and the violence, the reason and the muddle, which is the outcome of the struggle between the politic and anti-politics of the city. This is *the third city*—the city in which we all live and with which we are too familiar."[37] We cannot bypass this city in our pilgrimage to the New Jerusalem, for "to oppose the new ethics to the old city, Jerusalem to Athens, is to succumb to loss, to refuse to mourn, to cover persisting anxiety with the violence of a new Jerusalem masquerading as love."[38] In a "fourth city," what could be termed the "new Auschwitz," the rivalries of the third city will have to be (to recall the Christian conception of remembrance) remembered and forgiven. For Europe, Auschwitz is essential in this process.

Wells speaks of the Christianity that he believes has a place in the new Europe: it can't, he says, "be claiming Constantinian dominance or cultural superiority or historical entitlement. It must prove itself by acts of mercy, peace and grace, by evident wisdom, understanding and love, by facilitating

---

36. Rose, *Mourning*, 21.

37. Ibid., 34, Rose's emphasis.

38. Ibid., 36.

education, reconciliation and healing."[39] Like Gorringe's picture of the church, Europe can be a network of local communities facing outward, each shaped by and shaping its topography, each community a home in its own right, aware that other local communities are also home, and that all communities belong to the *oikoumene* that is home to us all.

An ultimate home

It was not, ultimately, in Worcester, any more than the Somme, that Studdert Kennedy found his true home. "On two points I am certain: Christ and His Sacrament; apart from those I am not sure I am certain of anything"—so he said to his fellow-chaplain Douglas Carey after the action on the Messines Ridge in 1917 for which he was awarded the Military Cross.[40] These words express precisely where Studdert Kennedy was at home. His rootedness was in Christ, and Christ himself became present in the sacrament. This home in Christ enabled him to minister to the deprived homes of his parishes and serve the uprooted, disorientated soldiers of the trenches. It was in Christ that suffering was and is redeemed.

It was more than in the teaching, healing Christ that Studdert Kennedy found his home. For him, it was Christ in a particular place that captured his heart and attention: Christ on the cross at Calvary. It was Calvary that demonstrated most fully the intersection of the best and the worst of humanity. The divine life, lived out in human form, met the sort of violent, disruptive, horrific nature of humanity that Studdert Kennedy witnessed in his own time. The cross at Calvary was "home," in the sense that it was the point at which the best and worst experiences could be distilled and understood.

In this light, it is unsurprising that Studdert Kennedy clung to the sacrament. If Christ on the cross was the place of home, then the sacrament of the broken bread was a re-stating, a re-enacting of that place of shared memory. As Brant Pitre has convincingly argued, when Jesus said "It is finished" on the cross, he was not just referring to his life or his messianic mission, for he did not say it until his request for a drink had been answered: he only said it "when he had received the wine."[41] His vow at the Last Supper not to drink of the fruit of the vine until he drank it in the kingdom and his prayer about not "drinking the cup" in Gethsemane (a strange metaphor to use for one's death), make the meaning clear.[42] Of the four cups of the Jewish

39. Wells, *How Then Shall We Live?* 48.

40. Carey, "War Padre," 154.

41. John 19:30; Pitre, *Jesus*, 147–70.

42. Mark 14:25, 36.

Passover, he drank the final one on the cross, not in the upper room.[43] He did it at the very moment of his death.

In so doing, Jesus extended his last Passover meal to include his own suffering and death. This means that the Last Supper was not just a symbolic enactment of how he was going to die, it was a prophetic sign that actually set his passion and death in motion, a sign that was not totally complete until his life had come to an end. Further, by praying three times in Gethsemane for the cup to be taken from him, Jesus revealed that he understood his own death in terms of Passover sacrifice, for, when the final cup of the meal was drunk, his own sacrifice would be complete, and his blood would be "poured out" like that of the Passover lambs.[44] The order would be reversed—in the old Passover, the sacrifice of the lamb would come first, and then the eating of its flesh. In this case, because Jesus had to institute the new Passover before his death, he pre-enacted it, as both host and sacrifice of the meal.

Most importantly, by waiting to drink the fourth cup of the Passover until the very moment of his death, Jesus united the Last Supper to his death on the cross. By refusing to drink of the fruit of the vine until he gave up his final breath, he joined the offering of himself under the forms of bread and wine to his offering of himself on the cross. Both actions said the same thing: "this is my body, which is given for you."[45] Both were done "for the forgiveness of sins."[46] In short, by means of the Last Supper, Jesus transformed the cross into a Passover, and by means of the cross, he transformed the Last Supper into a sacrifice.

Thus, receiving the sacrament is for Christians an entering into that sacrifice and a prefiguring of our heavenly home. For Studdert Kennedy, Calvary was a place of hope and glory, as it is in John's gospel. For there the love of God is revealed in its fullness, overcoming the destruction and death of which human beings were capable, and have since been capable. By giving people the sacrament, which Christians refer to as "the bread of life," whether in Worcester or France, Studdert Kennedy was drawing them into a different place, a transfigured place, and enabling them to find a way of working out their experiences for themselves within the "home" of Christ's body.

Outside the Church of St. Paul in Worcester, there is a memorial to those of the parish who lost their lives in the First World War, which

43. At the time of Jesus, four cups of wine were used at the Passover: the cup of sanctification, the cup of proclamation, the cup of blessing (cf. 1 Corinthians 10:16), and the cup of praise, normally drunk at the conclusion of the meal.

44. Matthew 26:36–46.

45. Luke 22:19.

46. Matthew 26:28.

Studdert Kennedy, as vicar, designed and erected. It shows the figure of Christ with head not bowed but raised. Studdert Kennedy said at its dedication: "[I] could not bring [myself] to have a Calvary made where Christ looked broken and dead."[47] So in the city which Studdert Kennedy made his home, in which he integrated the pain of his experiences with the love of God, he left a tangible sign of his—and our—ultimate home, in which all suffering is transfigured into glory.

Figure 6: The "Calvary" on the First World War memorial outside
St. Paul's Church, Worcester

47. As reported in *Berrow's Worcester Journal*, 16 April 1921, 7.

4

Poets in Wartime

A Study of Geoffrey Studdert Kennedy and Geoffrey Dearmer

Peter G. Atkinson

Geoffrey Studdert Kennedy: a real poet?

THE MEMORIAL TO GEOFFREY Studdert Kennedy in Worcester Cathedral describes him as "a poet, a prophet, a passionate seeker after truth, an ardent advocate of Christian fellowship."[1] The calendar of *Common Worship* in the Church of England, which commemorates him on 8 March, describes him as "priest and poet."[2] Both statements make Studdert Kennedy's standing as a poet a distinctive mark of his legacy, and there is no doubt that the "rough rhymes," together with the cigarettes, are a central element of the story of "Woodbine Willie."

Was Geoffrey Studdert Kennedy a poet? In the foreword to his collection of poetry *Lighten Our Darkness*, he wrote: "I have always wanted to be a poet. It is the only private ambition I have ever cherished. It is never likely to be fulfilled."[3] Another collection, *Peace Rhymes*, was dedicated to "that great host of ordinary men and women who, like the author, have always

---

1. The memorial is found in St. George's Chapel.

2. *Common Worship: Services and Prayers*, 7. The calendar of the Episcopal Church (of the United States) describes him simply as "priest."

3. Studdert Kennedy, *Lighten Our Darkness*, v.

longed to be real poets, and always known that they could never be—quite."[4] The second quotation is instructive in several ways. First, despite the self-deprecation of his poetic talent, Studdert Kennedy was confident enough to address "a great host" of readers; indeed, his first volume of poetry, *Rough Rhymes of a Padre*, published in 1918, sold 30,000 copies in the first weeks of publication, and 70,000 by 1924.[5] A large readership evidently took his verse seriously; a readership much larger than that enjoyed by many poets, at least in their own lifetimes. Secondly, he recognised in this "great host" a widespread desire not only to read poetry, but to write it. The First World War generated a vast quantity of poetry. It has been estimated that in Germany in the first month of the war, up to 50,000 poems were written *every day*.[6] Poetry was written as propaganda, as protest, as subversion, as exclamation, as consolation, and as quest for meaning.[7] There was nothing extraordinary about Studdert Kennedy's wanting to express himself in verse. But, as the quotation makes clear, he wanted to be a "real" poet, a poet of distinction. And here, opinion is divided.

Figure 7: The memorial to Geoffrey Studdert Kennedy in St. George's Chapel, Worcester Cathedral

Unlike Geoffrey Dearmer, a poet whom I shall consider in the second part of this essay, Geoffrey Studdert Kennedy never made it into the

4. Studdert Kennedy, *Peace Rhymes*, 5.

5. Studdert-Kennedy, *Dog-Collar Democracy*, 56.

6. Buelens, *Everything to Nothing*, 55.

7. Gary Sheffield describes the most frequently quoted British poets of 1914–18—Wilfred Owen, Siegfried Sassoon and others—as a "small and unrepresentative group of junior officers" who only emerged after the war as voices of pacifism and protest (*Forgotten Victory*, 17–24 at 18).

anthologies of war poetry. His reputation survives mainly in English-speaking Christian circles. Two quite long poems, "High and Lifted Up" and "The Eucharist," together with an extract of prose, "The Cross Set Up in Every Slum," are included in the magisterial anthology of Anglican spiritual writings, *Love's Redeeming Work* (2001);[8] but this is where his name is re-membered, not in the classrooms of schoolchildren or students who study "war poetry." And even in Christian circles, we may ask whether his poems by themselves, apart from the story of the priest who faced the horrors of the trenches, and won the Military Cross for bravery, and shared with the troops his doubts as well as his faith, would still be remembered. They are referred to (as, for example, in *Love's Redeeming Work*) as illustrative of a more general questioning of the traditional doctrine of God's impassibility, a tendency given sharp focus by the suffering of the First World War. In this sense, Studdert Kennedy's poems may be said to have a minor place in the history of theological thought. But taken simply as poetry, no critic has come forward to claim for them a place among those whom he himself described as the "real poets." The matter might be left there, were it not for the fact that such reputation as he had was savaged by two distinguished literary critics, and most unfairly. It is worth re-visiting this episode and at least asking the question whether his poetic reputation deserves, if not rehabilitation, then at any rate some positive re-adjustment.[9]

First offensive: I. A. Richards

Ivor Armstrong Richards (1893–1979) was a founder of, and formative in-fluence upon, modern literary criticism. He taught at Cambridge, and later at Harvard. In 1929, he published *Practical Criticism: A Study of Literary Judgment*, which appears to have remained in print ever since. The main thrust of his theory of literary criticism was that a literary product—in this case, a poem—should be read as a self-contained work of art, not for any insight which it might give to the mind of the writer, or to the times in which it was written, or to any philosophy of life in which either the writer or the reader might be interested. The particular method that he adopted for teaching his students was to provide them with unseen samples of poetry, of different eras, from which he had removed all references to authorship and date. The student had to react simply to the words on the page. Richards

---

8. Rowell et al., eds., *Love's Redeeming Work*, 595–98.

9. The episode discussed here was briefly aired in Studdert-Kennedy, *Dog-Collar Democracy*, 109–11, but the matter deserves fuller discussion.

found that this produced a startling variety of responses among his students, which in turn led to illuminating discussion.[10]

Richards collected thirteen such case-studies for *Practical Criticism*, printing the selected poems, and a range of his students' responses gathered over the years, which form the first half of the book; in the second half, Richards developed his theory of "self-referential" criticism, and drew conclusions from it for the teaching of literature in schools and universities. Included in his selection were poems by Donne, Rossetti, Longfellow, Lawrence, Hardy, and Hopkins, as well as some now less familiar names—together with Geoffrey Studdert Kennedy. In order to preserve as far as possible the same laboratory conditions in the book that he imposed in the classroom, Richards only revealed the identity of the thirteen authors in an appendix.[11] Before introducing the poems, Richards explained that the experiment would uncover certain main issues of critical reading: among them, the difficulty of making out the plain sense of the text, dealing with stock emotional responses, sentimentality, and the "troublesome problem" of what he called "doctrinal adhesions."

The poem of Studdert Kennedy which Richards chose for the book was "Easter," and it is important to see the text in full:

> There was rapture of spring in the morning
> When we told our love in the wood,
> For you were the spring in my heart, dear lad,
> And I vowed that my life was good.
>
> But there's winter of war in the evening,
> And lowering clouds overhead,
> There's wailing of wind in the chimney nook,
> And I vow that my life lies dead.
>
> For the sun may shine on the meadow lands,
> And the dog-rose bloom in the lanes,
> But I've only weeds in my garden, lad,
> Wild weeds that are rank with the rains.
>
> One solace there is for me, sweet but faint,
> As it floats on the wind of the years,

10. It will be apparent that what was possible in the 1920s would be quite impossible today, when students would only have to "google" the text to discover who wrote it, and when, and what other readers had said about it.

11. Even then he printed them back-to-front so that the book has to be held up to a mirror.

A whisper that spring is the last true thing,
And that triumph is born of tears.

It comes from a garden of other days,
And an echoing voice that cries,
"Behold I am alive for evermore,
And in Me shall the dead arise."[12]

In the appendix, where he identified his thirteen authors, Richards paid tribute to Studdert Kennedy's generosity. The latter had replied to Richards's request, "You can use any of my poems for any purpose you like. The criticisms of them could not be more adverse and slaughterous than my own would be."[13] But Studdert Kennedy did not live to see the use that Richards made of them. The preface to the first edition of *Practical Criticism* is dated April 1929, a month after Studdert Kennedy's death. Had he seen Richards's book, he might have felt less conciliatory. Not only did Richards print the poem without giving the author or the title (which was part of the experiment), he also altered one line of the second stanza ("but there's winter *now* in the evening") and omitted the fifth stanza altogether. He cheerfully admitted to the alterations (in the appendix) without giving a reason, and left the readers of *Practical Criticism* no means of deciding what effect these alterations might have on the poem.

In fact, the effect on the poem is crucial. Without the reference to "war" in the second stanza, the reader misses the only clue that this is a poem about lovers in wartime. It therefore becomes a love poem in general. Indeed, Richards explicitly stated that the "subject or theme of the poem" is "*a girl bewailing her lost or absent lover*."[14] Even more serious is the omission of the final stanza. For all the readers of *Practical Criticism* can know, this is a poem which asserts that spring—any spring—is "the last true thing," and that that is sufficient consolation for any loss, "triumph born of tears."

It is Studdert Kennedy's poem that Richards used for a study in the latter part of the book of the problem of sentimentality (still without admitting the violence that his alterations had done to the poem). What perhaps *is* surprising is that among the students, a selection of whose unattributed comments Richards supplied with each poem, there were those who were favourably impressed. Indeed, it is this poem, of all the thirteen selected by Richards, which seems most to have divided his students, with comments ranging from "absolute tripe" to "this is a fine poem written with

12. Studdert Kennedy, *Unutterable Beauty*, 63–64.
13. Richards, *Practical Criticism*, 366.
14. Ibid., 263, Richards's emphasis.

deep, emotional feeling and a choice of words that is only possible for the genuine poet."[15] Studdert Kennedy might have appreciated the compliment, but not at the cost of the omitted final stanza, which he would surely have said was the point of the poem, and to which the title of the poem draws attention. He might also have been flattered to be mistaken for Housman by one of Richards's students (no doubt the word "lad" was the misleading clue). Housman, however, would not have written a poem that ended with the fifth stanza—or the fourth; nor could Studdert Kennedy have written Housman's poems of bleak despair.

It is not that the final stanza makes "Easter" a "better" poem (what makes a poem better or worse will be discussed below) but simply that it makes it a different poem from the one that Richards criticised. Studdert Kennedy's poem is not just about "a girl bewailing her lost or absent lover," nor does it suggest that springtime is consolation for any loss, which is a sentimental idea by anyone's standards. The poem is a platform from which Studdert Kennedy proclaimed the Christian doctrine of the resurrection, which, far from being a sentimental idea, is one that provides the "solace" that "floats on the wind of the years" from that "garden of other days." It is the resurrection that is indicated by each returning spring, and it is the resurrection that is the "triumph born of tears." It is the allusion to the garden of the resurrection in the final stanza that makes sense of the images of gardens, woods, and meadows in the earlier stanzas, which on their own were understandably criticised by some of Richards's readers as hackneyed. It is the fifth stanza that gives them a purpose. And in any case, the whole effect of the poem is weakened by omitting the reference to "the winter of war," which gives to the grief of the young lovers a sharply specific setting.

When Richards discussed the poem in the second half of *Practical Criticism*, he made clear that Studdert Kennedy's poem fails on the test of sentimentality. Sentimentality was an important matter for Richards, for his critical theory was based on the assumption that the purpose of poetry is to excite emotion. It must, however, he thought, be the right *sort* of emotion, and of the right quantity. "Sentimentality," for Richards, meant an *inappropriately or excessively* emotional response to the subject of the poem, on the part either of the poet or of the reader; and this is what he found in (his version of) Studdert Kennedy's poem. The purpose of the poem, he thought, is to excite a general feeling of regret. But, he went on, "most people will not find it difficult, if they so desire, to sit down by the fireside and concoct a precisely similar emotion without the assistance of any poem whatsoever—merely by saying Oh! to themselves in various tones of sadness, regret and

15. Ibid., 53–61.

tremulous hope."[16] The fault of a bad poem, such as he took Studdert Kennedy's to be, is that it merely dips into an existing supply of melancholy that any reader can summon up for themselves without making of it something new or fresh or original—which would be the mark of a good poem. And if the poem that Richards condemned were the poem that Studdert Kennedy wrote, then I should agree.

The effect of Richards's alterations is not only that we have both his and his students' criticisms of the poem that Studdert Kennedy did *not* write; we do not have their criticisms of the poem that he *did* write. We can glimpse something of what the students might have made of it in the comments made of another of Richards's selected "unseens," which turns out to be Donne's *Holy Sonnet VII*, "At the round earth's imagined corners blow."[17] It seems scarcely credible today that none of the students was able to identify the author, but the Metaphysical Poets had long been in eclipse.[18] Thus it was an unfamiliar poem, on an explicitly Christian theme, with which the students were faced. In general, they didn't like it: "I can't make out what all the shouting is about"; "mouthfuls of words . . . has no appeal whatsoever . . . too religious for one who doesn't believe in that way." Perhaps the most startling comment is from the student who thought "the lines . . . express the simple faith of a very simple man."[19] It is clear that many of the students either reacted against, or had difficulty in relating to, the Christian content of the poem. No doubt they would have reacted in the same way to Studdert Kennedy's final stanza. But it is their comments on Donne that led Richards, in the second half of *Practical Criticism*, to use the sonnet as the basis of a discussion of what he called "doctrinal adhesions."[20]

In this chapter, Richards raised the perennial question, for all readers of literature, of how far they can enjoy a work that expresses or implies a religious or philosophical outlook different from their own. He offered, obscurely, a distinction between "intellectual belief" and "emotional belief." "Intellectual belief" is what a Christian would give to Donne's sonnet (or indeed to Studdert Kennedy's "Easter"), but that, according to Richards's

---

16. Ibid., 266.

17. Donne, *Complete Poetry*, 282.

18. Donne had no entry in Palgrave's *Golden Treasury*, first published in 1861 and frequently republished. Herbert Grierson's *Metaphysical Lyrics and Poems of the Seventeenth Century* was published in 1921 (and famously reviewed by T. S. Eliot—see his *Selected Essays*, 281–91), but evidently had not yet turned the tide in favour of Donne. Sir Arthur Quiller-Couch included seven poems by Donne in his enormously influential *Oxford Book of English Verse*, but only one sonnet ("Death be not proud").

19. Richards, *Practical Criticism*, 43–46.

20. Ibid., 271–91.

theory of what a poem is for, is irrelevant. The important thing is "emotional belief," an entering into the emotion of the poem, considered for its own sake, irrespective of whether one shares the religion or the philosophy of the poet. This is an odd use of the word "belief," and it draws too sharp a distinction between an emotional and an intellectual response. There are poems—many, but not all of them, explicitly religious—in which the emotional and the intellectual responses are inseparable. How can one read the final lines of Wilfred Owen's "Dulce et Decorum Est" without being emotionally affected, but also without asking oneself: do I agree?[21] Studdert Kennedy would have wished the same to be said of the closing lines of "Easter"; but since Richards excluded those lines, we do not have his commentary on them.

Studdert Kennedy deserved better treatment at the hands of so formidable a critic. Richards's students and readers deserved the opportunity to respond to the poem he wrote, not the text that Richards adapted for his own purposes. It is, however, good to know that Richards acknowledged Studdert Kennedy's generosity, not only in the appendix to *Practical Criticism* noted above, but also before his own death fifty years later, when he said in correspondence with Geoffrey's nephew Gerald Studdert-Kennedy that he had included this note in order "to indicate my admiration and regard for his generosity of spirit."[22] Apparently, another of Richards's selected poets had threatened legal action.

Second offensive: Roy Fuller

Both I. A. Richards's critical theory and Geoffrey Studdert Kennedy's poetry were discussed by Roy Fuller, in the first series of his lectures given as professor of poetry at Oxford in the academic year 1969–70, and published as *Owls and Artificers*.[23] Fuller entitled his second lecture "Woodbine Willie lives!" but in fact the lecture is a discussion of Richards's notion of sentimentality. Nonetheless, Fuller was determined to have some fun with Studdert Kennedy along the way. He began by reading the fourth stanza (only) of "Easter," noted that he had taken it from "Richards's celebrated

21. "My friend, you would not tell with such high zest / To children ardent for some desperate glory / The old Lie: Dulce et decorum est / Pro patria mori" ("Sweet and fitting it is to die for one's country"—Quintus Horatius Flaccus [Horace], *Odes*, III, ii, 1–3). Owen's poem "Dulce et Decorum Est" is printed in many anthologies, for example, in Stallworthy, ed., *New Oxford Book of War Poetry*, 204–5.

22. Studdert-Kennedy, *Dog-Collar Democracy*, 111.

23. I went up to Oxford in 1971, and heard Roy Fuller's second series of lectures. I don't remember him mentioning Studdert Kennedy again.

book *Practical Criticism*," reminded his audience of Richards's practice of placing unattributed texts in front of students, and went on to quote the one who found it "a fine poem written with deep, emotional feeling." Fuller commented that "forty years on," we "aren't likely to say the same." No doubt there was a ripple of amusement in the lecture-hall, and no doubt more amusement when Fuller went on to say that "few or none would be greatly surprised to learn that the piece comes from a book called *More Rough Rhymes of a Padre,* by the Reverend G. A. Studdert Kennedy, 'Woodbine Willie' of the First World War."[24] Few in the audience would know anything of Studdert Kennedy, and Fuller didn't take the trouble to enlighten them further. "Rough rhymes," "padre," "reverend," "Woodbine Willie," "First World War"—any one of those phrases was sufficient to raise a laugh in an Oxford lecture-hall in 1969. Fuller quoted no more than the fourth stanza, and he didn't explain that Richards had already significantly altered the meaning of the poem. Thus, when Fuller asked rhetorically "what on earth" Studdert Kennedy's line "the wind of the years" can mean, the answer should have been, "Read the poem!" The "wind of the years" may not be a very good line, but in the context of the poem it means *something*: it refers to the message of the resurrection blowing from the Easter garden to the bereaved lover in her "winter of war."

Fuller was fulsome in his praise for Richards ("one of the great men of my time"),[25] but the real target of his second lecture was not Studdert Kennedy but Richards himself. Fuller took issue with Richards's notion of sentimentality, and, more fundamentally, with his theory that a poem should be valued "on its own terms." He agreed with the Marxist critic Alick West who wrote: "When Dr Richards wishes to preserve the emotional value of poetry by isolating it from beliefs about objective reality, he isolates it from the social reality which tests the objective truth of utterances by practice; he is destroying the possibility of any response to poetry by isolating the response from its only source."[26] West, followed by Fuller, dismissed Richards's treatment of sentimentality, because for both of them, a poem must be "about" something. From this it follows that to judge a poem as "sentimental," account must be taken of that objective "something" that is what the poem is about. Building on this, Fuller offered his own three-fold definition of sentimentality, which is diametrically opposite to Richards's definition. Fuller defined sentimentality as, first, "reactionary feeling," secondly, "anti-scientific feeling," and thirdly, "deficiency of realism." There

24. Fuller, *Owls and Artificers*, 28.

25. Ibid.

26. As quoted in ibid., 33.

is no great surprise that a Marxist-sympathising critic should take offence at these. Perhaps the surprise is that the word "sentimental" can be made to mean all those things.

At this point in the lecture, Fuller had almost lost interest in Studdert Kennedy, and he did not spell out his new definition of sentimentality in terms of Studdert Kennedy's poem, though perhaps we can guess what he would have made of it. No doubt he would have found it "reactionary" in ascribing significance to an individual love-affair, "anti-scientific" in supposing that springtime represented hope, and "deficient in realism" in finding a triumph in tears. And had he bothered to include the fifth stanza of the poem, its explicit Christianity would doubtless have proved to be "sentimental" on all counts. Despite the fact that Fuller turned Richards's definition upside-down, he still held Studdert Kennedy guilty of sentimentality. Those opening remarks—"rough rhymes," "padre," "reverend," "Woodbine Willie," "First World War"—were sufficient to condemn him, practically unheard. At the end of the lecture, Fuller did admit that he "rather regrets using Woodbine Willie as a whipping-boy," and went on to acknowledge Studdert Kennedy's generous reply to Richards.[27] The amends come too little and too late. Fuller forgot that a whipping-boy was one who was punished for an offence which he had not committed.

What is a good poet?

Geoffrey Studdert Kennedy was savaged by these two distinguished and influential critics on the basis of a single poem, shorn of its significant title, shorn of the single word which located it in a specific setting that was vital for its interpretation, and shorn of its even more significant final stanza, which conveyed the actual message of the poem. Instead, the altered text was made to bear the brunt of both critics' indictment of "sentimentality," despite their giving the word contradictory definitions. If we conclude from this that the case against Studdert Kennedy as a "real poet" is so far unproven, that he was indeed a whipping-boy, then can a more positive case be made in his defence?

My defence, such as it is, begins by questioning Studdert Kennedy's stated ambition to be a "real poet." I do not question the modesty of his conviction that he would never become one, but I do question the assumption that the placing of poets in an order of importance, or drawing a line between the "real" poets and the rest, is a useful activity or even a practicable one. I turn in support to a late book by C. S. Lewis, *An Experiment in Criticism*,

27. Ibid., 43.

published in 1961.[28] This is not one of his religious books. It is written in his capacity as a professor of English literature, and it is a trenchant counterblast to the assumptions that had dominated the teaching of literature in universities throughout his working life. Many of those assumptions can be traced to I. A. Richards, who is one of the implicit (and sometimes explicit) targets of the book. In short, Lewis had had enough of evaluative literary criticism, the tiresome and, as he saw it, entirely unproductive business of deciding whether Dickens was "good" or Milton "bad," whether Tennyson was "worse" or Kipling "better." As A. N. Wilson remarked in his biography of Lewis, this may seem to some readers now to be a statement of the obvious, but it was not obvious at the time.[29] Lewis detected among the critics whom he called the "Vigilants" a campaign to operate a virtual index of prohibited authors: "Under Vigilant criticism a new head falls every month. The list of approved authors grows absurdly small. No one is safe."[30]

Lewis also objected to the assumption (and here the target is Richards) that the purpose of literature is moral improvement, and that it should be taught with that in view. "One sad result of making English Literature a 'subject' at schools and universities is that the reading of great authors is, from early years, stamped upon the minds of . . . young people as something meritorious,"[31] and he went on to trace this out in a host of consequential assumptions about literature, such as tragedy being intrinsically more important than comedy, or farces, fantasies, fairy-tales, and adventure-stories being unworthy of "serious" readers. The main argument of the book is a glorious affirmation of the joy of reading, not for instruction, or self-im-

---

28. For those who do not know the book, a warning is necessary. As is often the case with Lewis (and I write as a very great admirer), his writing, though not necessarily his argument, is marred by incidental prejudices. When he mentions "unliterary" people, they generally turn out to be women. The extraordinary fact is that Lewis wrote *Experiment in Criticism* soon after the death of his very literate and literary wife, Joy Davidman. He published his stark chronicle of bereavement, *A Grief Observed*, in the same year. All I can say is that the central argument of *Experiment in Criticism* is fundamentally anti-elitist. Rowan Williams addresses some of Lewis's tiresome prejudices in his commentary on the Narnia stories, *Lion's World*, 33–46.

29. Wilson, *C. S. Lewis*, 289.

30. Lewis, *Experiment*, 127. His target was F. R. Leavis (1895–1978), a prominent literary critic who taught at Cambridge from 1931 to 1964. He was made a Companion of Honour in the year before his death. Wilson describes the atmosphere in the English faculty at Cambridge, dominated by Richards and Leavis, when C. S. Lewis took up his chair in medieval and renaissance literature in 1954: "whole categories of book, and the works of authors hitherto considered great (like Dickens or Milton), were dismissed as valueless. This was particularly true in the case of Dr Leavis, who had some of the fanaticism of a Savonarola or a Robespierre" (Wilson, *C. S. Lewis*, 287).

31. Lewis, *Experiment*, 10.

provement, or discovering a congenial philosophy of life, but for its own sake. Lewis did not suggest that any work of literature is as good as any other, nor that there are not many different types of enjoyment. Ultimately, he insisted, a great work of art, be it painting or music or text, requires a kind of contemplative response which is the opposite of much that passes for criticism. "The first demand any work of art makes upon us," he wrote, "is surrender. Look. Listen. Receive. Get yourself out of the way. There is no good asking first whether the work before you deserves such a surrender, for until you have surrendered you cannot possibly find out."[32] The *greatness* of a work of art, according to Lewis, is measured by the extent to which it can sustain prolonged and repeated contemplation by large numbers of people who are prepared to make that surrender. "The prima facie probability that anything that has ever been truly read and obstinately loved by any reader has some virtue in it is overwhelming."[33] Conversely, a bad work of art is one that does not admit of that enraptured and repeated surrender: "a bad book is one of which a good reading is impossible. The words in which it exists will not bear close attention, and what they communicate offers you nothing unless you are prepared either for mere thrills or for flattering day-dreams."[34]

From this it follows that professional critics are no more qualified to judge greatness in a work of art than any other enraptured reader (or listener, or viewer); indeed, Lewis suggested that readers are now "drenched, dizzied and bedevilled by criticism to a point at which primary literary experience is no longer possible."[35] It also follows that the collective judgment of greatness is necessarily provisional. "We start from the assumption that whatever has been found good by those who really truly read probably is good."[36]

It further follows from this that Lewis was vastly unperturbed by a poet whose beliefs differed from his own. In a direct allusion to Richards, he wrote: "In good reading, there ought to be no 'problem of belief.' I read Lucretius and Dante at a time when (by and large) I agreed with Lucretius. I have read them since I came (by and large) to agree with Dante. I cannot

32. Ibid., 19. Cf. Iris Murdoch's treatment of the same contemplative approach to art in *Sovereignty of Good*.

33. Lewis, *Experiment*, 111.

34. Ibid., 114.

35. Ibid., 128.

36. Ibid., 112.

find that this has much altered my experience, or at all altered my evaluation, of either."[37]

And what, for Lewis, of sentimentality, that grave offence of which Studdert Kennedy was convicted by both Richards and Fuller? Lewis took the example of Landseer's (then) popular painting, *The Old Shepherd's Chief Mourner*, depicting a faithful sheepdog grieving at the deathbed of his master, a picture that most people would agree is a masterpiece of sentimentality. "To be moved by the thought of the solitary old shepherd's death and the fidelity of his dog, is . . . not in the least a sign of inferiority. The real objection to that way of enjoying pictures is that you never get beyond yourself. The picture, so used, can call out of you only what is already there. You do not cross the frontier into that new region which the pictorial art as such has added to the world."[38] So far as this goes, it is not very different from Richards. Both agree that a great work of art is not there to be made use of, or to be a means of self-indulgence, or to engineer a congenial emotion. Both agree that great art takes a person beyond themselves. But Lewis put it better. At the end of the book, he offered his *credo* for literature: "Literary experience heals the wound, without undermining the privilege, of individuality. There are mass emotions which heal the wound; but they destroy the privilege. But in reading great literature I become a thousand . . . and yet remain myself. Like the night sky in the Greek poem, I see with a myriad eyes, but it is still I who see. Here, as in worship, in love, in moral action, and in knowing, I transcend myself; and am never more myself than when I do."[39]

It will be objected that by invoking so much literary theory to answer the simple question of whether Geoffrey Studdert Kennedy was a good poet, I have used the proverbial hammer on a nut. But the hammer (or rather two hammers) had been wielded already by Professors Richards and Fuller. The fact that the critics were themselves the object of some hammering from so formidable a counter-critic as C. S. Lewis is relevant to a fresh reading of Studdert Kennedy. So how might Studdert Kennedy's "Easter" fare in Lewis's "experiment in criticism"?

Following Lewis's criteria, the question is whether disciplined and experienced readers have found in practice that they can surrender themselves to the words of the poem with a contemplative attention; that the poem does not in their experience wear itself thin by repetition; and that by entering into the poem they have found themselves "enlarged." The tens of thousands

37. Ibid., 86.
38. Ibid., 21–22.
39. Ibid., 140–41.

of people who bought copies of *Rough Rhymes* in the immediate aftermath of the war certainly count in its favour, but the demand has not evidently been sustained. The attacks by Richards and Fuller might be blamed for that, but equally it might be thought that the added exposure that they gave the poem might also have won it some fresh admirers. It would be hard to make out a case, on Lewis's criteria, that the poem is a missing masterpiece.

If we ask why the poem has not won that larger and sustained readership, then we must consider that final stanza, the one that makes sense of the poem. Are the closing words, placed on the lips of the risen Christ, sufficient to "cross the frontier into that new region" where readers find themselves "enlarged"? I cannot but think that the end of the poem would have been more effective had it been understated. Think of the final line of George Herbert's sonnet "Redemption": "Who straight, *Your suit is granted*, said, and died";[40] or of "Prayer": "something understood";[41] or, in a different vein, the closing line of poem "XXXIX" in *More Poems* of A. E. Housman: "remembered and remain."[42]

Geoffrey Studdert Kennedy *could* achieve effective endings. I think he has one in "Woodbine Willie": "For the men to whom I owed God's peace / I put off with a cigarette."[43] The simple line "because of him" that closes each of the three verses of "Good Friday Falls on Lady Day" is also good.[44] But the one word "War!" that ends the poem "Waste" is too obvious; the reader will already have worked out what the subject of the poem is.[45] We could go on. The point, however, of considering Studdert Kennedy in the light of Lewis's "experiment in criticism" is not to rank him "good" or "bad," but to allow readers to find out for themselves whether his poems do indeed carry one across the frontier into a "new region." And though the effect may not have been sustained down the generations, at any rate thousands of people who read him during and after the war, did find a path into the "new region" of a long-forgotten Christian faith.

The last poet of the First World War

By way of both comparison and contrast, and to salute another voice, I should like to set alongside Geoffrey Studdert Kennedy another Christian

40. Herbert, *Works*, 40.

41. Ibid., 51.

42. Housman, *Collected Poems*, 200.

43. Studdert Kennedy, *Sorrows*, 1.

44. Studdert Kennedy, *Songs of Faith*, 44.

45. Studdert Kennedy, *More Rough Rhymes*, 80.

who began to write poems during the First World War. Geoffrey Dearmer was born in 1893, and lived to the magnificent age of 103. He was the eldest son of Percy Dearmer, the distinguished liturgist and hymnographer, founding editor of the *English Hymnal* and the *Oxford Book of Carols*, vicar of St. Mary's, Primrose Hill, in north London, and later canon of Westminster Abbey and professor of ecclesiastical art at King's College, London.[46] The parallels between Geoffrey Studdert Kennedy and Percy Dearmer, who were close but not exact contemporaries, are many. Both were parish priests who served as chaplains in the First World War. In Percy Dearmer's case, this was in Serbia, where his first wife Mabel served as a nurse and died of enteric fever in 1915. Both Studdert Kennedy and Percy Dearmer had acute social consciences, fired by their experience of the war. Both struggled with the challenge of communicating the Christian faith to soldiers under fire, and found themselves compelled to re-examine their own beliefs. Both believed in the "beauty of holiness" and were convinced that art could communicate Christian truth in a way that goes beyond words. Both returned home after the war, ill-at-ease with much in the Church of England, and both spent some post-war years outside the formal ministry of the church. Percy Dearmer wrote some verse: mostly hymns and translations of hymns.

Geoffrey Dearmer, on the other hand, served as a soldier, and it was as a soldier and not as a chaplain that he began writing poetry. The small quantity of verse that he published was well received in the post-war years and some appeared in various anthologies.[47] His most-quoted poem, "The Turkish Trench Dog," appeared in *Anthem for Doomed Youth*, the anthology of First World War poetry edited by Lyn MacDonald and published by the Folio Society in 2000. That was four years after his death, and seven years after the publication of *A Pilgrim's Song*, a selection to mark his hundredth birthday, both of which events revived public interest in the last surviving poet of the First World War.

Geoffrey Dearmer's wartime poetry was a personal response to the world in which he found himself. Unlike Geoffrey Studdert Kennedy, he was under no obligation to make sense either of the war, or of his Christian faith, to anyone but himself. Nonetheless, his poems did speak to others; his faith was evident and his admirers found it attractive. He struck a different note from the better-known "war poets." In his obituary of Dearmer in the *Independent*, Laurence Cotterell observed that

---

46. See Gray, *Percy Dearmer*.

47. Two poems, "Birds" and "Unseen," were published in Squire, ed., *Second Selections*, 155–58.

Dearmer saw at least as much action as Owen or Sassoon, yet his verse contains none of the inspired bitterness (amounting to sheer genius) that invested their poetry and the work of other notable contemporaries. They were long in a muddy world of war, and men could not be blamed for looking down and seeing realism in mud. Dearmer tended to look up and see the stars, as real as the bloodied mud of the battlefields swirling around his boots. His religious faith remained unwavering and he never allowed the horrors of war or the disillusionments of so-called peace to lead him into the iconoclastic (sometimes nihilistic) cynicism that beset so many minds during and after the First World War.[48]

Jon Stallworthy, poet and biographer of Wilfred Owen, who wrote the foreword to *A Pilgrim's Song*, probed further. He noted that like Wilfred Owen (Dearmer's exact contemporary) and Edmund Blunden, Dearmer identified with Keats ("under sentence of death the celebrant of life").[49] But unlike Owen and Blunden, Dearmer's poem "Keats, Before Action," insists on discovering a transcendent beauty that even battle could not quench:

> Enough—enough—let lightning whip me bare
> And leave me naked in the howling air
> My body broken here, and here, and here.
> Beauty is truth, truth beauty—that is all,
> The very all in all.[50]

In October 1915, Geoffrey Dearmer's younger brother Christopher was killed at Gallipoli, three months after their mother had died in Serbia. In the poem that he wrote in response to this, Geoffrey returned to the image of beauty again, and coupled it with that of blood:

> O beauty scarce unfurled,
> Your blood shall help to purify the world.[51]

Stallworthy commented that Siegfried Sassoon had used similar words in response to the death of his brother, also at Gallipoli, but that Sassoon and Owen would "later come to a more desolate vision, articulated in a language that rejected the old pieties," but went on to say that "one does not have to share Geoffrey Dearmer's beliefs to respect them and to recognize

---

48. 19 August 1996: http://www.independent.co.uk/news/obituaries/obituary-geoffrey-dearmer-1310563.html.

49. Dearmer, *Pilgrim's Song*, vi–viii at vi.

50. "Keats, Before Action," in ibid., 24.

51. "To Christopher, Killed, Sulva Bay, October 6th, 1915," in ibid., v.

that he speaks for many less articulate victims of the Western Front."[52] I am not, however, convinced that "your blood shall help to purify the world" is exactly one of the "old pieties." Many were grasping at similar phrases, some of which had the resonance of religion. The German poet Ernst Wilhelm Lotz, killed in 1914 at the age of twenty-four, wrote in one poem of the war "washing away the wreckage of the shattered world."[53] W. B. Yeats famously greeted the Easter Rising in Dublin in 1916 with the words, "a terrible beauty is born."[54] Such phrases were not meant to articulate an exact theological system, and it would be a mistake to assume that Geoffrey Dearmer, simply because he was a Christian, was investing his reference to blood and purification with a precise religious significance. His authentic voice is more clearly heard when he wrote of nature reclaiming the beauty of a world devastated by war. For him, the "common grass still breathed of Paradise," in the aftermath of the battle at Gommecourt.[55] For him, the "poppy-mantled meadows blow / In murdered Picardy."[56] He told how the Turkish trench dog ("an open ally of the human race") licked the face of the terrified soldier in the trench at Gallipoli.[57] These are images that in the wrong hands would fail the test of sentimentality. But as Stallworthy pointed out in a consideration of the American poets of the Vietnam era, there is a difference between what is written by poets who were "there," and those who were not.[58] Having "been there" does not guarantee a better poem (as Stallworthy said, Tennyson did not witness the charge of the Light Brigade), but some poems are the worse for the poet *not* having been there. Stallworthy criticised a poem by Robert Lowell, who never served in Vietnam,

52. Ibid., vii.

53. Ernst Wilhelm Lotz, "Aufbruch der Jugend," quoted in Buelens, *Everything to Nothing*, 87.

54. Yeats, "Easter 1916," in *Collected Poems*, 202–5 at 203 and 205. Compare also Sir Arthur Conan Doyle, who gives Sherlock Holmes this final speech in "His Last Bow": "There's an east wind coming all the same, such a wind as never blew on England yet. It will be cold and bitter, Watson, and a good many of us may wither before its blast. But it's God's own wind, nonetheless, and a cleaner, better, stronger land will lie in the sunshine when the storm has cleared" (Doyle, *Sherlock Holmes*, 1086). Conan Doyle wrote "His Last Bow" in 1916. He was passionately concerned for the welfare and morale of the British Army. In July 1915, he began a campaign to provide infantry soldiers with body armour, an idea which Lloyd George made some effort to implement in the following year. Holmes's famous last words, set retrospectively on 2 August 1914, were certainly intended to boost public morale in 1916.

55. "Gommecourt," in Dearmer, *Pilgrim's Song*, 15–19.

56. "The Somme," in ibid., 25–27 at 27.

57. "The Turkish Trench Dog," in ibid., 3.

58. Stallworthy, ed., *New Oxford Book of War Poetry*, xxxv–xl.

but whose poem purported to be a recollection of the My Lai massacre.[59] Dearmer's "Turkish Trench Dog," by contrast, is moving because the poet could give it the ring of personal authenticity. The same story, made up by a poet at home, would have been mawkish.

There are moments when Geoffrey Dearmer's Christian faith is explicit. In "The Dead Turk" (set in the Dardanelles), he reached for a Christian image with urgency and conviction. This had nothing to do with "old pieties"; it is an old image, but one treated with freshness and vigour:

> Dead, dead, and dumbly chill. He seemed to lie
> Carved from the earth, in beauty without stain.
> And suddenly
> Day turned to night, and I beheld again
> A still Centurion with eyes ablaze:
> And Calvary re-echoed with his cry—
> His cry of stark amaze.[60]

At other times, and more characteristically, Dearmer's Christian faith is implicit: implicit in his joyfulness, implicit in his belief that the returning spring has a significance and redemptive power beyond itself, implicit in his conviction that war cannot have the final word.

Poets and apologists

One of the paradoxes of Christian poetry is that the implicitly Christian poet may articulate Christian truth more effectively than the poet whose Christianity is explicit. Indeed, this is a paradox that applies to other kinds of Christian discourse as well. Geoffrey Studdert Kennedy was nothing if not an explicitly Christian poet: he entitled his first collection, *Rough Rhymes of a Padre*. He wished to be read as an army chaplain whose poetry was part of his struggle to make sense of the war; part, indeed, of his preaching. What he said in his sermons, he could say better in his poems. His poetry was no private thing, a personal struggle at odds with his official calling. By his poems, he made his personal struggle a part of his official calling, a public demonstration to the soldiers in his care that he too struggled. This gave his

---

59. Ibid., xxxvi–xxxviii. On 16 March 1968, soldiers of the US army massacred between 347 and 504 unarmed Vietnamese men, women, and children. Twenty-two soldiers were charged with criminal offences, but only a platoon commander was convicted and he served three-and-a-half years of a life sentence under house arrest. The episode provoked worldwide condemnation, and increased resistance to the Vietnam War in the United States.

60. "The Dead Turk," in Dearmer, *Pilgrim's Song*, 7; cf. Mark 15:39.

poetry its authority, but it imposed limits as well. He could speak in certain registers, but not others. If Geoffrey Studdert Kennedy lacked a certain joyfulness in temperament, a consistent note of joy in his poetry would have diminished his authority.[61] "Well, he would say that, wouldn't he?" was the response that his poetry was striving to avoid.

Geoffrey Dearmer also wrote poems to articulate his personal struggle for meaning, but he did so in a private capacity. He was not preaching; he was not an official spokesman of religion. If he discovered light even in his darkest moments, thought his brother's death was redemptive, or contemplated the timelessness of a starlit night, there was no one to say, "Well, you would say that, wouldn't you?" With the authority of a bereaved, fighting, private soldier, he was free to find his own sense of peace and joy.

The point has a wider application in the field of Christian apologetics. To return to C. S. Lewis, one of the most effective Christian apologists of his generation: his authority as an apologist was derived at least in part because he was "unofficial": his arguments were the ones that had compelled him, unwillingly, from his one-time atheism to the faith in which he came to rejoice. On the lips of an official representative of the Christian church, those arguments would have seemed predictable, and carried less weight. On the other hand, there is another sort of apologetics that can be all the more effective, precisely when it comes from an "official" source, and that is the apologetics of personal doubt and struggle. The Anglican theologian Austin Farrer compared the effect of his friend Lewis with that of his fellow-ecclesiastic, John Robinson, the bishop of Woolwich:[62]

> The Bishop of Woolwich captures the attention of his readers by showing them that he is as intellectually worried, as dissatisfied with orthodoxy, and as unable to reconcile conflicting insights as they are themselves. They are consoled to think that there is

---

61. See the discussion of his melancholy below, 89.

62. John Robinson (1919–83), a New Testament scholar, was the bishop of Woolwich from 1959 to 1969, after which he returned to academic life in Cambridge. In 1963, he published a popular book, *Honest to God*, in which he sought to bring to a wider audience the New Testament studies of Rudolf Bultmann, the systematic theology of Paul Tillich, and the speculative later writings of Dietrich Bonhoeffer. Eminent as these theologians were, Robinson's book struck an unsuspecting British public with the force of a meteor, and seemed to show that the "anything goes" mood of the 1960s had hit the Church of England. There were calls for Robinson to be tried for heresy. It created the caricature of the "unbelieving bishop," still a stock-in-trade of the conservative press. In fact, in his own academic field of New Testament studies, Robinson was decidedly conservative. He died from cancer after months of illness in which his personal faith was transcendently clear. See Brierley, "Panentheism: The Abiding Significance of *Honest to God*."

not that iron curtain between the official Church and the contemporary mind which they had supposed; they are free to hope
that Christian faith can be had on tolerable terms and without
achieving any strict coherence of ideas. Lewis's appeal was just
the opposite. Muddled minds read him, and found themselves
moving with delight in a world of clarity.

What are we to say of the two approaches? Perhaps they are
adapted to different [people], or to different times. But supposing that either is equally practicable, there is no question which
takes us further. The one opens the hope of thinking towards
belief, the other supplies an exercise in believing thought. It is
not, of course, fair to make a direct comparison between men so
differently placed: Lewis's approach is not open to Robinson. A
lay professor and one-time atheist can say to the world, "Look
and see that such a man as I am can be an orthodox Christian."
What can a prelate say? "Look and see that a struggling enquirer
can be a suffragan bishop."[63]

There is something of John Robinson about Geoffrey Studdert Kennedy, "intellectually worried, dissatisfied with orthodoxy, and unable to
reconcile conflicting insights." But he could say to the troops, "Look and
see that a struggling enquirer can be an army chaplain." And therefore there
is something of Lewis in Geoffrey Dearmer, whose readers can find themselves "moving with delight in a world of clarity." He was in the position to
say, "Look and see that a private soldier in the trenches can be a Christian."
And as Farrer pointed out, at different times and with different audiences,
each approach has its place.

The editors of *Love's Redeeming Work* remarked "how close is the connection between literature and Anglican spirituality," and Geoffrey Studdert
Kennedy, as we have seen, is one of their twentieth-century examples of
an Anglican poet, "expressing in passionate poetry the dilemma of believing in a God who permitted such appalling suffering, and found that only
in the cross was any possible answer to be found."[64] It is sad that a space
was not found in that volume for Geoffrey Dearmer as well, for as we have
seen, his was a poetry no less deeply felt, whose search for meaning amid
the meaninglessness of slaughter found a voice which has won the respect
of believers and unbelievers alike. Good poetry, as we have seen, should
not deter readers whose beliefs differ from those of the poet. Good poetry,

---

63. Farrer, "Christian Apologist," 29–30. Austin Farrer (1904–68) was a priest,
preacher, philosophical theologian and New Testament scholar, chaplain of Trinity
College, and later warden of Keble College, Oxford.

64. Rowell et al., eds., *Love's Redeeming Work*, 374.

written from whatever faith or lack of faith, enlarges the mind and enriches the imagination of the attentive reader. Good poetry written in wartime will outlive that specific historic moment and speak to readers in different times and places of the tragedy of human suffering and needless death. And good *Christian* poetry written in wartime offers the opportunity to reflect in depth on the only place where "any possible answer" is to be found.

5

"There Ain't No Throne"
Geoffrey Studdert Kennedy
and the Doctrine of God

Michael W. Brierley

If the Christian religion means anything, it means that God
is Suffering Love.[1]

OVER THE COURSE OF the last eighty-five years, the life of Geoffrey Studdert
Kennedy has been the subject of a number of studies. Some have considered
his poetry.[2] Others have examined his politics.[3] Still others have explored
his work for its insights into evangelism, prayer, or preaching.[4] Most of all,
his writings have been mined for what they have to say about the nature and

---

1. Studdert Kennedy, *Hardest Part*, 44.

2. See Mursell, *Out of the Deep*, 143–57, and the essay by Peter Atkinson in this
volume and the studies cited therein.

3. See Studdert-Kennedy, "'Woodbine Willie,'" and the essay by Mark Dorsett in
this volume.

4. On evangelism, see Strachan, "Studdert Kennedy"; on prayer, Sinclair, *When
We Pray*; and on preaching, Jeffs, *Princes*, 152–68, Davies, *Varieties*, 107–15 (cf. Davies,
Worship and Theology, 237–44), Bell, "Patriotism and Sacrifice," and the essay by Geor-
gina Byrne in this volume.

character of God.[5] Those who have undertaken such excavation have often come to regard Studdert Kennedy's theological doctrine as the jewel in the crown of his contribution to the contemporary church. This is because they have discovered in his work a "new vision" of God.[6] As the concept, model, or image of God that people hold lies at the heart of theology and faith, so the "new vision" proffered by Studdert Kennedy's thought has accordingly exercised a profound effect on those who have engaged with his writings.

This essay seeks to do three things. First, it outlines the understanding of God that was proposed by Studdert Kennedy. Secondly, it analyses this account, and endeavours to establish precisely that which was "new" in it. Thirdly, it develops his doctrine, by taking the biblical motif within his writing about God as a shepherd ever seeking the lost (encapsulating the characteristics of the divine that Studdert Kennedy held to be fundamental), and combining it with an image that he himself embodied in his ministry as a chaplain on the front line, in order to produce an image of God—God as eternal rescuer of the wounded—that symbolises the "new vision" that Studdert Kennedy offered, and which thereby may enable that same "new vision" to be of fresh help to people of faith today.

The doctrine of God in the writings of Studdert Kennedy

When Studdert Kennedy first began to write for a public audience, the notion of God preoccupied him. His three earliest prose publications—an essay for the edited collection *The Church in the Furnace* (1917), *Rough Talks by a Padre* (1918), and *The Hardest Part* (1918)—all venture to communicate a different model of God from the one hitherto received.[7] The prompt for writing them was theodicy, that is to say, the question of how to reconcile suffering with the inherited conception of God. The question was given "terrible urgency" by experiences of the First World War.[8] "A million mothers sitting weeping all alone" and "a host of English maidens making pictures in the fire, / While a host of broken bodies quiver still on German

---

5. See, for example, Vines, "Theological Struggle"; Walker, "Pastoral Theology"; Ellis, "Geoffrey Studdert Kennedy"; Bell, "Theology"; and Slocum, "Geoffrey Studdert Kennedy."

6. Matthews, "Studdert Kennedy," 317; Sinclair, *When We Pray*, 25.

7. Studdert Kennedy's other publication that focused on doctrine was *Food for the Fed-up*, consisting of reflections on the creed.

8. Purcell, *Woodbine Willie*, 31.

wire" came between the old, unhelpful doctrine of God and a more constructive alternative.[9]

Why didn't God stop the war? That, claimed Studdert Kennedy, "is the big question that, deep down within him, every man is asking."[10] The perception was that Christianity and the war contradicted one another.[11] In his essay for *The Church in the Furnace*, he suggested that, for the soldier, "the Front is one vast contradiction": "I believe in God the Father Almighty, and a trench mortar has just blown my pal, who was a good-living lad, to pieces, and God is Love, and they crucified the sergeant-major, and peace on the earth, good will towards man, and I stuck my bayonet through his belly . . . Christ, there's the —— tea up; where's my —— dixie?"[12] This incompatibility between war and faith could be provoked by particular occasions. For example, shortly after coming across the body of an innocent-looking German in June 1917, Studdert Kennedy asked, "How can a man believe in an absolute Almighty God?"[13] The war seemed "to scupper all one's ancient understandings."[14] "Here is the case in a nutshell. Does God will War?"[15]

It is the problem of evil in classic form: if God is both almighty and good, then he would "put a stop to this whole beastly business";[16] but, since the whole beastly business continues, then God is either non-existent, or not almighty, or not good. If God was indeed almighty, then his goodness would be compromised: "If this word 'Almighty' means that the Father could have made this world, and obtained the results He desires, in a thousand other ways, but that He deliberately chose this, that makes my gorge rise. Why in thunder choose this one? It is disreputable if He could have done it otherwise, without this cruelty and wrong. It is not commonly respectable. . . . I cannot get up any reverence for such a being."[17] Indeed, Studdert Kennedy

9. Quite literally came between, in Studdert Kennedy's poem "High and Lifted Up": see *Peace Rhymes*, 80–87 at 83. The poem thus implied that such scenes accounted for the move from an old doctrine of God to a new one.

10. Studdert Kennedy, *Rough Talks*, 210.

11. Ibid., 208.

12. Studdert Kennedy, "Religious Difficulties," 379. The crucifixion of a sergeant-major was an alleged German atrocity: see Fussell, *Great War*, 117–20.

13. Studdert Kennedy, *Hardest Part*, 11.

14. Ibid., 8.

15. Studdert Kennedy, *Lies!* 5.

16. Studdert Kennedy, *Rough Talks*, 210.

17. Studdert Kennedy, *Food*, 54. Thus (55), the way in which God has created the world can have been the only way: God was constrained to create this way.

could put this in characteristically robust language: "I cannot and will not worship Him. I hate Him."[18]

Studdert Kennedy was keen to state that the problem of evil is insoluble:[19] it is not susceptible to rational solution, for then evil would be rational, something "of order"; whereas for Studdert Kennedy, evil was irrational, not part of God's creative activity, which brings order or reason out of chaos.[20] Yet at the same time, Studdert Kennedy did not wish to use the "mystery" of God as an excuse for not taking thought as far as it could be taken. One of his poems amounted to a scathing attack on the suggestion that God was inscrutable, and that therefore suffering was something that people just had to put up with.[21] The dilemma of sacrificing God's existence, almightiness, or goodness had to be faced. Given this dilemma, and "the inner ruminations of an incurably religious man under battle conditions,"[22] Studdert Kennedy felt that the "almightiness" of God was the weakest link, the aspect of divinity that needed to be qualified or re-interpreted. "There is one main idea in [The Hardest Part:] . . . We must make clear to ourselves and to the world what we mean when we say 'I believe in God the Father Almighty.'"[23] "I don't believe there is an absolute Almighty Ruler. I don't see how any one can believe it."[24]

The common conception of almightiness was God's ability to do anything that God chose. Studdert Kennedy reacted strongly against this. He called the unmoved God "a fiend of Hell infernal."[25] People, he said,

> have at the back of their minds the ancient misconception of an absolutely almighty being who can do anything he chooses. They think that just as God spoke the word and the stars came out, spoke yet again and the flowers grew, waved His wand and made a universe, as Cinderella's Fairy Godmother made coaches out of pumpkins, so this Almighty God has nothing else to do but touch men's lips and from their mouths perfect truth in perfect words will flow like golden rivers. That idea is as impossible

18. Studdert Kennedy, Hardest Part, 36–37.

19. See, for example, the preface to the second edition of Hardest Part (1925), ix.

20. Cf. John 1:1–3. Studdert Kennedy seems, with Augustine, to have regarded evil as privative: see Wicket Gate, 136, and Word and the Work, 37.

21. See "A Sermon," in Studdert Kennedy, More Rough Rhymes, 32–37.

22. Studdert Kennedy, Hardest Part, 189.

23. Ibid., 190.

24. Ibid., 12.

25. Studdert Kennedy, Rough Rhymes, 60.

and absurd with regard to the Bible as it is with regard to the universe.[26]

Studdert Kennedy found at least three problems with this sort of conception. First, he did not regard there to be any evidence at all that God had or exercised power of this kind; that is to say, he held it to be metaphysically unsubstantiated.[27] Secondly, he thought that a God who controls everything induced a kind of religious and political paralysis: "Christianity became static instead of dynamic, because it taught men to worship a passive and submissive Christ, bowing to the will of an incomprehensible God."[28] A "tyrant God" freezes people into subservience, and reinforces earthly despotism.[29] "It has led to the easy tolerance by Christian people of social wrongs," causing an "orthodox infidelity," as church people sacrificed their moral standards to their religion.[30] Thirdly, moreover, "it has led to the abandonment of religion by many noble souls who sacrificed their religion to their moral standards."[31] That is to say, a "false conception of God" keeps people from the church, because it is inferior to their own morals:[32] it is missiologically disastrous. "We can no longer interpret ultimate reality in the terms of absolute monarchy if we are to reach the heart of [people]."[33] In summary: "So comes about the awful state of things that God's foes are often those of His own household—narrow-minded, ignorant, conventional Christians— while His firmest friends are too often found among [people] outside the pale who do not call upon His Name."[34] Part of the barrier between the church and people at large "can be removed if the barricade of false conceptions and old outworn ideas could be broken down."[35]

The root cause of the difficulty was the worldly notion of power, which humanity had projected onto God. "To the making of gods there is no end;

---

26. Studdert Kennedy, *Lies!* 174.

27. Studdert Kennedy, *Rough Talks*, 211; cf. *Hardest Part*, 41–42, *Lies!* 149 and 195, *Food*, 57, and *Warrior*, 228.

28. Studdert Kennedy, *Hardest Part*, 157.

29. Cf. Studdert Kennedy, *Food*, 36. For the effect which the doctrine of God and political systems have on each other, see Nicholls, *Deity and Domination*, and cf. Davies, "Divine Kenosis."

30. Studdert Kennedy, *Hardest Part*, 198; *Food*, 66.

31. Studdert Kennedy, *Hardest Part*, 198.

32. Studdert Kennedy, *Food*, 91. On the moral repugnance of the monarchical God, see 85–88; cf. *More Rough Rhymes*, 67.

33. Studdert Kennedy, *Hardest Part*, 97.

34. Ibid., 88.

35. Studdert Kennedy, *Food*, 93.

and most of them are devils."[36] Studdert Kennedy regarded absolute power as an "easy omnipotence."[37] People longed for it, and in their desire, made God in their own (flawed) image, rather than the other way round.[38] "Our ideas of perfection are wrong. They are not the ideas that God has revealed to us, but our own," writ large.[39] The God whom we worship "is an infinite extension of ourselves—a God Who is what we would be if we could have our way—and so we make Him an absolute Monarch."[40]

The clearest way of tracing and illustrating this projection was in terms of the imagery used by Christian faith. Christian faith, indeed Scripture, envisaged God as decked in the trappings of earthly kingship. Christ, according to the creed, "ascended into heaven, and sitteth on the right hand of the Father." Stained-glass windows depict him with crown, orb, and sceptre. Christianity had turned God into a passionless potentate.[41] Studdert Kennedy's critique, in a poem about judgment day which opened his collection *Rough Rhymes*, was short, sweet, and devastating: "There ain't no throne."[42] It was one of the lies that had to be dismantled. "It's a wrong idea of God. It's a lie—an idol."[43] In his *Rough Talks*, he said, "I can neither respect nor worship this Heavenly King who sits upon a throne up in the skies, with Christ at His right hand, and calmly contemplates this world as it is. . . . I can't respect Him because He does nothing."[44] A similar sentiment was expressed in poetry: "I hate the God of Power on His hellish heavenly throne, / Looking down on rape and murder, hearing little children moan."[45] *The Hardest Part* contained what was perhaps his bluntest statement: "I want to kill the Almighty God, and tear Him from His throne."[46]

---

36. Studdert Kennedy, *Wicket Gate*, 133.

37. Ibid., 48; cf. *Warrior*, 229.

38. Cf. Genesis 1:26–27.

39. Studdert Kennedy, *Food*, 58.

40. Studdert Kennedy, *Word and the Work*, 79; cf. 78. Cf. also *Peace Rhymes*, 85: "All that showy pomp of splendour, all that sheen of angel wings, / Was but borrowed from the baubles that surround our earthly kings. . . . / But the word that Thou hast spoken borrows nought from Kings and thrones, / Vain to rack a royal palace for the echo of Thy tones."

41. Or, to use another of Studdert Kennedy's phrases, a "glorified policeman" (2nd ed. of *Hardest Part* [1925], ix).

42. Studdert Kennedy, *Rough Rhymes*, 16; cf. *Food*, 286.

43. Studdert Kennedy, *Lies!* 205. Cf. *Rough Talks*, 245, and *Peace Rhymes*, 81: "God, I hate this splendid vision—all its splendour is a lie."

44. Studdert Kennedy, *Rough Talks*, 244.

45. Studdert Kennedy, *Peace Rhymes*, 83.

46. Studdert Kennedy, *Hardest Part*, 40–41.

Indeed, to Studdert Kennedy's satisfaction, the enthroned figure seemed to be being deposed by the war, both literally and spiritually: "We are witnessing the passing of the monarch absolute from the world in a flood of blood and tears, and all the metaphors supplied from absolute monarchy must pass too."[47] He was, perhaps, being optimistic: "Never again, I believe, will men bow down and worship this majestic tyrant who sits upon a throne and wields as weapons pestilence, disease, and war. Such a vision of God rouses in the best of men, not reverence, but revolt; not loyalty, but contempt; not love, but bitter hatred."[48] The de-throning of this idol was of paramount importance for the survival of the church. If the church persisted with the distorted image of God, if it continued to "Caesarise the Christ," then it would die.[49] "Omnipotence absolute and unlimited" required "repeated and constant denial."[50] To the charge that this God of absolute power was not what classical theology had necessarily taught, Studdert Kennedy could respond with the telling criticism that this was nonetheless the model that it had imparted and that had been popularly received; and yet from which people, at their deepest level, recoil.[51]

Again, it was the "problem of power" that was at the very heart of the trouble. "We have not grasped God's Truth revealed in Christ, because our idea of power is essentially wrong": humanity has a "chronic disposition to confuse Power with Force."[52] Studdert Kennedy told retreatants, "God is unarmed, harmless, and men have never been able to grasp that truth. . . . We shall not disarm men, until we disarm God in our thoughts."[53] The vision of God in Christ "is obscured by that other vision which we set up beside it, the vision of the regnant God upon a throne, calm, serene, and passionless, ruling the world with a wave of the hand."[54] The orbed and sceptred God was, for Studdert Kennedy, disarmed by Christ, who applies the principles of the Magnificat to God himself: it is not so much God who puts down the mighty from their seat, as Jesus who puts down the mighty God from his

47. Studdert Kennedy, "Religious Difficulties," 390; cf. *Hardest Part*, 90.

48. Studdert Kennedy, *Hardest Part*, 91.

49. Ibid., 159, 155, and 92.

50. Ibid., 194–95 and 190. Alas, this task was compromised, not least by the liturgy: "the shadow of those old beliefs . . . lies over the liturgies and forms of service that I am obliged to use . . . and I have to spend so much of my time explaining that the words of the Prayer Book do not mean what they say, but something different" (Studdert Kennedy, *Food*, 225–26).

51. Studdert Kennedy, *Hardest Part*, 195 and 193; cf. Moore Ede in his preface, x.

52. Studdert Kennedy, *Food*, 60 and 58.

53. Studdert Kennedy, *New Man*, 44–45.

54. Studdert Kennedy, *Hardest Part*, 147.

seat, and the church must beware of rearming one whom Christ has dis-armed.[55] "The doom of all Kaisers, Czars, snobs, and autocrats is recognised as inevitable, and with them must go the old God. The Sultan of the universe has been slain."[56] One of Studdert Kennedy's earliest formative experiences in the war was in February or March 1916, before he had been to the Front, when he encountered an officer in hospital, who asked him what God was like—a question that *The Hardest Part* was effectively written to answer. "All my experience has grouped itself round and hinged itself upon the answer to this question . . . because it appears to me to be the only question that ultimately and really matters."[57] In reply to the officer, Studdert Kennedy pointed to a crucifix on the wall, and suggested that God was Christlike; his theology is essentially an exposition of the effect of the cross on the doc-trine of God.[58] Studdert Kennedy could very easily have written, "God is Christlike and in him is no un-Christlikeness at all," while Michael Ramsey actually takes the credit for doing so.[59]

The *Rough Talks* contain a section that discerns the activity of God in three areas: nature (or science), history, and Scripture.[60] Studdert Kennedy expanded this in *The Hardest Part*, each area being treated in a separate chapter.[61] The argument was that in both nature and history, a spirit of good-ness could be seen, striving and struggling for beauty and wholeness; and that Christ revealed this world process in a concentrated way. "As one reads the story of science and the struggle of nature towards perfection, one sees staring up . . . the face of Christ patient, pain-pierced and powerful."[62] There is thus a consonance between Christ and the natural creative process. "One sees in Christ the Revelation of suffering, striving, tortured, but triumphant Love which Nature itself would lead us to expect."[63] More than consonance,

---

55. Cf. Luke 1:52; Studdert Kennedy, *Warrior*, 231 and 281; *New Man*, 83; and *Word and the Work*, 79–80, where Studdert Kennedy suggested that humanity enthrones and enrobes Christ, makes him a "super-super-Napoleon," because it cannot accept the message that Christ forsakes such garb: "it is not Christ that changes His glory but we that must change ours" (79).

56. Studdert Kennedy, *Lies!* 211.

57. Studdert Kennedy, *Hardest Part*, xi and xvi; cf. *Rough Talks*, 129–30.

58. Cf. Studdert Kennedy, *Rough Talks*, 219, 232–34, and 245; *Rough Rhymes*, 60; and *Lies!* 196.

59. Ramsey, *God, Christ and the World*, 98.

60. Studdert Kennedy, *Rough Talks*, 213–34.

61. Studdert Kennedy, *Hardest Part*, 15–72. The areas were treated again in *Lies!* 137–97.

62. Studdert Kennedy, "Religious Difficulties," 382–83.

63. Studdert Kennedy, *Hardest Part*, 28.

then: Christ *reveals* the struggle that is at the heart of nature and history. "The life and death of Christ are the epoch-making events in that great story of Divine patience and pain, and in the light of the Cross all history becomes luminous. In the Cross God gathers up all history into a moment of time, and shows to us the meaning of it. It is the act in time which reveals to us the eternal activity of suffering and redeeming love all down the ages."[64] And what Christ reveals, the eternal activity that Christ shows, above all on the cross, is not being-in-control, but operating-under-limitations. Christ is not able to do anything he chooses; his power, rather, is the power of service, and this is none other than the power of love. "Force is weakness, and only Love is power."[65] People seem willing to respect love as long as there is force behind it, but that is a denial of the cross.[66] The divine power is not compulsion, but persuasion. "That is the very essence of the Christian Truth, and it is because we have failed to grasp it that we crave for a God with what we call 'absolute power,' Who is Master in His own universe, and are too blind to see that the foolishness of God is wiser than men, and the weakness of God is stronger than men."[67] This, ultimately, is the vision that people find attractive. "The only thing we can respect, and remain self-respecting, is loving service. . . . [People] do not, and will not, believe in the monarch on the throne; they do, and will, believe in the Servant on the Cross."[68]

This, then, was Studdert Kennedy's "master-theme."[69] Christ's suffering love shows the suffering God at the heart of the universe. The revelation of God in Christ "finally tears the Almighty God armed with pestilence and disease from His throne, and reveals the patient, suffering God of love Who endures an agony unutterable in the labour of creation, but endures on still for love's sake to the end. It is the final truth, but it was miles beyond the world of His day, and it is miles beyond us still. . . . The furnace of this world war is burning out the dross of dead conventions from the Christian creed, and showing up the pure gold of the Cross."[70] The revelation by Christ of the nature of God thus answers the problem of theodicy as far as it can be

---

64. Ibid., 61–62.

65. Studdert Kennedy, *Wicket Gate*, 86; cf. *Rough Rhymes*, 51, *Food*, 63, and *New Man*, 107.

66. Studdert Kennedy, *Food*, 59.

67. Ibid., 63.

68. Studdert Kennedy, *Hardest Part*, 95–96; cf. 94, and *Lies!* 193 and 211.

69. Purcell, *Woodbine Willie*, 222.

70. Studdert Kennedy, *Hardest Part*, 69–71.

answered.[71] God doesn't stop the war, "because He can't."[72] God does not will the war, just as God did not will the cross.[73] God operates under limitations, limited by the world's response to divine love.[74]

> So, at last, the great suffering, striving God of service and of love is coming to His own, and as He comes into His own, so the High and Mighty Potentate, King of kings and Lord of lords, Almighty God, powerful, passionless, and serene, is being deposed from His throne in [people's] hearts . . . and in His place there standeth one amongst us Whom we knew not, with bloody brow and pierced hands, majestic in His nakedness, superb in His simplicity, the King Whose crown is a crown of thorns. He is God.[75]

Little wonder, then, that readers have found in Studdert Kennedy a new vision of God. "Two utterly incompatible visions of God" are at stake.[76] "I don't know or love the Almighty potentate—my only real God is the suffering Father revealed in the sorrow of Christ."[77] And it was to the worship of that God that Studdert Kennedy wanted to win the world.[78]

God "endur[ing] on . . . for love's sake to the end": herein lies the final point to be made in this explication of Studdert Kennedy's doctrine of God, namely, the answer to the question, "What do you mean by 'Almighty' then?"[79] Is God almighty at all? As has been seen, the power of Love is not the power to do anything it wishes; the power of Love is, rather, the power to persist until it wins a loving response.[80] The power resides in this persistence; and thus almightiness is reconceived in terms of infinite patience. God "is strong enough and patient enough to overcome all obstacles, solve all problems, and endure all pain, and prove Himself Almighty in the end."[81]

71. Ibid., 34–35.

72. Studdert Kennedy, *Rough Talks*, 210.

73. Studdert Kennedy, *Hardest Part*, 44 (cf. "Religious Difficulties," 387) and 107 (cf. 156, and *Wicket Gate*, 213).

74. Studdert Kennedy, *Lies!* 153.

75. Studdert Kennedy, *Hardest Part*, 95; cf. *Lies!* 196–97.

76. Studdert Kennedy, *Hardest Part*, 41.

77. Ibid., 10.

78. Ibid., 41.

79. Studdert Kennedy, *Rough Talks*, 211.

80. Studdert Kennedy, "Religious Difficulties," 382.

81. Studdert Kennedy, *Rough Talks*, 212; cf. 213, *Hardest Part*, 28 and 154, and *Lies!* 201. The resurrection is the "promise" and "guarantee" of this triumph: Studdert Kennedy, *Food*, 26–27, and *Hardest Part*, 89–90 and 200–201; cf. "Religious Difficulties," 382.

God's power is the power, to use a phrase from H. G. Wells's novel of 1916, to "see it through."[82] The persistence of God provided Studdert Kennedy with confidence that love will win, that the agony will issue in victory; it enabled him to talk, almost like a mantra, of God not only suffering, struggling and striving, but also unbeaten, insuperable, and unconquerable.[83] "I see [the Spirit] thwarted, hindered, baffled in its task, but never stayed or stopped; always it begins again, always it persists."[84] The reconception of divine omnipotence in terms of what might be called the endurance or persistence of God is one of Studdert Kennedy's most significant and original doctrinal points.

An evaluation of Studdert Kennedy's doctrine of God

The idea that God suffers ("passibility") was not new to Studdert Kennedy; it had been occurring in British theology since the latter part of the nineteenth century, and in German theology before then.[85] But Studdert Kennedy's popular style meant that of all the early British passibilists, he gave the doctrine new exposure and new strength, rendering it a "new vision" to those (then or since) who had not encountered it before. While Stuart Bell has claimed that Studdert Kennedy's passibilism was of limited influence in inter-war theology[86]—a claim that needs more research, as the inter-war surveys of the doctrine pay tribute to Studdert Kennedy's contribution[87]—Studdert Kennedy's views receive repeated attention in

82. Wells, *Mr. Britling Sees It Through.* Cf. Studdert Kennedy, *Rough Rhymes,* 34–35: "the only God that a true man trusts / Is the God that sees it through" (35). H. G. Wells, during his brief, wartime theistic phase, had advocated a doctrine of the "finite God," a more exaggerated version of the limited God (see further, Brierley, "Panentheist Revolution," 8, n. 27). Studdert Kennedy saw the similarities of his thought to that of Wells, but could also see how Wells left God too excoriated ("Religious Difficulties," 380–81 and 384).

83. See, for example, Studdert Kennedy, "Religious Difficulties," 385–86, and *Hardest Part,* 28, 42–43, 69, 71, and 160.

84. Studdert Kennedy, *Lies!* 151; cf. *Rough Talks,* 219.

85. See Brierley, "Introducing the Early British Passibilists," and "Panentheist Revolution," 43–80.

86. Bell, "Theology," 96–97 and 110, and Bell, "Faith in Conflict," 26, 214–15, and 308. Cf. Bell, "Patriotism and Sacrifice," 197 and 206.

87. See Mozley, *Impassibility of God,* 157–59, and Horton, *Contemporary English Theology,* 50–56. For surveys after the Second World War, see Mozley, *Some Tendencies,* 52, Ramsey, *Gore to Temple,* 58, House, "Barrier," 409–10, and Bauckham, "'Only the Suffering God," 9.

contemporary theological literature.[88] The veteran commentator on English church life, David Edwards, wrote that Studdert Kennedy did "more than any other Englishman to teach . . . God's suffering love."[89] Indeed, Jürgen Moltmann likened *The Hardest Part* to Barth's "bombshell" commentary on the letter to the Romans, which was published within six months of *The Hardest Part*: "in fact it deserved even greater attention than Barth's book, for the theology of the suffering God is more important than the theology of the God Who is 'Wholly Other.'"[90] Moltmann studied *The Hardest Part* alongside Clarence Rolt's *The World's Redemption*, and the parallels between the two books are striking.[91] Where Rolt wrote, "Love is, in fact, the only real power, and force is not power at all," Studdert Kennedy wrote, "There is, and can be, only one Power, and that is Love. For that purpose force is not power, it is weakness."[92] Where Rolt wrote, "God *is* Love, and this Love is itself His Power," Studdert Kennedy wrote, "God is Love, and all power belongs to Love."[93] There is no evidence that Studdert Kennedy read Rolt— ironically, between Studdert Kennedy's ordination in 1908 and Rolt's death a decade later, Studdert Kennedy was out of the diocese of Worcester, in Leeds, for precisely the same two years (1912–14) that Rolt was in the diocese of Worcester—but the extraordinary similarities in their reconceptions of divine omnipotence make one wonder.

If Studdert Kennedy was an advocate of passibilism for a popular audience, it can be argued that he exercised a similar, implicit role for modernism. He was too much of an independent thinker to have been a member of the Modern Churchmen's Union, but he was quite ready and willing to expose "false teaching in the past" and re-interpret the Christian faith,[94] and it is interesting to note his proximity to modernist thinkers at each stage of his life to 1918: when he was at Leeds Grammar School, he was taught by Cyril Norwood, later president of the Modern Churchmen's Union;[95] when at Ripon Clergy College, he was taught by the emerging arch-modernist

88. In addition to the studies cited in n. 5 above, see Woollcombe, "'Fiery Glow'" (cf. Woollcombe, "Pain of God"), Goldsborough, *Where Is God*, Williams, "Sermon," Brant, *Running*, and Paul, *Evil*.

89. Edwards, "'Woodbine Willie,'" 11; cf. Wilkinson, "Searching," 14.

90. Moltmann, *Trinity*, 35.

91. Ibid., 31–34. For Rolt, see Brierley, "Panentheist Revolution," 61–71.

92. Rolt, *World's Redemption*, 15; Studdert Kennedy, *Food*, 60 (cf. *Lies!* 193).

93. Rolt, *World's Redemption*, 16 (Rolt's emphasis); Studdert Kennedy, *Food*, 65.

94. Studdert Kennedy, *Hardest Part*, 44. See, for example, 82–84, and *Lies!* 116–36; cf. *Food*, 199.

95. Mozley, "Home Life," 29. For Norwood, see Brierley, "Ripon Hall," 141, n. 328, and his entry in the *ODNB*.

Henry Major;[96] while at Rugby (1908–12), he would have come across the headmaster of Rugby School, Albert David, whose sermon of 1911 on "a suffering God," "a new idea of God" in place of "an inadequate, a worn-out conception of God," was included in the first volume of the *Modern Churchman*;[97] and at Worcester he knew the formidable progressive partnership at the cathedral of Moore Ede and James Wilson.[98] In the 1920s, Studdert Kennedy told one of his contemporaries at Ripon, Woodman Dowding, that "the thought of which his life and services were expressions, and of which his books are illustrations, was in the first instance derived from Dr. Major's lectures on the Philosophy of Religion."[99] Indeed, in a review of the 1929 memoir of Studdert Kennedy, Dowding called Studdert Kennedy "the greatest of popular expounders of Modernism."[100]

In some respects, Studdert Kennedy's thought was ahead of its time. His claim that "the doctrine of the sovereign Kaiser-God . . . is dead, as dead as cold mutton,"[101] could be said to pre-figure the essence of the "death of God" movement of the 1960s.[102] His emphasis on the Christlikeness of God anticipates that theme in the work of John V. Taylor.[103] His insistence that God be seen in terms of a creative "process" preceded the movement

96. For Major, see above, 21, n. 15. Around the same time, Studdert Kennedy was also attracted to R. J. Campbell's *New Theology* (Mozley, "Home Life," 50; cf. Brierley, "Panentheist Revolution," 8, n. 24, and 126).

97. See David, "Loving God?" 522–23; cf. Stephenson, *Rise and Decline*, 103. Albert Augustus David (1867–1950) was headmaster of Clifton (1905–9), headmaster of Rugby (1909–21), bishop of St. Edmundsbury (1921–23), and bishop of Liverpool (1923–44); see further, the entry by Matthew Grimley in the *ODNB*. For the first volume of the *Modern Churchman*, see Brierley, "Panentheist Revolution," 128–29, and Pearson, "Henry Major."

98. For Moore Ede, see above, 26, n. 44. For James Maurice Wilson (1836–1931), see his *Autobiography*; Beeson, *Canons*, 68–81; and his entry in the *ODNB*. A mathematician and liberal theologian of some standing (Stephenson, *Rise and Decline*, 64), Wilson was headmaster of Clifton (1879–90) and archdeacon of Manchester (1890–1905). He became a residentiary canon of Worcester at the age of sixty-eight, and retired in 1926 at the age of eighty-nine.

99. Mozley, "Home Life," 53. For Major's recollection of Studdert Kennedy as a student, see Pearson et al., *Scholarship*, 157: "he struck me then as a man resolved to get at the truth and to preach it, and he possessed a power of pungent repartee."

100. Dowding, Review of G. A. *Studdert Kennedy*, 668. For Studdert Kennedy's concern for the popular rather than the academic side of theological debate, see his *Wicket Gate*, 25–30.

101. See the preface to the second edition of *Hardest Part* (1925), viii.

102. See Brierley, "Panentheist Revolution," 422.

103. Taylor, *Christlike God*; cf. Woollcombe, "'Fiery Glow,'" 10.

known as process theology[104]—Studdert Kennedy was influenced by Henri Bergson,[105] and approved of what he read in the 1920s of Alfred North Whitehead.[106] It would be claiming too much to say that Studdert Kennedy's work articulates a developed panentheism; but it would be true, and would also explain his affinities with both modernism and process thought, to say that his work displays incipient panentheistic tendencies.[107]

He was also an unusually "sensual" theologian, in the sense that he was highly aware of the human body (including physical/sexual attraction),[108] seeing at first-hand what war (and slums) did to bodies;[109] and he had a rare (at that time) theological eye for the perspective of women, for example, the mothers of those who were fighting at the Front.[110] The two concerns came together in a remarkable poem that takes its title from Mary Magdalene's words at the empty tomb, "They have taken away my Lord, and I know not where they have laid him," referring to those missing in action, and the pain of not having a body to bury and a grave to visit.[111] Studdert Kennedy appreciated the depth of connection between mothers and children, and the acuteness of the pain of those who have given birth to those whose bodies rotted unburied. Another poem suggests that for that very reason, mothers might take comfort in the "broken body" of the sacrament.[112] His thoughts on gender, which came together in the last book that he himself published, *The Warrior, the Woman and the Christ*, have in no way stood the test of

104. Studdert Kennedy, *Food*, 33–36, where, unhelpfully, he used the term "progress" more than "process" (cf. vii–xiv). He ascribed a level of freedom to even inanimate matter (*Wicket Gate*, 140).

105. Studdert Kennedy, *Hardest Part*, 177: "Bergson taught me much." Cf. *Wicket Gate*, 177; *Word and the Work*, 53; *Food*, 151, 214, 218, and 223; and *Warrior*, 257.

106. Studdert Kennedy, *Warrior*, 172, 217, and 239.

107. Panentheism is the doctrine that the cosmos exists "within" God, and that God, in turn, pervades the cosmos. It is often contrasted with pantheism, which *identifies* God with the cosmos, and "classical theism," which tends to view God and the cosmos as separate entities. Process theology is a particular type of panentheism, and English modernism acted as a conduit for panentheistic ideas within British theology. For two introductions, see Brierley, "Panentheism," and Clayton, "Panentheism."

108. See Studdert Kennedy, *Sorrows*, 21, and *Lighten Our Darkness*, 62.

109. See, for example, Studdert Kennedy, *Hardest Part*, 2. His unusual sensitivity in this area may have stemmed from work that he undertook on venereal wards at Netley and at York during the Boer War (Studdert Kennedy, *Rough Talks*, 104).

110. Studdert Kennedy, *Rough Rhymes*, 19.

111. John 20:13. "I Know Not Where They Have Laid Him" appeared in Studdert Kennedy, *More Rough Rhymes*, 17–21. Cf. Studdert Kennedy, *Hardest Part*, 163, and *Rough Talks*, 24: "They have taken away my *lad*, and I know not where they have laid him" (my emphasis).

112. "A Mother Understands," in Studdert Kennedy, *Rough Rhymes*, 41.

time, but in 1928, they were a brave and pioneering theological foray into the area.

It would be easy to think that the "new vision" of God was suggested to Studdert Kennedy by the war. In fact, the war played a more subtle role in the formation of his theology, and the previous "slum" context of his work is rather its primary inspiration. Studdert Kennedy grew up in the vicarage of the slum parish of Quarry Hill.[113] This gave him his "profound affection for the poor,"[114] and he ministered in places of a similar nature until 1921: he gravitated as a curate to the poorest parts of Rugby, and after returning to Quarry Hill as a priest, he was attracted to St. Paul's, Worcester, primarily because of its poverty.[115] This is a likely source of the melancholy that some commentators have observed in Studdert Kennedy's life and appearance (see figure 8).[116] He attributed his concern for the poor to his always having

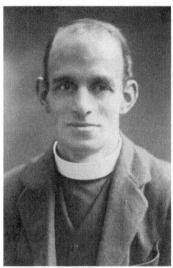

Figure 8: Postcard of Geoffrey Studdert Kennedy printed after his death

lived among them.[117] Studdert Kennedy has accordingly been viewed in the late nineteenth-century Anglo-Catholic "slum priest" tradition of Arthur Stanton and Robert Dolling;[118] and it was in this context that his doctrine of the suffering God began to be forged. It may have been the case for other revisionists that their "religious revolution started on the Somme and the Salient,"[119] but in Studdert Kennedy's case, the war had a more nuanced effect: "The Vision of the Suffering God revealed in Jesus Christ, and the necessary Truth of it, first began to dawn on me in the narrow streets and shadowed homes of an English slum. All that War has done is to batter the essential Truth of it deeper in, and cast a fiercer light upon the Cross."[120] There can be little doubt

113. Moore Ede in Studdert Kennedy, *Hardest Part*, vii; cf. Mozley, "Home Life," 70 and 31.

114. Mozley, "Home Life," 33.

115. See above, 25.

116. Jeffs, *Princes*, 160 and 167–68; Purcell, *Woodbine Willie*, 15–16; Edwards, "'Woodbine Willie,'" 11; and Holman, *Woodbine Willie*, 155.

117. Studdert Kennedy, *Rough Talks*, 169.

118. Moore Ede, "His Life in Worcester," 95; cf. Reckitt, *Maurice to Temple*, 164.

119. Barry, *Period*, 56.

120. Studdert Kennedy, *Hardest Part*, 193–94.

that Studdert Kennedy is referring here to Quarry Hill, where he discussed theology with his friend, the opponent of passibility, Kenneth Mozley.[121] It is difficult, of course, to compare Studdert Kennedy's pre-war and post-war theology when there are no extant samples of the former, but given Studdert Kennedy's pre-war willingness to explore radical theological ideas, there is no reason to demur from his own suggestion that his passibility first arose from reflection on Edwardian poverty. Thus, Studdert Kennedy's doctrine of God was not a product of the war; there is more continuity between his pre-war and post-war thought than that.[122] The role that the war played in his theology was one of clarification and emphasis: its contradictions provoked his thinking,[123] and "open[ed] his eyes to the vision which was already there within his soul."[124] The moment which seems to have opened his eyes more than any other was his running across the body of a young German soldier, mentioned earlier. "From that moment on I never saw a battlefield as anything but a Crucifix. From that moment on I have never seen the world as anything but a Crucifix. I see the Cross set up in every slum, in every filthy over-crowded quarter, in every vulgar flaring street."[125] The war also had the more practical effect of giving Studdert Kennedy wider opportunities of writing, oratory, and pastoral care, such as to establish his national reputation.

The relation of Studdert Kennedy's pastoral experience to his doctrine of God is not simply one of cause and effect: there is, rather, a fundamental alignment of their content. It is no coincidence that from his pastoral ministry with the poor and the suffering, arose a doctrine of God who is not aloof from people's suffering, but very much "with" them in it. "It's funny how it is always Christ upon the Cross that comforts; never God upon a throne."[126] The importance of "being with" for Christian theology has recently been expounded by the contemporary theologian Sam Wells, and it is borne out in Studdert Kennedy's life and theology.[127] He instinctively recognised the importance of being physically with, and spending time with, those for

---

121. Mozley, "Home Life," 42–43.

122. Ibid., 58; cf. Kirk, "I. C. F. Crusader," 167.

123. Studdert Kennedy, *Warrior*, 18. Cf. 21: war "shouts and bawls its questions at you. It throws them at you stark, raw, quivering, and all shot through with pain."

124. Mozley, "Epilogue," 244.

125. Studdert Kennedy, *Word and the Work*, 58; cf. *Hardest Part*, 10–11 and 44.

126. Studdert Kennedy, *Hardest Part*, 10; cf. 12.

127. Wells, *Nazareth Manifesto*: "what humanity needs is a love that abides, perseveres, remains present to us whatever happens, however bad things are, for however long it takes" (244). "God's action, it seems, is not to make bad things not happen. God's glory is revealed in that God does not leave us alone when they do" (213).

whom he cared. As the pastoral theologian Alastair Campbell put it later in the century, "pastoral care is grounded in mutuality, not in expertise."[128] In his *Rough Talks*, Studdert Kennedy mentioned that on his first posting to the Front, there not being any orders, he went up to the Front with his men—after all, "these men were my parish"—a move which was much appreciated.[129] He wished to be "a real good, pukka padre," and amplified what that entailed: such a padre "ought to share your danger, and he ought to share your life."[130] The classic expression of this was the advice that he gave Theodore Hardy, a new chaplain who, following the death of his wife, had signed up for ministry in the forces at the age of fifty-three.[131] Studdert Kennedy, whose attachment to the line is shown not least in his annoyance at being withdrawn to preach for the National Mission,[132] met Hardy for an hour at Étaples towards the end of 1916:

> Live with the men. Go everywhere they go. Make up your mind that you will share all their risks, and more if you can do any good. You can take it that the best place for a Padre (provided he does not interfere with military operations) is where there is most danger of death. Our first job is to go beyond the men in self-sacrifice and reckless devotion. Don't be bamboozled into believing that your proper place is behind the line; it isn't. If you stay behind you might as well come down, you won't do a ha'porth of good. Your place is in front. The line is the key to the whole business. Work in the very front, and they will listen to you when they come out to rest, but if you only preach and teach behind, you are wasting time, the men won't pay the slightest attention to you.[133]

---

128. Campbell, *Rediscovering*, 15.

129. Studdert Kennedy, *Rough Talks*, 18–20.

130. Ibid., 203 and 205; cf. *Hardest Part*, xiv and 153–54. Studdert Kennedy attributed this approach to advice from his own divisional chaplain: see the press report of a meeting with parishioners in November 1916, in Worcester Cathedral Library, Muniments Add. Mss. 480.

131. For Hardy, see Hardy, *Hardy VC*, Raw, *"It's Only Me,"* and Hypher, "Compassionate Hero," as well as his entry in the *ODNB*.

132. Hardy, *Hardy VC*, 20 and 24; cf. Carey, "War Padre," 130, and Studdert Kennedy's letter to parishioners of 5 February 1917, printed in the *Worcester Daily Times*, 13 February 1917, 2 (and quoting Matthew 6:21): "the trenches are the heart of England. There is the treasure of her manhood—and where your treasure is there will your heart be also."

133. Hardy, *Hardy VC*, 20–27 at 25; cf. 53–58, Carey, "War Padre," 138–41, and Parker, *Whole Armour*, 34.

The advice had a profound effect on Hardy, who took it to heart: he was awarded the Distinguished Service Order for staying, under fire, for over thirty-six hours with a man trapped in mud until he died, and he threw himself into all manner of dangerous situations, becoming one of three First World War chaplains to be awarded the Victoria Cross, until he died of wounds less than four weeks prior to the armistice.[134] "Being with" people was effective because it reflected the relation between God and the world; and thus it was possible to use human "being with" relationships as an analogy for relationship with the divine. So Studdert Kennedy likened the old concept of the far-off God to a remote commander, the "bad staff officer who wears red tabs and spurs and never sees the trenches," and the new vision revealed by Christ was comparable to the "comrade" who gets muddy and bloody.[135]

The relation between God and the cosmos is not quite as straightforward as a person "being with" a friend; for Studdert Kennedy also talked of God being "in" the world. Precisely how "being in" relates to "being with" was not worked out in his theology; his sense of "immanentism" was not developed.[136] Sometimes, "being in" did not seem to amount to much more than a "being with": Studdert Kennedy was aware, for example, that God could suffer as a parent suffers the failings of a child.[137] In other places, however, Studdert Kennedy alluded to a closer relation between God and the suffering of the world.[138] He held to a broad sacramentalism—an ability to see God "in" the universe in general[139]—such that, at times, there was something about him of the mystic.[140]

---

134. Raw, *"It's Only Me,"* 53–55.

135. Studdert Kennedy, "Religious Difficulties," 390–91; cf. 404, and *Rough Talks,* 213, which talk of "Christ the Captain"; Parker, *Whole Armour,* 83; and Slocum, "Geoffrey Studdert Kennedy."

136. Studdert Kennedy, *Rough Talks,* 190 and 245.

137. Cf. Studdert Kennedy, *Rough Talks,* 127–28, and *Hardest Part,* 134.

138. See, for example, God knowing the "feel ov a bullet," a statement that Studdert Kennedy justified on the basis of Christ's words in Matthew's Gospel (25:40): "'Inasmuch as ye did it to one of these / Ye 'ave done it unto me'" (*Rough Rhymes,* 24; cf. *More Rough Rhymes,* 10, and *Lies!* 6).

139. See Studdert Kennedy, *Food,* 30; *Wicket Gate,* 167; and *Word and the Work,* 72. Cf. Mozley, "Home Life," 65–66, and Temple, "Man," 214–15 and 218.

140. Cf. Mozley, "Home Life," 67; Studdert Kennedy to Battersby Harford, 20 November 1908 (Ripon College Cuddesdon, Ripon Hall archives, Mo/3); and Dick Sheppard's tribute in *St. Martin's Review* (May 1929), 256–58 at 257–58.

God the "rescuer of the wounded"

It has been seen above that Studdert Kennedy interpreted the almightiness of God in terms of the power to "see it through"—what could be termed the infinite "persistence" of God. The resurrection demonstrated that Jesus was "unbeaten" or "undefeated" on the cross, and thus revealed God's triumph, just as the crucifixion revealed God's suffering.[141] If William Temple thought that the final triumph of love and goodness in Studdert Kennedy's theology was insufficiently expressed, the difficulty, perhaps, was how to frame that triumph pictorially.[142] If the cross and empty tomb are inseparable, how can the triumph of suffering Love be portrayed within one symbol? Christianity has always struggled with this problem. An empty cross has sometimes been preferred to a crucifix, in order to suggest that Christ is risen, but that can leave the triumph too implicit. Studdert Kennedy preferred to depict Christ on the cross with his "chin up," that is to say, with an undefeated head.[143] Some churches drape a cast-off grave-cloth across a cross to symbolise the resurrection, at the risk of it looking like a scarf with a dinner suit. Others depict an empty tomb behind the cross.[144] It is not an easy dilemma to resolve.

There are some images in Studdert Kennedy's writings that offer a constructive way forward. If, in his earliest essay, he wrote of God as "a gallant and fatherly Colonel who goes over the top with His men,"[145] in subsequent publications, he went further: God is undefeated, so God is more like unbeaten soldiers who have emerged from conflict; injured but resolute troops who have come out the other side. Thus, the image of God was to be found in "a procession of wounded that comes in after a battle."[146] In his poem "Solomon in All His Glory," Studdert Kennedy went beyond Christ's suggestion that Solomon's glory was no match for that of the lilies of the field,

141. Studdert Kennedy, *Hardest Part*, 92; *Rough Talks*, 233.

142. Temple, "Man," 220–21.

143. See below, 169–70.

144. Cf. Studdert Kennedy, *Hardest Part*, 199.

145. Studdert Kennedy, "Religious Difficulties," 391. Cf. the parallel between preparation for going "over the top" and Christ praying in the garden of Gethsemane (Studdert Kennedy, *Rough Talks*, 262, and *Hardest Part*, 105–6, and Studdert-Kennedy, *Dog-Collar Democracy*, 67).

146. Studdert Kennedy, *Hardest Part*, 93. Cf. 72: "Beside the wounded tattered soldier who totters down to this dressing-station with one arm hanging loose, an earthly king in all his glory looks paltry and absurd."

venturing that even the fairest of lilies had nothing on the glory of "tattered, torn, and bloody khaki."[147]

This can be taken further by another image from Studdert Kennedy's writing, an image derived from Scripture, from the Gospels of Matthew and Luke: that of a shepherd, seeking out a lost sheep. In Matthew's version, there is a chance that the shepherd finds the sheep: "if he finds it, truly I tell you, he rejoices."[148] Luke, by contrast, refers to the finding as a certainty, rather than as a possibility: not "if" the sheep is found, but "when." The shepherd seeks *until* the sheep is found; the possibility of the shepherd returning to the fold empty-handed is excluded.[149] In this tiny difference between two Greek words, *ean* and *heōs*, "*if* he finds it" and "*until* he finds it," lies the triumph of God, Studdert Kennedy's notion of "almightiness," and indeed his whole doctrine of God. God is involved in an "everlasting search"; God is *ever* seeking out lost sheep.[150] God is one who will not rest until every last sheep is found, and the whole world thereby redeemed. "The essence of the Christian revelation is that revelation of God as a coming God, a seeking God, a Good Shepherd Who seeks His sheep, . . . a Love that never ceases, and by its nature never could cease. . . . God is for ever coming to us—He is the coming God."[151] "Advent," or the Coming (of God), thus describes the whole creative process.[152]

So in the poem "Come Unto Me," Studdert Kennedy reacts against Jesus's words "Come unto me . . . and I will give you rest," because they imply that humanity comes to Jesus, when, in the shepherd/sheep analogy, Jesus comes looking for humanity;[153] and also because it might induce inactivity when there is still redemptive work to be done. Christ "calls us not to rest

---

147. Matthew 6:29; Studdert Kennedy, *More Rough Rhymes*, 45. Cf. the claim of the writer to the Hebrews that of those who were stoned to death, sawn in two, and killed by the sword, who "went about in skins of sheep and goats, destitute, persecuted, tormented," the world was not worthy (11:38–39).

148. Matthew 18:13.

149. Luke 15:4–5.

150. Studdert Kennedy, *Word and the Work*, 68; cf. *New Man*, 43, 74, 100–101, and 127.

151. Studdert Kennedy, *Wicket Gate*, 177–78.

152. Studdert Kennedy, *Word and the Work*, 53.

153. Matthew 11:28; Studdert Kennedy, *More Rough Rhymes*, 62–71. "Come Thou to us, O Lord. / Come Thou and find us. / Shepherd of the sheep / We cannot come to Thee" (71).

but to more toil."[154] Studdert Kennedy was not one for sitting down, and neither was his God.[155] After all, "there ain't no throne."

> It is not thus I deem
> Life should be lived;
> It is not that I crave,
> Not Rest, but strength to save
> The wounded and console their pain,
> To strive with evil and then strive again,
> Until the far off victory is won . . .
> To seek, to help, to save
> The wandering and restore the lost,
> Bring back to shore the tempest-tossed
> And set their hungry bodies down to feast.[156]

Similarly, Christ's descent into hell was not a one-off event between Good Friday and Easter Day: "He *for ever* descends to the depths to seek and to save that which is lost."[157]

If the element of "eternal search" that Studdert Kennedy found essential to this image of the shepherd, is translated into the context of "tattered, torn, and bloody khaki," then the resulting image of God is not one that Studdert Kennedy committed to writing, but one that he actually *embodied*, namely, in repeated efforts to rescue the wounded—the action for which he was awarded the Military Cross. Studdert Kennedy's action in June 1917 of persistent attempts to bring in the wounded from No Man's Land, offers an image of God that encapsulates his theology. God is the Eternal Rescuer, the one who ventures into the world gone wrong, into No Man's Land (that place where indeed full humanity is not to be found), and ceaselessly seeks out its casualties, and will not rest until every last one has been brought in. I once took a funeral on 8 March (Studdert Kennedy's "feast-day") of someone who had died tragically young, and, reflecting on that loss in the context of Studdert Kennedy's life, found myself saying to the mourners at the service that the protection of God consists not in preventing tragedies from happening, but in something far more powerful—in not ceasing or resting until every tragedy in the history of the universe has been redeemed.

154. Studdert Kennedy, *Lies!* 155.

155. God is "ever active" (Studdert Kennedy, *Word and the Work*, 69); God's "wrath" can only ever be "an increased activity" (*Warrior*, 231).

156. Studdert Kennedy, *Peace Rhymes*, 62–64. In these last two lines, the imagery of a shepherd and sheep from the previous lines is mixed with that of sitting down at a banqueting table (cf. the same mix in Psalm 23), and with sailors, mid-storm, reaching the haven that they desire (Psalm 107:30; cf. John 6:21).

157. Studdert Kennedy, *Food*, 250 (my emphasis); cf. 301.

I am not saying that images of God drawn from military contexts are unproblematic (though arguably, in a context in which shepherds have all but disappeared, they are more culturally relevant than the pastoral motif); nor am I saying that there are no alternatives to the image of God as the Rescuer of the Wounded from No Man's Land. What I am saying is that this image is consonant with the theology of Geoffrey Studdert Kennedy; that it is an image that he himself embodied; that those images which construe omnipotence in terms of persistence or "eternal searching" have the most healthy and accurate interpretations of divine power; and that therefore those images hold most promise for the church and faith today.

6

Prophecy or Propaganda?
Preaching in a Time of War

Georgina A. Byrne

He is a speaker of extraordinary power, and I know none so effective with men. His powers of vivid description, his absolute naturalness and manifest sincerity attract and interest.[1]

SO WROTE THE DEAN of Worcester, William Moore Ede, of Geoffrey Studdert Kennedy's preaching. Paying further tribute to the popular and well-known priest on 10 March 1929, the Sunday after Studdert Kennedy's death, the dean preached a sermon in Worcester Cathedral, which, as well as reminding readers of Studdert Kennedy's wider ministry, was clearly full of admiration for the man as a public speaker. In the early days of the war, when Worcester was a training centre for the army, around two thousand men were arriving at the cathedral on Sundays. When Moore Ede invited Studdert Kennedy to preach, he spoke to the men and "held them spell-bound—not a cough, no shuffling of feet. What he said became the main topic of conversation during the ensuing week." This was not unusual; on one occasion, preaching in Rouen on Good Friday, he had men "carried

1. Moore Ede's preface in Studdert Kennedy, *Hardest Part*, xii.

97

away" by his words. At the end of the sermon "they rose and cheered Jesus Christ."[2]

It might be expected that the dean of Worcester would be quick to point out the attributes of a fellow priest who had become one of Worcester's favourite sons, but Moore Ede was not the only one to acknowledge the power of Studdert Kennedy's preaching. Canon Frederick Macnutt encountered Studdert Kennedy in Boulogne, describing him as "quite one of the best Missioners I have ever known." It was his preaching that most impressed Macnutt: "He is an Irishman, as charming and as amusing and as eloquent as only an Irishman can be. . . . I never knew anyone who had such power in getting the goods delivered as he gives his message to the men. One moment he has them in fits of laughter; the next he has hold of their heart strings and is drawing those hearts to Christ and all that is good."[3]

"Dick" Sheppard, despite disliking the way that Studdert Kennedy "thought aloud" in his sermons, nevertheless admitted deep admiration for his ability as a preacher,[4] and Studdert Kennedy was numbered among Ernest Jeffs's "princes of the pulpit," where he was described as offering "pungent and explosive phraseology." His "breezy and banging words were a natural expression of the man; and the man was far more than a boisterous eccentric. He was a prophet."[5] Jeffs noted that Studdert Kennedy's easy, familiar style and occasional lapses into slang were not always appreciated, but that, for all the "breeziness," there was "an undercurrent of pain, sorrow and gloom" in his preaching that seemed at one with human suffering and the cross of Christ.[6]

Regardless of the gifts of a preacher, it is the content of a sermon that is crucial. A powerful speech—and a powerful speaker—can move, challenge, encourage, or unsettle the audience, stimulating thought and changing opinion. This chapter examines the Church of England's response to the First World War through its sermons. Any brief perusal of sermons or

2. As reported in the *Worcestershire Echo*, 11 March 1929 (cutting held in Worcester Cathedral Library, Muniments Add. Mss. 480); cf. Carey, "War Padre," 124.

3. F. B. Macnutt, "Vicar's Letter from France," 20 February 1917 (Worcester Cathedral Library, Muniments Add. Mss. 480). Frederick Brodie Macnutt (1873–1949) became incumbent of St. Martin's, Leicester, in 1918, and thereafter the first provost when that church became Leicester Cathedral. By "missioners," Macnutt meant those who led the National Mission of Repentance and Hope.

4. See Roberts, *H. R. L. Sheppard*, 189. Hugh Richard Lawrie "Dick" Sheppard (1880–1937) was vicar of St. Martin-in-the-Fields from 1914 until 1926 and dean of Canterbury from 1929 until 1931. He was himself a noted speaker, giving the first sermon broadcast by the BBC.

5. Jeffs, *Princes*, 154–55.

6. Ibid., 160.

opinion pieces of the time will quickly reveal that the church's reaction to war was neither united nor monolithic. Instead, what emerges is a more nuanced variety in theology, theory, and practical advice to the Christian in the pew, as well as marked "phases" of response as the war progressed. Moreover, preachers were obliged to balance their personal thoughts—and the war experiences that shaped those thoughts—with a sense that they, from the pulpit, spoke with the authority of the church. Throughout the war and beyond its conclusion, it is clear that preachers and writers sought to deliver a narrative to answer questions (real or imagined) from the general public to whom they ministered: why was the war happening and for what purpose did loved ones die?

While many sermons were preached concerning the war—and many words written by Anglican thinkers of the day—this chapter focuses on three well-known preachers, noted for their flair and ability. The first is Geoffrey Studdert Kennedy, the vicar of St. Paul's in Worcester and the subject of this book. He presents an interesting subject not only because of the power of his delivery and his talent for engaging with soldiers, but because his attitude to the war shifted as a direct result of his experiences as a chaplain. After the end of the war, he spoke against conflict. As Moore Ede put it, "he became an ardent apostle for peace and often here, in Worcester, dwelt on the wickedness and folly of war."[7]

The second preacher is Arthur Foley Winnington-Ingram, bishop of London. He was born, the fourth child of ten, in Stanford-on-Teme in Worcestershire, where his father was the rector; his mother was the daughter of Henry Pepys, the bishop of Worcester.[8] His preaching style was direct and straightforward, and he was a popular preacher in every sense of the word. When he was preaching in St. Paul's Cathedral, latecomers were often faced with a large placard saying "church full"—meaning that there wasn't even standing room.[9] When preaching at Winchester College, he "was in a class by himself in his influence on the boys. He was the only preacher who really cut any ice with them."[10] Such was his passionate and encouraging style, he drummed up not only recruits for the army during the war, but vocations to ordained ministry before and after it.

---

7. Sermon reported in the *Worcestershire Echo*, 11 March 1929 (Worcester Cathedral Library, Muniments Add. Mss. 480). For details of this change, see Bell, "Collusion to Condemnation."

8. For Winnington-Ingram (1858–1946), see the *ODNB* and Carpenter, *Winnington-Ingram*. His name does not always carry a hyphen. I am following the practice of his biographer and the *ODNB*.

9. Carpenter, *Winnington-Ingram*, 73.

10. Ibid., 226.

He is remembered, perhaps unfairly, for his bellicose preaching during the war. The most infamous anti-German sermon has, recently, been proven to have been heavily edited to his discredit.[11] That said, he was intensely patriotic and, as his biographer suggests, "sometimes he incautiously expressed himself in striking phrases, which were afterwards remembered against him."[12]

The third preacher is (Agnes) Maude Royden (1876–1956). Royden was a suffragist campaigner, the editor of *Common Cause*, the suffragist newspaper, and a gifted speaker who drew crowds not only because of the unusual fact that she was a woman who preached, but because she was eloquent, challenging, and passionate in her delivery. As one commentator noted, "Putting aside the question of sex as an irrelevance, it would not be denied by anyone who has followed her career that she is singularly equipped with the gifts of preacher and teacher."[13] She was the youngest child of Sir Thomas Bland Royden, the chairman of the Cunard Line, and his wife Alice. After education in Cheltenham and Oxford, she decided to devote her life to social work in the slums, but was soon encouraged to speak by the parish priest, George William Hudson Shaw, who saw her potential. Her talent was quickly noted and, as she spoke for the cause of women's suffrage, she gathered admirers and spoke at larger venues. One admirer was the bishop of Winchester, Edward Talbot, who invited her to speak to two thousand men at the Church Congress in Southampton in 1913 on the subject of the white slave trade. Her speech there, and the manner of her delivery, made significant impact on those who heard her.[14] Her voice was described by Alfred Gardiner as "musical and resonant" and "the vehicle of a mind that is fresh and vigorous, and of an emotion that is sincere and never extravagant."[15]

Preaching at the outbreak of war

Britain's declaration of war on Germany on 4 August 1914 was met with dismay by many in the church. As Alan Wilkinson has noted, senior figures wrote of their personal abhorrence of war in general, their concern for the inevitable loss of life, and their desire not to be drawn into the language of blame. Henry Scott Holland (1847–1918), theologian, social reformer, and

11. Bell, "Malign or Maligned?"

12. Carpenter, *Winnington-Ingram*, 281.

13. Gardiner, *Certain People*, 237.

14. Fletcher, *Maude Royden*, 102–7. See this book also for a full account of Royden's life.

15. Gardiner, *Certain People*, 238.

canon of St. Paul's, for example, wrote in a letter that speaking of Germans or the Kaiser as "the devil" was the sort of thing that made war inevitable—although he himself used exactly that language only a month later.[16] Charles Gore (1853–1932), bishop of Oxford, did not think that war could ever be a Christian weapon. He hated war "with all his heart." Nevertheless, he was convinced that participation in the war was the right course of action.[17] The archbishop of Canterbury, Randall Davidson (1848–1930), was "very depressed by the tragedy and waste of it all."[18]

Whatever their personal feelings and misgivings about the war, disclosed in letters and diaries, the fact remained that a call to arms had been issued and thousands of British men were signing up and committing themselves to combat overseas. Far more than the South African wars, the First World War involved a greater personal commitment from the population, whether as combatants or civilians. Those whose profession compelled them to speak in public were required to balance abhorrence of war as theory with the reality of parishioners engaging in action. Their task was to help people make sense of the situation in the light of the gospel.

The primary question that preachers needed to answer, therefore, was why Britain was involved in the war at all. It is important to note that the vast majority of the British public supported action against Germany and Church of England clergy who also supported it were reflecting a wider mood.[19] Those who were clear that Britain had no choice but to honour its pledges to Belgium by engaging in conflict needed to convince themselves, however, as well as the general public, that actively supporting war was consistent with Christian teaching. Thus, the focus of the positive support was grounded in three key themes: in the first place, there was a pressing need to counter "German aggression"—which was set out without any real self-examination of British aggression. Secondly, the importance of "freedom" was stressed as a Christian (and British) characteristic, which Germany was seeking to diminish or contain by its desire for global domination. Thirdly, by engaging in war, however tragic and distasteful it was, Britain was securing a greater, lasting peace for the future.

Winnington-Ingram, speaking at London's Guildhall, made it clear that soldiers were fighting for national freedom. The expansionist actions

16. Wilkinson, *Church of England*, 14–15.

17. Ibid., 16. Gore had become bishop of Worcester in 1902, bishop of Birmingham in 1905, and then bishop of Oxford in 1911. See his entry in the *ODNB*.

18. Bell, *Randall Davidson*, 738.

19. Stuart Bell, for example, notes that the vast majority of people, as well as the mainstream churches, supported British involvement: Bell, "'Patriotism and Sacrifice,'" 193.

of the Germans—of which the invasion of Belgium was only part—needed
to be halted. Defending Belgium was an act of national security: "I would
rather die than see England a German province."[20] In vivid language, he laid
out the difference between the militaristic Germans and the freedom-loving
British. Having lived in Germany for a year, he claimed some knowledge
of the German character, suggesting that its people were being tightly ordered and governed by an aggressive regime, their freedoms curtailed. "It's
all very well for them, but no Englishman would stand being overridden
and downtrodden by policemen every moment of his life. It would stifle
a child of freedom. . . . We are the children of the salt spray and the wild
wind."[21] Germany wanted to conquer the world with its own *Kultur*, but
"fortunately the British Empire stands in the way."[22] Prussian dominance
would be "crushed" and "when, please God, we have won the victory, our
England will be free with a freedom that it has not known for years, and will
have the liberty which the world can neither give nor take away."[23]

The theme of German aggression as the chief reason for the war was
common. William Temple (1881–1944), for example, then the rector of St.
James's, Piccadilly, noted that German soldiers were guilty of atrocities and
spoke of the need to resist evil.[24] Scott Holland, who had despised language
that denounced Germany, wrote that "every day reveals the black blind horror of Prussianism. It is the very devil. It has to be fought and killed. It is the
last word in iniquity."[25]

Geoffrey Studdert Kennedy, like Winnington-Ingram and most clergy,
approved of the war and encouraged men to join up.[26] He became a chaplain
in late 1915 and was in France just before Christmas. Speaking to soldiers at
the camps of northern France, he claimed that Britain had not wanted war
and was not "spoiling for a fight," but entered into it to put an end to German dominance and militarism.[27] Unlike Germans, who were militaristic,
the British, he argued, were "pugnacious" and stood for "honour and civilisation. We stand for peace."[28] Studdert Kennedy articulated another of the

20. Winnington-Ingram, *Church in Time of War*, 6.

21. Ibid., 7.

22. Ibid., 8.

23. Ibid., 17.

24. Temple, *Christianity and War*. Temple became bishop of Manchester in 1921,
archbishop of York in 1929, and archbishop of Canterbury in 1942. See Iremonger,
William Temple, and his entry in the *ODNB*.

25. Wilkinson, *Church of England*, 15.

26. Holman, *Woodbine Willie*, 31.

27. Studdert Kennedy, *Rough Talks*, 36.

28. Ibid., 60.

familiar reasons for fighting that was offered in justification: that the allies fought in order to work for a greater peace. Even as soldiers stood "armed to the teeth," they were scheming for peace.[29] War, a necessary evil in this generation, needed eliminating and it would be the task of the nations to "work out a plan" to eliminate it.[30] He saw no difficulty in claiming that, as they fought for peace, the soldiers were fighting for Christ.

Although war was generally undesirable, then, it was necessary. William Temple asked, "May not force be used to hinder the evil-doer precisely in order that spiritual power may have free course?"[31] After all, it had not been possible to act fully in accordance with the mind of Christ on 4 August, so with penitence and prayerfulness and a hope in the overthrow of military might, it was a Christian's duty to engage.

Not everyone agreed with the need for war, nor accepted the reasons given for engagement. Maude Royden certainly thought otherwise. If war was undesirable for Christians, then it was always undesirable. She had been told, she said, that now "was not the time" to be preaching ideals. She countered, "Is there ever a time not to preach the ideal?"[32] In a pamphlet distilling her mission talks, *The Great Adventure: The Way to Peace*, she dismissed the argument of German militarism by pointing out Britain's own record for empire-building, and caricatured the popular opinion that the defence of Belgium was enough of a reason to enter into conflict. "We were pledged to the defence of Belgium and Belgium was attacked by Germany. We had arms and we must use them. To refuse meant national dishonour and dishonour is worse than the worst of wars."[33]

Of course Britain had tried to avoid war. Britain had, she knew, attempted to halt German expansion by conversation and diplomacy. She pointed out, however, that when Germany was invited to desist from oppression and trampling on treaties, the Germans might well have pointed out that this is what Britain had done in Egypt and South Africa. Only when Britain's own interest was threatened, did the British then rush to champion treaties and defend "little" nations. Some said that Germany wanted war and was preparing for it, but so had Britain—on the grounds that this is the way to secure peace.[34] Writing in the *Challenge*, a liberal church newspaper, she said that although she could well believe that Sir Edward Grey had striven to

29. Ibid., 64.
30. Ibid., 62.
31. Temple, *Christianity and War*, 12.
32. Royden, *Great Adventure*, preface.
33. Ibid., 3.
34. Ibid., 5.

prevent war, a small glance at a map would reveal that Britain's aim for years had been to isolate Germany. How could Britain claim to be championing the little people of Belgium: "Do we expect to be taken seriously after the example we set in South Africa?"[35]

If Royden was to argue against British involvement in the war, then she needed to offer an alternative. For her, the only alternative was pacifism. To stand by and remain neutral would be worse than war, she thought. War is better than neutrality—if these are the only options. "But is it not tragic that, nineteen hundred years after the Crucifixion, we Christians should still conceive of peace in terms of *neutrality*? Was Christ, then, 'neutral' on the cross? Or was his life one long act of 'non-resistance'? . . . He chose another alternative—He made peace."[36]

Royden made a direct appeal to Scripture. "I am aware as I write it that the proposal to disarm and appeal to the love and pity of humanity sounds strange today. Yet not stranger surely than the Sermon on the Mount, still read aloud in our churches, by apparently serious priests, to seemingly receptive congregations."[37]

Against the prevailing notion that, by engaging in conflict, Britain would secure a greater peace, she asked, "Is it not time that we abandoned the hope of exterminating heresies by killing heretics?"[38] Even victory would not demonstrate the over-arching virtue of the enterprise for "if and when we have succeeded to the limit of our hopes, when we have Germany beaten, what shall we have proved? That we were stronger than Germany! . . . And when we have done it, shall we have proved that we were right? By no means; only that we are more numerous and more rich."[39]

In a blistering attack against those who argued that war would lead to peace, she suggested that they were being led by a force other than God.

> There is only one way to kill a wrong idea. It is to set forth a right idea. You cannot kill hatred and violence by violence and hatred. You cannot make men out of love with war by making more effective war. Satan will not cast out Satan, though he will certainly seek to persuade us that he will, since of all his devices this has been throughout the ages the most successful. To make war in order to make peace! How beguiling an idea! To make Germans peaceable by killing them with torpedoes and

35. *Challenge*, 21 August 1914, 509; Fletcher, *Maude Royden*, 110.

36. Royden, *Great Adventure*, 4, Royden's emphasis.

37. Ibid., 7.

38. Ibid., 9.

39. Ibid., 10.

machine-guns—that does not sound quite so well. Yet this is what we set out to do when we "fight German militarism" with the weapons of militarism.[40]

The remedy was, she argued, for one nation to be a "martyr" in the cause of peace; to lay down its arms. This was real peace—and the great adventure. "Who is the great adventurer—he who goes out against the enemy with swords and guns, or he who goes out with naked hands? Who is the mighty hunter—he who seeks the quarry with stones and slings, or he who, with St. Francis, goes to tame a wolf with nothing but the gospel? We peace people have made of peace a dull, drab, sordid, selfish thing. We have made it that ambiguous, dreary thing—"neutrality." But Peace is the great adventure, the glorious romance."[41]

Her approach won her few friends. Kinder critics pointed out that it was fanciful to expect a nation to martyr itself. An individual might rise to that supreme sacrifice, but no whole nation, collectively, would be prepared to face poverty and slavery in order to follow Christ.[42] Newspapers were quick to mark her out as a "crank" and described her, and women who shared her pacifist views, as "peacettes" or "crankettes."[43] Her bold views came at a personal cost, as she felt isolated and unable to share fully in the suffering of her fellow citizens.

Preaching during the war

As the war continued, the questions of why Britain was at war gave way to other concerns—namely what those at home were to make of the rising number of casualties and how a victorious war might be fought in the light of Christian values.

For Studdert Kennedy, the course of the war brought about profound spiritual and theological questions that he wrestled with and spoke about. Initially, he had been ready to fall in with maintaining morale among the troops, challenging their personal morals at the same time. British soldiers were to uphold the Christian (sic) value of sportsmanship, putting right

---

40. Ibid., 11. "Satan will not cast out Satan" is a biblical reference (Mark 3:23).

41. Ibid., 12.

42. This was the view taken, for example, by B. H. Streeter, in *War, This War and the Sermon on the Mount*. Winnington-Ingram wrote to her in friendly terms that she was trying to "hurry God," who could only get out of each age the morality of which it was capable (Fletcher, *Maude Royden*, 126).

43. Fletcher, *Maude Royden*, 124.

before might and not hitting "below the belt."[44] They were to avoid temptation back at the camp, particularly drink and women, remembering their
loved ones at home and remaining "pure." "Better the guns of the Germans
than the temptations of the Devil!"[45]

Experiencing the horrors of trench warfare close at hand, however, he
found himself challenged by the questions that soldiers put to him, needing
to rethink for himself what human suffering meant and where God was
within it. Here it was that the prophetic passion, with which he became
associated, emerged. It was not an easy rhetoric to voice in time of war,
especially as he worked it out in the context of conflict and death. He seems
to have become uneasy about his earlier sermons and the enthusiasm for
war that they had contained.

In *The Hardest Part,* he offered a glimpse into the experiences that led
to such soul-searching. The sight of a dead German, only a young man,
who lay "like a tired child that has cried itself to sleep," and the questions of
a sergeant as to the whereabouts in battle of God the almighty gave rise to
existential and theological questions: "Do I believe in Him? How can I find
Him in this welter of sin and cruelty."[46]

The war, which in the beginning had received his support, was now
the crucible of his anger. "War is only glorious when you buy it in the Daily
Mail and enjoy it at the breakfast-table. It goes splendidly with bacon and
eggs. Real war is the final limit of damnable brutality, and that's all there is
in it. It's about the silliest, filthiest, most inhumanly fatuous thing that ever
happened. It makes the whole universe seem like a mad muddle. One feels
that all talk of order and meaning in life is insane sentimentality."[47]

In contrast to his sporting references in earlier sermons, he said that
"[Christ] gave us chivalry, and produced the sporting soldier; but even that
seems dead. Chivalry and poison gas don't go well together. Christ himself
was turned into a warrior and led men out to war."[48] He became uncertain
of the reasons for the war, noting mixed views among the men.

> Some came because they were not going to stand bullying,
> and they regard the Prussian as a bully. Some fight because
> they think liberty as they know it and understand it is at stake;

44. Studdert Kennedy, *Rough Talks,* 27. Sporting references were not unusual in the
early stages of the war; cf. below, 122, n. 39.

45. Letter to parishioners preserved in a press cutting in Worcester Cathedral
Library, Muniments Add. Mss. 480.

46. Studdert Kennedy, *Hardest Part,* 11 and 7–8.

47. Ibid., 30.

48. Ibid., 31.

others because they are Englishmen, and they are not going to see their side defeated if they can help it. Some enlisted because their pals did, or their girl said they ought.... Everywhere I find among the men of the army that this is the one great thing that touches them and rouses real enthusiasm. They do believe in Democracy. They are not quite sure what it means, but whatever it means, they believe in it.[49]

Most of all, the war challenged his belief in God as "almighty," a notion that became more unpalatable to him as time went on.

One of the ablest and most energetic of our bishops at the outbreak of the war started a campaign, the watchword of which was "the majesty of God." God was King, and by the horrors of Pentecostal calamity strove to turn men back to Him. At the time, staggered by the immensity of the evil, I simply did not think; I submitted. Now, after three years of it, I believe that this teaching is liable to be utterly misunderstood, and does but give occasion to the enemies of the Lord to blaspheme. Never again, I believe, will men bow down and worship this majestic tyrant who sits upon a throne and wields as weapons pestilence, disease, and war.[50]

The abhorrence of such a majestic God led him to the suffering God, who not only stood alongside the troops in the midst of their trials, but was also the suffering Christ on the cross.

Winnington-Ingram did not change his views about the war as it progressed. His sermons suggest that he believed his role to concern the encouragement of both troops at the Front and families at home rather more than the nature of God. This is not to say that he was unconcerned with God, rather that he was thoroughly convinced by the righteousness of the cause and the belief that, in some way, God had everything under control.

This meant that, if there were hardships, they were there for a reason. God, he believed, was "purifying" the nation. In a sermon at Westminster Abbey on Advent Sunday 1916, he noted a "wave of pessimism" over the land: a latent disbelief in God who ought to be doing something to end the war. Had it ever occurred to those who criticised God, he wondered, how much they had served and trusted God before the war began? "What

49. Ibid., 71.

50. Ibid., 86. Winnington-Ingram certainly held this view. At the beginning of the war, he wrote to Maude Royden that "this is the last Armageddon of the world, and when the great storm cloud has burst and spent itself, the great sun of Love which has been growing in intensity behind it, will shine out in its permanent strength" (Winnington-Ingram to Royden, 13 August 1914, in Fletcher, *Maude Royden*, 112).

right has a man who has never prayed to God before the war for years, or a woman who has made her own pleasure and comfort her God, to expect God, while they have not changed, to make them his special favourites and the choice instruments of his will?"[51] However righteous the cause it fought, the nation was called to repent.

His particular causes were immorality and drunkenness. From the outset, he preached to troops against vices, doing so outdoors and standing on a wagon at Bulswater Camp in August 1914.[52] He spoke to two thousand women at Church House in October of the same year and charged them to befriend the wives of soldiers who, now receiving more money than they had ever known, were wasting it on drink. At least the public house opening hours had been shortened; even so, women had taken to drinking in the mornings.[53] He estimated that 10 percent of the population were "afflicted with immorality,"[54] and he deplored the conduct of "thousands of girls" in London and the soldiers who allowed themselves to "fall."[55]

Steering clear of suggesting that immorality was the theological reason for war, he claimed that, by war, God was "refining" the nation. Little by little, the "dross" would be purged away. War, he argued, recognised the beauty of things, such as the treasure of city clerks offering themselves for service, or girls giving up their men. The mourning of mothers (of which he encountered plenty) was "too beautiful for words."[56]

At the same time, he offered words of encouragement to all, mixing biblical verses with Shakespearean oratory; a favourite was the "St. Crispin's Day" speech from *Henry V*. Popular English triumphs were invoked: on 25 July 1915, he addressed three thousand troops from the steps of St. Paul's concerning "the soul of the nation":

> Can we admit for a moment that the soul of the nation which won Agincourt, which flung back the Armada, which withstood for many years the armies of Napoleon, is not as great as the soul of any other nation? . . . As I stand in front of this great cathedral I cannot forget the cathedral of Ypres and others on the Continent which are now in ruins. We are fighting for the right for all to live free. It is a glorious time in which to be living.

51. Winnington-Ingram, *Rays of Dawn*, 39–40.

52. Winnington-Ingram, *Day of God*, 25.

53. Ibid., 62.

54. Winnington-Ingram, *Rays of Dawn*, 41.

55. Winnington-Ingram, *Victory and After*, 125.

56. Winnington-Ingram, *Rays of Dawn*, 47.

> You soldiers in front of me have the chance of taking part in the
> second Battle of Waterloo.[57]

As Carpenter says of him, "He had the power of divining, and expressing, the sentiments of the ordinary Briton, and he gave them the most Christian complexion of which they were capable."[58]

Unlike the bishop of London and Studdert Kennedy, Maude Royden could not venture out onto battlefields, even had she wished to. As war progressed, she moderated her pacifism in public, possibly as a result of a near-disastrous instance of mob violence that she encountered while attempting to speak about peace.[59] In a sermon at the City Temple, she described herself as a pacifist, but owned that the word could be claimed by all who worked and hoped for a time when international dispute would be settled without war. By implication, she was, potentially, drawing alongside herself those who claimed that this particular war was necessary for the greater peace that would come.

In the meantime, she turned her attention back to her primary concern: the role and treatment of women. She took to pointing out the double standards of morality among parliamentarians and prelates when it came to women's causes, using the suffragist newspaper *Common Cause* as her vehicle. Her anger revolved around both the treatment of women in practical terms and the demeaning of women in language and trope. Women who were married to foreigners, for example, were to register and report to police, confining their movements to a five-mile radius; men married to foreign wives had no such restrictions. She took issue with the way in which the violation of women by German soldiers was vividly reported in the press: why was the violation of women unique when men suffered too, except to define women purely in terms of their sex? She queried the popular trope of "women" as being a cause for temptation and "wastage" in the army. An MP had said that there were only two causes of wastage from the army: women and drink. Women, Royden argued, resented the word "woman" being synonymous with vice.[60] At the same time, soldiers were encouraged to

57. Winnington-Ingram, *Church in Time of War*, 305.

58. Carpenter, *Winnington-Ingram*, 283.

59. In 1915 she set out, with others, to convert England to pacifism. They travelled through the Midlands in caravans and preached in the open air—sometimes in churchyards opened by suspicious clergy. At Hinckley, the group was physically attacked by a mob, after newspapers had claimed that they were spies, financed by Germany, whose real motivation was to frustrate recruiting. The group was unharmed, but Royden was badly shaken by the experience, not least discovering what it meant to be an "object of hate . . . cut off from people." For a full account, see Fletcher, *Maude Royden*, 129–32.

60. Ibid., 116–17.

"forgo no opportunity for paternity"—by implication fathering illegitimate children—despite the common opprobrium heaped on unmarried mothers. Not only was this simply a crude way of filling future factories and armies, she argued; it reduced women to the status of "mere breeders of the race."[61]

Preaching beyond the war

As the war came to an end, all three preachers looked towards the future with hope and a sense of the great amount of work that needed to be done; this was a time when the nation might breathe again with fresh purpose.

Winnington-Ingram, by virtue of his episcopal office, found himself speaking at large memorial services and offering words of comfort to the bereaved. He reassured them that their husbands, brothers, and sons had not died in vain. The language that he employed for such occasions was vivid and energising, if theologically questionable. Preaching at a Canadian memorial service at St. Paul's, during the war, he suggested that soldiers had won everlasting life by virtue of their service: "They did not want to die; they loved life; they looked forward to a happy life here; they were planning out a useful and interesting future; they were not soldiers in the ordinary sense, though they died a soldier's death; THEY ASKED LIFE 'AND THEY WILL HAVE IT.' *He has given them a long life, even for ever and ever.*"[62]

He told the Upper House of Convocation that he was prepared to admit that he regularly referred to departed soldiers as "saints" because they had died "so gloriously" and were a lesson to all of "purity and devotion."[63] The cause for which they had died, namely the fight against German militarism, had been just; therefore he could assure his hearers of their salvation and even their sanctity.

Nevertheless, for the rest of the nation, there was work to do. The war, he thought initially, had left people in a better place. Preaching at St. Paul's on 29 September 1918, he said, "In the main, we are a nobler nation than we were four years ago[;] . . . we have escaped from a pettiness of aim and a narrowness of outlook."[64] What was needed was a revival in spiritual life, but also in the social life of the nation. He was keen that the drinking hours in public houses did not increase, and that young people were saved from immorality, but also that there was opportunity available for every person. In

---

61. In *Common Cause*, 30 April 1915, noted in Fletcher, *Maude Royden*, 118.

62. Winnington-Ingram, *Church in Time of War*, 288; cf. Psalm 21:4. All emphasis is Winnington-Ingram's own.

63. Upper House of Convocation (Canterbury), 7 February 1918.

64. Winnington-Ingram, *Victory and After*, 37.

a sermon preached on Ash Wednesday 1919 at Holy Trinity, Sloane Street, he noted that, already, there were signs that "we are sinking back into the old life."[65] There was grasping, grabbing, and strife between employers and employees. The church, he said, would lead the way in a new vision for the country; one based on equality of opportunity and a spirit of brotherhood. He was not specific about how such a vision was to come about, but he saw the need for more housing, an end to industrial unrest, and a greater care for the poor. Having employed his enthusiastic oratory for the righteous cause of the war as the bringer of a greater peace and an end to militarism, he now applauded the ideal of the League of Nations as a way forward.[66]

Studdert Kennedy, demobilised in 1919 and made a king's chaplain in 1920, returned initially to his parish in Worcester, but his gifts as a preacher—and the demand for him to use those gifts widely—led him to leave his parish ministry to work for the Industrial Christian Fellowship (ICF) from 1921.[67] He was more animated in his concern for the social welfare of the masses than was Winnington-Ingram, and equally interested in their moral welfare, but, as will be seen, less overtly political than Royden, resisting the pull of socialism. The Christian faith evaded allegiance to one political movement or another; he was critical of any creed that did not have Christ at its centre.

He was saddened that some of the most principled and well-meaning people were not within the folds of the church. "Humanity is what they believe in and live for," an inspiration that was honourable in doctors, educationalists, scientists, and socialists, but which brought them only "near" to the kingdom of God in the eyes of Christ. They had a "false" conception of God and, although full of love, lacked faith and hope.[68] These were people whom the church would need to preach to and enfold if it was to save the world.

Studdert Kennedy saw that the world could only be changed by a deeper connection with Jesus Christ. The task of the church was to draw the world to the cross—which continued to feature strongly in his preaching and his poetry. People, he argued, needed redemption. The years of war had exposed the ugly reality of human nature and, even more than education, what people needed in order to overcome that ugliness was the power that

65. Ibid., 115.

66. Ibid., 130. This, however, should be set alongside his determination that the German nation should be "punished" for beginning the conflict: ibid., 54–56.

67. Taking a non-taxing cure at St. Edmund King and Martyr in the city of London to enable this.

68. Studdert Kennedy, *Food*, 91.

only Christ could offer: "In Jesus as God, I believe, lies the hope of the world and its only hope."[69]

His talks are imbued with a deep sadness at the waste of war and depravity to which humanity can sink, and his poems even more so. His answer to the sin of the world lacked the fiery determination of Royden and the breezy optimism of Winnington-Ingram; instead, he appeared to cling to the cross as the world's (and his) only hope. It is small wonder that in his assessment of Studdert Kennedy's preaching, Ernest Jeffs noted that he "lacked inward sunshine." Jeffs surmised, probably rightly, that the theological wrestling that had taken place through the war had left him battle-scarred in spirit and unable to share fully with his hearers the hope of which he was certain.[70] The power of Christ comes through in his writing, and the certainty of God's love for his creation, but there is little practical indication of how the world might be transformed for the good of all; his vision for the future was more spiritual than concrete.

Wide hopes for the future were embraced by Maude Royden, although, typically, she was prepared to be more specific—and more political—about her aims. At the end of the war, she was asked to go and preach about "purity" to a camp of 15,000 soldiers over the course of three nights. The men were being sent home slowly in phases and, in the meantime, were simply doing fatigues and extra drill practice. She discovered that they were army engineers but that they were not being trained to be engineers in civilian life because it was considered "not worthwhile" to spend money training them. She was furious at such lack of forethought, seeing that the men would end up unemployed. "And they had the effrontery to ask me to go down and preach purity to these men! I said I would rather go and preach to the War Office."[71]

It was important to enable soldiers to work again. Drawing on the parable of the labourers in the vineyard, she argued that a man could not be blamed for being unemployed if no one had hired him.[72] She was concerned that women were losing their employment as men returned home. A woman, she said, had as much right to work as a man. It was preposterous that an office in the north of England was discharging women who had no dependents—"as if a woman herself does not need food or clothing."[73] It was, she had been told, cheaper to provide dole than to create jobs—while at

69. Studdert Kennedy, *Democracy*, 173.

70. Jeffs, *Princes*, 167. See also above, 89.

71. Royden, *Political Christianity*, 62–64.

72. Ibid., 46; cf. Matthew 20:1–16.

73. Ibid., 49.

the same time working people complained of overwork! This, she thought, belittled the importance of valuable employment for every human being.

If the nation was properly to restore the life of its people, then money was needed to put families on a stable basis. She had a plan for this, but had been told it would cost £144 million and the money was not available. Yet, she argued, £50 million was being spent in Mesopotamia by Mr. Asquith because there were oil wells there. "The money is there. The trouble is that it is spent on the wrong thing."[74]

It was, to her mind, unacceptable to keep Christian principles out of economics and business matters; but, equally, these were places where the Christian needed to be. So, whereas Studdert Kennedy sought the salvation of humanity by returning to the Christian tradition, Royden's faith drove her out of the church in search of fresh ways to transform the world in the service of Christ. For her, Christ was not a mystic who withdrew from the world, but one who "came into the world and took material things to be the instruments of his triumph."[75] Thus, a Christian country should put Christ at the heart of its working life. She pointed her hearers to the work of the Cadbury family, who created a village for their workers and cut the working day to eight hours—which had been thought of as folly. Yet putting human life before business interests had hardly ruined their business. Doing the right thing for workers never harmed business. Taking children out of mines and mills, limiting the hours worked by children under the age of fourteen: these reforms had been challenged by business experts in their day as detrimental to England's commercial supremacy. In fact, business grew. Doing the right thing, seeking first the kingdom of God, was good for business as well as morally right.[76]

Her awareness of international affairs, drawn from her connections throughout the war with the Women's International League, meant that she was quick to condemn British policy that harmed other nations in Europe. In a sermon preached on Palm Sunday 1919, she argued that Britain was trying to "build our new civilization on hatred and revenge." Recriminations and punishment (such as advocated by the bishop of London) were having a disastrous effect in central Europe, where people were starving. "Do you think it belongs to peace to starve a generation of children in Austria? Does it belong to peace to try and hold Ireland against her will? Or to force from Germany what Germany cannot pay?"[77]

74. Ibid., 59.
75. Royden, *Christ Triumphant*, 105.
76. Ibid., 41–57; cf. Matthew 6:33.
77. Royden, *Political Christianity*, 37.

She believed that it was right for the church to engage on political matters, speaking about such diverse subjects as disarmament, British policy towards Russia, and mental health. Wherever possible, she encouraged dialogue, especially after she had preached (although she would deal with questions during her sermons if necessary), claiming that if most people believed that the church was disconnected from the world, it was important for the church to re-engage.[78]

Conclusion

Making sense of human conflict is never straightforward. Preaching in time of war is further complicated by the fact that the preacher speaks with a degree of authority as he or she attempts to help fellow Christians discern the things of God. There is a balance to be struck, even now, therefore, between "preaching the word in season and out of season," as the Church of England service for the ordination of priests puts it,[79] and being mindful of British military personnel who may be engaged in conflict at any point overseas. Preachers need to make sense of war in the light of the gospel for a congregation that may include convinced pacifists as well as soldiers and their families.

Britain has actively engaged in conflict several times since 1918, and preachers have been called upon to wrestle with their thoughts, feelings, and theologies to make sense of this. For some high-profile preachers, this has led to personal criticism. In 1982, at the end of the war with Argentina in the Falkland Islands, the archbishop of Canterbury, Robert Runcie (1921–2000), was criticised for including prayers for Argentinian soldiers who had died in the conflict and suggesting that no one country could lay claim to God, during the service of thanksgiving at St. Paul's Cathedral.[80] Ironically, Runcie had served as a tank commander in the Second World War, and had been awarded the Military Cross for two acts of bravery: he was not a pacifist and had supported the action against Argentina.

---

78. Sue Morgan makes explicit the interplay between Royden's politics and preaching, noting the "inability of the Established Church to benefit from [her] popularity and standing with socially radical groups" (Morgan, "'Feminist Conspiracy,'" 789).

79. *Common Worship: Ordination Services*, 37, drawing on 2 Timothy 4:2.

80. Moore, *Margaret Thatcher*, 757. Moore says that in interview, Runcie told him that Thatcher had "gripped his hand" and said "well done" for the service, but then also notes that the prime minister thought the service lacking in "thanksgiving." In her own autobiography, Thatcher (*Downing Street Years*, 235) doesn't mention the service at all. See also Mantle, *Archbishop*, 155–63, and Carpenter, *Robert Runcie*, 255–61.

More recently, another archbishop of Canterbury, Rowan Williams (b. 1950), publicly opposed Britain's involvement in Iraq in 2002, and continued to criticise the conduct of coalition troops and the treatment of military prisoners, writing to the prime minister to that effect on behalf of other bishops.[81] In a subsequent radio interview, he disclosed his anxiety that he had not done enough to prevent Britain's involvement in Iraq.[82] In 2007, he described the possibility of bomb strikes in Syria as "potentially murderous folly."[83] He, at least, was joined in his misgivings by large numbers of the public, representing serious concerns that engagement in Iraq and Syria was neither legitimate nor justifiable.

For Geoffrey Studdert Kennedy, Arthur Winnington-Ingram, and Maude Royden, war brought personal as well as public challenges. Each of them was faced with the reality of conflict: burying or remembering men known to them, and coming to terms with the vast loss of life that the war entailed. The tragedy of it touched each of them, and each sought solace in faith; in the case of Studdert Kennedy, wrestling with an inherited confident theology and emerging with something more resonant with his experience. They were not given the privilege of dealing with their thoughts in private. They were preachers who commanded large and attentive audiences, eager to know what they thought, whose duty it was, by their preaching, to enable others to grapple with the reality of war and how to make spiritual sense of it. Their differing approaches, styles, and theologies are indicative of three very different but equally passionate lovers of Christ. Whether we regard their sermons, from our comfortable distance, as prophecy or propaganda, the sermons came from the core of the preachers' personal conviction and faith. Ultimately, it is that very faith that emerges with energy—even from words in dusty books, for decades lying unspoken.

81. http://news.bbc.co.uk/1/hi/uk/3852127.stm; cf. Goddard, *Rowan Williams*, 246–49.

82. "Today Programme," BBC Radio 4, 29 December 2006.

83. *Guardian*, 6 October 2007: https://www.theguardian.com/uk/2007/oct/06/religion.usa; cf. Shortt, *Rowan's Rule*, 385.

7

"National Mission"?

Geoffrey Studdert Kennedy, Edward Lee Hicks, R. H. Tawney, and the Social Witness of the Church of England

Mark R. Dorsett

THERE ARE MOMENTS WHEN a specific crisis inexorably directs attention to a powerful historical undercurrent. The First World War, among many other disruptions, brought to an end the British social convention of fairly limited state intrusion into private life. Conscription and state intervention in industry challenged the very nature of Liberal society as the Edwardians had conceived it, and there was much soul-searching about the kind of society that was developing. Within the church, too, there was urgent debate about the future of society, and anguished self-examination about the role that Christian faith would play within it. Any constructive thought about the future demanded attention to the perceived absence, albeit mostly benign, of the working class from the Church of England. In his study of the two centuries of Christian life after the French Revolution, Hugh McLeod observes that in Britain, "the majority of working-class people were neither deeply committed church members, nor did they have strong radical or anti-religious convictions. Their religious ideas tended to be fluid, eclectic, and, from the point of view of churchman or militant unbeliever, incoherent."[1]

---

1. McLeod, *Religion and the People*, 124. While there were wartime worries about

116

Church of England clergy, and particularly those serving as chaplains on the Western Front, were confronted with the realisation that the mass of people were largely indifferent to the active practice of faith as they understood it. Chaplains were better placed than parochial clergy to reflect on this, as they often experienced intense exchanges with men in extreme situations. The ubiquity of sudden and violent death gave a certain urgent authenticity to the ministry of front-line priests. The National Mission of Repentance and Hope was one aspect of the institutional response to this situation. Though one of his biographers described it as "one of the most curious enterprises ever undertaken by a Church in the middle of a war," Geoffrey Studdert Kennedy played a key role within it.[2] One of the "Committees of Inquiry" set up in the wake of the Mission reflected that "the idea of fellowship which is an essential conception in . . . worship has largely been lost through the individualism and the antagonism of classes resulting from the competitive system."[3] In other words, no understanding of the church's mission could ignore the relationship between faith and prevailing socio-economic conditions, and the relative failure of the National Mission was one indication of the scale of the task.

Indeed, to reflect on the Mission after a century is to confront the very nature of Christian social witness. Peter Selby once wrote that the church is placed in the world "to express the longing of God."[4] It is always a counter-cultural struggle to do this and the Church of England has at times colluded with things that it should have challenged. The church cannot quite escape that longing for God, yet "it is that very longing which the Church forgets when it overrides the needs of those who long, and whom God longs, to be included. At such times the Church simply gives a higher priority to maintaining itself."[5] This urge to tribal self-defence lay behind what Selby called "the class captivity of the Church of England."[6] To what extent did the National Mission challenge this captivity? How far did Studdert Kennedy himself achieve a renewed vision of the church in his own ministry?

At the time of the Mission, the future was, of course, unknown, and it would be unfair to judge the Mission and the man by twenty-first-century

church attendance (cf. Machin, *Politics*, 310), attendance figures fell more sharply in later decades, and levels which dismayed church leaders in the First World War would have delighted later generations.

2. Purcell, *Woodbine Willie*, 109.

3. *The Worship of the Church: Being the Report of the Archbishops' Second Committee of Inquiry*, as quoted in Norman, *Church and Society*, 228.

4. Selby, *BeLonging*, 2. Selby was the bishop of Worcester from 1997 to 2007.

5. Ibid., 15.

6. Ibid., 12.

standards. Hensley Henson, then dean of Durham, complained with characteristic bitterness that the Mission brought into prominence "foolish persons, ardent, bigoted and ill-informed, who would not otherwise have gained a hearing."[7] This was an unfair judgment: none of these epithets applied to the Anglicans who are the main focus of this short study. They are all worth a hearing and none of them was foolish. Nonetheless, a critical perspective is required. After examining the impact of the Mission, attention will turn to Studdert Kennedy and two Anglican contemporaries, Edward Lee Hicks, bishop of Lincoln,[8] and R. H. Tawney, one of the most influential economic historians of the twentieth century.[9] These comparisons will illuminate the relative failure of Studdert Kennedy fully to understand the class captivity of his church, and thus the wider limitations of the mission of the wartime church.

Studdert Kennedy and the National Mission

In March 1915, the bishop of Worcester, Huyshe Yeatman-Biggs,[10] wrote to the archbishop of Canterbury, Randall Davidson,[11] to express his concern that the spiritual opportunities that the war presented were not being seized. He had previously written to the *Times* in the same vein.[12] Yeatman-Biggs was only one voice among many urging the archbishops to action, and in November 1915, Davidson made public his desire for a great national spiritual initiative. Earlier in the year, a group had been convened that would, in Davidson's words, consider "ways in which we can effectively 'buy up the

7. As quoted in Neville, *Radical Churchman*, 261. Henson (1863–1947), politically conservative but theologically liberal, was controversially appointed bishop of Hereford in 1917. He was translated to Durham in 1920 and remained there until his retirement in 1939.

8. Edward Lee Hicks (1843–1919) was a residentiary canon of Manchester Cathedral, and then bishop of Lincoln from 1910 until his death.

9. Richard Henry Tawney (1880–1962) was a lecturer (1917–31) and professor (1931–49) in economic history at the London School of Economics. His best-known work was *Religion and the Rise of Capitalism*, published in 1926.

10. Yeatman-Biggs became bishop of Worcester in 1905 and went on to become bishop of Coventry in 1918. A bronze effigy of him was one of the few things to survive the bombing of Coventry Cathedral in 1940.

11. Born in a year of revolutions, 1848, Randall Davidson was a notably cautious archbishop of Canterbury from 1903 to 1928. For a very fair assessment of Davidson, see Edwards, *Leaders*, 232–67. Lloyd George's mistress, Frances Stevenson, called him "God's own butler" (234).

12. See Thompson, "War, the Nation, and the Kingdom of God," 339.

opportunity' which the War affords . . . to bring good out of manifold evil."[13]
The group met in Beaconsfield in early October 1915 and were unanimous
in recommending that "there should be a National Mission led by the Archbishops; that it should be on a scale such as we have never yet contemplated,
and should extend throughout all the cities and towns of the land."[14]

The archbishops, welcoming the proposals, made a public declaration
of intent in November 1915, and later that month, under the chairmanship
of Arthur Winnington-Ingram, bishop of London, the group and four bishops agreed that: "the present emergency demands some special action on
the part of the Church to bring home to the Nation the call of God in War."[15]
Despite some unease about the title "National Mission," Davidson proceeded with the next step, which was to set up a central council of seventy with
the bishop of London as "chief of staff." Alan Wilkinson summarised the
matter thus: "The National Mission of Repentance and Hope in the autumn
of 1916 was an attempt by the Church of England to respond to the spiritual
needs of the nation in wartime; an attempt to discharge its sense of vocation
to act as the Christian conscience of the nation."[16]

Unfortunately, as David Thompson's account makes very clear, there
was a "fatal confusion over the Mission's purpose."[17] For Winnington-
Ingram and those on the evangelical wing, the Mission was seen as an
occasion for traditional "missionary" activity, with a call to sinners to individual repentance and a renewal of life, which was quite compatible with
a fervently patriotic commitment to the war and, effectively, indifference to
social questions. Bishop Moule of Durham, for example, expressed the aims
of the Mission "almost exclusively in terms of the deepening of individual
spirituality."[18] For William Temple and others on the Left who were imbued
with the spirit of the Christian Social Union, matters were otherwise.[19] A
concern for social questions was not "an extra added on to an evangelistic

13. As quoted in ibid., 340.

14. Ibid.

15. Ibid., 341. Worcestershire-born, Winnington-Ingram died in Upton-upon-
Severn after being taken ill while playing golf. In between times, he was bishop of
London from 1901 to 1939. For a challenge to the standard account of Winnington-
Ingram, see Bell, "Malign or Maligned?"

16. Wilkinson, *Church of England*, 70.

17. Thompson, "War, the Nation, and the Kingdom of God," 347.

18. Wilkinson, *Church of England*, 74. Handley Moule (1841–1920) became bishop
of Durham in 1901 after an academic career at Cambridge, and died in office. His great-
nephew C. F. D. Moule became a distinguished biblical scholar.

19. A full, if partisan, account of the Christian Social Union tradition is given in
Norman, *Church and Society*, 221–78. For a critique of his account of the Union, see
Studdert-Kennedy, *Dog-Collar Democracy*, 14–15.

campaign," but the heart of their enterprise.[20] John Kempthorne, bishop of Lichfield, wrote to the archbishop of Canterbury to express his anxiety that "the *social* aspects of a National Mission were not adequately emphasised."[21] Given this division, it is little wonder that historians have judged the Mission a failure. Wilkinson wrote: "In retrospect, the remarkable thing is not the comparative lack of success of the National Mission (though it is difficult to know what the best hopes of the organizers really were) but that it should have been mounted at all."[22]

This is a fair verdict, but in the dark days of 1916, there were more urgent things to attend to than the judgment of posterity, and the question of who should take the Mission to the troops was pressing. There was one obvious answer. Geoffrey Studdert Kennedy, an outstanding pastor in deprived parishes, had established a justified reputation as a chaplain who could speak to soldiers on the Western Front in their own language. This involved a good deal of swearing that made some uncomfortable. Nonetheless, the deputy chaplain general, Bishop Llewellyn Gwynne, was not afraid to consider unconventional options and he chose Studdert Kennedy for a leadership role. When Studdert Kennedy expressed some reluctance, it is said that Gwynne replied: "It does not matter what you want; . . . as you have been given by the Almighty the gift of the gab, you have to do what you are told."[23]

For a man with precarious health, Studdert Kennedy's work-rate was characteristically extraordinary. In one short spell, he preached over thirty sermons to congregations of up to fifteen hundred soldiers, and by the spring of 1917, he had visited all the British bases.[24] The talks are preserved in his first prose work, *Rough Talks by a Padre*, published in 1918.[25] He was not just a theological Missioner, he was also instructed to raise morale and strengthen the fighting spirit of the men. It is not obvious that these tasks were the same. As Callum Brown has observed: "The churches took it upon themselves to be part of the propaganda machine of the day, bolstering the recruitment posters, government newsreels and the calls to duty. . . . Clergy were saying things they later regretted."[26]

20. Thompson, "War, the Nation, and the Kingdom of God," 346.

21. As quoted in ibid., 350, emphasis in the original. Kempthorne was bishop of Lichfield from 1913 until his retirement in 1937.

22. Wilkinson, *Church of England*, 71.

23. Carey, "War Padre," 130. For a sympathetic appraisal of Gwynne, see Parker, *Whole Armour*, 79–81. See also the entry by Peter Howson in the *ODNB*.

24. Holman, *Woodbine Willie*, 40.

25. Studdert Kennedy, *Rough Talks*, 11.

26. Brown, *Religion and Society*, 89.

After a century, some of Studdert Kennedy's words are indeed unsettling, as they apparently collude with a view of Christianity that asks no questions about the moral priority of the nation state, while uncritically accepting a nationalistic account of the origins and conduct of the conflict.[27] He changed over time, but the language of his early sermons still has the power to disturb. He could, for example, speak of Germans as the "enemies of God."[28] This matters because, as Jonathan Gurling has observed, "it is obvious . . . that his real impact was through the spoken word rather than through his writing."[29] Another chaplain, F. B. Macnutt, said, "Several times I had seen the extraordinary effect his addresses had upon the men."[30] A sermon is an event, not a text, and even if we could actually *listen* to Studdert Kennedy we could not *hear* him with the sensibilities of 1916 because our perceptions would inevitably be those of the twenty-first century. His manner of speech, perfectly natural in its day, jars: who now, for example, would describe a child sex offender as "a damned blackguard"?[31] His words simply do not live on the page.

To begin with, he was confident of both British innocence and German barbarity. He seemed simply to ignore the fact that for centuries, British imperialism had been sustained by force, whereas he was keen to pronounce that Germany was driven by "unadulterated Barbarism."[32] German intellectuals had created a philosophy that "Might is always Right."[33] According to Wilkinson, across the trenches Studdert Kennedy "purveyed a highly-coloured version of German history and their national characteristics,"[34] and so he was able to speak of the Germans as a backward people who did not believe in freedom. All of the German people had rejected Christian civilisation.[35]

Many Anglicans, such as Randall Davidson, were careful throughout the entirety of the war to avoid such rhetoric, but Holman defended Studdert Kennedy on the grounds that he was trying to maintain the fighting spirit and morale of the troops. Arguably, however, the archbishop and the

27. For trenchant criticism, see Louden, *Chaplains*, 60–68.
28. Studdert Kennedy, *Rough Talks*, 72.
29. Gurling, "Padre," 21; cf. Purcell, *Woodbine Willie*, 34.
30. Carey, "War Padre," 132.
31. Studdert Kennedy, *Rough Talks*, 104.
32. Ibid., 57.
33. Ibid., 55.
34. Wilkinson, *Church of England*, 210.
35. Studdert Kennedy, *Rough Talks*, 60.

chaplain had the same basic Christian responsibility to eschew what we would now term racist language and ethnic stereotyping.

Holman considers it "odd" that Studdert Kennedy should be so pre-occupied by the issue of "sportsmanship" in his preaching.[36] Along with many others, Studdert Kennedy imbibed the ethos of faith-as-sportsman-ship. Thus, "the great German crime is the denial of this sporting spirit."[37] Kerry Walters, who rightly admired Studdert Kennedy, found it painful to contemplate the fact that in Studdert Kennedy's eyes, "the Tommy was mor-ally superior to the Hun because of the British 'sporting tradition.'"[38] Painful or not, Studdert Kennedy's apparent fixation with sport was not nearly as odd as Holman supposed. In fact, it gives an important insight into his basic thinking about the relationship between faith and culture.[39]

In the short-term, however, Studdert Kennedy was simply uncritically reflecting the spirit of the time when he so forcefully assumed that faith was to be equated with manliness, sportsmanship, and patriotism. There was, in that sense, nothing original in his message to the troops and there is little that remains that could be relevant to the church's mission today. Studdert Kennedy's power lay in the quality of his personal example rather than in what he offered by way of social commentary. What compelled people was

36. Holman, *Woodbine Willie*, 42.

37. Studdert Kennedy, *Rough Talks*, 28.

38. Walters, "Introduction," 10. He points out that Studdert Kennedy was later to be embarrassed by this jingoism.

39. In his survey of the religious scene between 1850 and 1914, Hugh McLeod talks of a leisure revolution which saw the "emergence of sport as a national obsession" (*Religion and Society*, 196). This had religious implications because "sport was becoming the emotional centre of many people's lives" (ibid., 199). Sport and Christianity were linked in a variety of ways. The ideal of "muscular" Christianity grew in importance in the latter part of the nineteenth century and it became a powerful influence in public schools. This in turn led to a rise in the acceptance of militarism as an expression of Christian manliness, and so late Victorians sang "Fight the good fight" and "Onward Christian soldiers," whereas military language had played little part in the hymnody of the late eighteenth and early nineteenth centuries. The rise of uniformed organisations for youngsters from the Boys' Brigade to the Scouts reinforced the link between sport, manliness, patriotism, and religion (ibid., 150–54). The effect of this leisure revolution was curious because while churchmen were often passionate about sport, they did not see that changing patterns of leisure activity would weaken the churches in the longer run, as there simply became other things for people to do. It is plausible to suggest that, though a few Edwardians lost their faith through encountering Darwin, Marx, and Nietzsche, vastly more simply drifted away because of the variety of alternative activi-ties open to them during the limited time that they were free of the workplace. In a sense, the churches were paradoxically engines of this change, as they often set up the very organisations that became autonomous rivals for people's leisure time. This all helped to change the face of twentieth-century Christianity as the practice of faith be-came one option among many.

his transparent compassion, unselfishness, and sincerity, but, while these qualities are rightly celebrated, his surviving prose works cannot be any kind of model for social witness today.

Edward Lee Hicks

While Studdert Kennedy was serving in the trenches, Edward Lee Hicks was contemplating the war from the bishop's palace in Lincoln. In his diocese, the National Mission was discussed and carefully planned, and Hicks approached the task with enthusiasm. He wrote in his diary: "The extraordinary feature of it is that its aims and scope exactly correspond with what I have been always insisting upon as the duty & call of the Church, viz, to appeal not only to individuals for their conversion to God, but to appeal to the Collective Church to take collective action in Xt's name in order to remedy the national evils and social sins of England. God help us in this great endeavour."[40]

When he addressed the Lincoln Diocesan Conference in 1916, he focused on the purpose of the National Mission and stressed its social implications: "To shelter the weak, to raise up a barrier against organised selfishness, to storm the citadels of legalized vice, to fight for municipal righteousness, to agitate for wholesome legislation, to use the vote for promoting good government, to help the weak against the strong, and to make the ways of the world a little less thorny for the wayward."[41]

From the beginning, Hicks recognised that a truly Christian mission could not simply be about individual conversion, nor could patriotism ever be enough, as it was more likely to disfigure the life of the nation than ennoble it. The collective good of the people was never ultimately served by war. He wrote: "Nations have not only their pacific moods; they have their warlike moods also. I was a boy at the time of the Crimea campaign. But I recollect distinctly the war-fever of the time. It swept through the country like a prairie fire. And yet as we look back on it, what a ridiculous war it was—how heedless its inception, how incompetent its carrying out."[42] He also had clear memories of the Boer War and the reasons he had opposed it. Preaching in Manchester Cathedral in 1899, he observed: "Prejudice and passion have prevailed instead of calm and collected reasoning. . . . Statements of the wildest sort, pleas wholly groundless, have taken hold of the

---

40. Evans, *Edward Lee Hicks*, 232.

41. Neville, *Radical Churchman*, 263.

42. Ibid., 247.

popular mind."[43] He continued to be uneasy about any kind of association of religion with militarism. In 1904, he reflected: "Would it not be well if those of us who are entrusted with the care of the large industrial populations were to try more regularly to remind the working men that the great interest of labour is Peace? That war selects chiefly the workers as its victims in the field and the hospital abroad, and its victims in taxation, dear commodities and unemployment at home?"[44]

In 1910, Hicks became president of the Church of England Peace League and remained so until his death in 1919. It was a small organisation, but its aims expressed very clearly his personal convictions, particularly "to keep prominently before the members of the Church of England the duty of combatting the war-spirit as contrary to the spirit of Christianity."[45] It also stressed international co-operation as the key to a world free of war. Small wonder, then, that when war broke out in 1914, Hicks found himself conflicted. He had never been a complete pacifist, but he was a profound sceptic about the need for war and his first instinct was to urge British neutrality, though this was to change. As Gillian Evans remarks, he found it difficult to be consistent in his approach,[46] and the war changed him in a number of significant ways. As Graham Neville wrote, Hicks "hated so much about it, yet was spurred to fresh initiatives, as he became involved in the unexpected ministry of the church."[47] He supported the work of chaplains, he helped refugees, he re-thought the role of women in church and society, he defended conscientious objection and he continued to challenge anything that smacked of false nationalistic pride. All of this was admirable, particularly in a man who was sixty-seven years old before he became a bishop. Evans writes that: "Edward Hicks may have been against war in principle, but he liked people. . . . Those whose consciences prompted them to become soldiers he treated kindly. He shunned no one. It was one thing to disapprove of war in general and try to live as a man of peace. It was another to do the duties of a bishop in a country at war."[48]

Hicks can be seen as an advocate of what Giles Ecclestone would later term "critical solidarity" between church and state.[49] He offered an impres-

43. Evans, *Edward Lee Hicks*, 64.

44. Neville, *Radical Churchman*, 247.

45. Evans, *Edward Lee Hicks*, 124.

46. Ibid., 181.

47. Neville, *Radical Churchman*, 252.

48. Evans, *Edward Lee Hicks*, 209.

49. Ecclestone (1936–90) was the son of the radical Anglican priest Alan Ecclestone, and secretary to the General Synod's Board for Social Responsibility during the Thatcher years. He thus had pressing reasons to think about the relationship between

sive pastoral ministry to his diocese, including the military, but he was not prepared to equate British success with the triumph of morality. His broader mission was to demand a society that was fairer and more equal, and he had a strong sense of political reality. Neville is right to say that there was "a coherent basis . . . to his particular social and political commitment."[50] He was grounded in an incarnationalist theology which expressed itself pragmatically in a demand for practical reform. By contrast, as will become more apparent in comparison with Tawney, Studdert Kennedy seems to have ended up as a sort of warm-hearted but bewildered Tory radical. The socially conservative aspects of his character are often underestimated because of his populist appeal. According to Wilkinson, Studdert Kennedy "was curiously unquestioning about being a priest in uniform. . . . He could on occasion sound like any other conventional patriotic preacher of the period."[51] Nobody could say that of Hicks.

Richard Henry Tawney

If it seems unfair to compare a man who knew the horror of the trenches with an aging bishop who had no such experience, it is instructive to compare Studdert Kennedy with a Christian contemporary who fought and was badly wounded on the Western Front. Born in 1880, Richard Henry Tawney was an Oxford-educated scholar with a passionate commitment to social justice and a lifelong devotion to the Workers' Educational Association (WEA).[52] He was a distinguished economic historian and a close friend of William Temple, a towering influence in twentieth-century Anglicanism, who was to become archbishop of Canterbury in 1942. In November 1914, Tawney joined the Seventh City Battalion of the Manchester Regiment as a private soldier, and though he rose to the rank of sergeant, he never sought a commission. As a private in one of the so-called "Pals" battalions, he was perfectly placed to see at first hand the war that the working class fought.

In February 1916, the Manchesters arrived on the Somme opposite the German-held town of Mametz in preparation for a major assault. So it was that on 1 July 1916, Tawney became one of the regiment's three-hundred-and-fifty casualties. He was hit "in the first wave of the attack by bullets which went clean through his chest and abdomen and took away part of one

church and state.

50. Neville, *Radical Churchman*, 293.

51. Wilkinson, *Church of England*, 136.

52. The most recent biography is Goldman, *Life of R. H. Tawney*. It is both a judicious life of Tawney and a fair evaluation of his overall significance.

of his kidneys."[53] He spent more than a day lying in No Man's Land before he was finally taken to hospital. The experience only reinforced his passionate commitment to democracy and social justice. The following year, while recuperating, he wrote to a friend: "This war seems to have caught us halfway in transition to democracy. We have not the kind of strength we should have if the mass of working people felt that this war was their war, not an enterprise for which their rulers want their arms but not their hearts and minds."[54]

After the war, he served on the Sankey Commission which attempted to reform the dismal state of the coal industry, he was tireless in his support of the WEA, and he wrote a classic work of history, *Religion and the Rise of Capitalism* (1926). As his biographer Goldman has observed, "it is the religious foundation of his social thought which counts,"[55] and he could speak and write "about morality, spirituality and transcendence because he had the linguistic resources within himself to do so, based on the Bible."[56] He was a man whose social concern always had a moral imperative: he thought that "modern society is sick through the absence of a moral ideal" and "the industrial problem is a moral problem."[57] There could never be purely instrumental solutions to social ills because there "was no certainty that when we have cured poverty we shall be better pleased with ourselves."[58] Tawney was rightly dismissive of any attempt to argue that faith was a non-political matter. "The criticism which dismisses the concern of the Churches with economic relations and social organization as a modern innovation finds little support in past history. What requires explanation is not the view that these matters are part of the province of religion, but the view that they are not."[59]

Tawney never wavered in his belief that the Church of England should take a clear moral stance on social questions. As for the belief that it was vain to pursue equality because it could never be fully achieved, that was "like using the impossibility of absolute cleanliness as a pretext for rolling in a dung heap."[60] Tawney was a life-long socialist whose core belief was that practical measures were needed to change the living conditions of the

53. Goldman, *Life of R. H. Tawney*, 98.
54. Ibid., 94.
55. Ibid., 183.
56. Ibid., 312.
57. Ibid., 170.
58. Ibid., 174.
59. Ibid., 184.
60. Ibid., 312.

people. He was a natural democrat with a theologically-grounded belief in the presumption of equality. "The necessary corollary, therefore, of the Christian conception of man is a strong sense of equality. Equality does not mean that all men are equally clever or equally virtuous, any more than they are equally tall or equally fat. It means that all men, merely because they are men are of equal value."[61]

This guiding principle made him a practical reformer who sought direct involvement in social change. At this point, by comparison, the relative incoherence of Studdert Kennedy's post-war thinking becomes very apparent. He gave way to what I will call the "Brownlow fallacy," after Dickens's character of that name. Holman offered the following observation:

> Father Geoffrey and Tawney had similar beliefs. Both asserted that all people were of equal value to God and therefore all had a claim to God's resources. However, they differed on how the end of poverty and other social injustices was to be achieved. Tawney argued that the rich and powerful would never voluntarily agree to share their incomes and wealth more fairly and that therefore the Labour Party had to seek change through politics and trade union activities which complied with the law. Father Geoffrey considered that this meant class warfare and put his faith in all people accepting "The truth that the Secret of Life is service." This could only come about by widespread acceptance of Christianity.[62]

This highlights the core weakness of Studdert Kennedy's thinking. For all his extraordinary personal courage and compassion, he never developed any coherent thoughts about how real change might be brought about. He once told Ernest Bevin that "class hatred" was created by the Labour Party, and he seems never to have contemplated the idea that, from a different perspective, this was simply the poor attempting to defend themselves in a profoundly unequal society. During the war, he demanded that Britain must "secure leaders who have no party to serve, and no axe to grind, no class to consider—men wholly devoted . . . —men who are clean at heart."[63] On the subject of where such men were to be found, he had nothing to say. Thus, Gerald Studdert-Kennedy was right to say of Geoffrey that "his general orientation had little in common with Tawney's."[64] Tawney was "unromantic about the working classes" and had an "unpatronising sense of the human

---

61. Ibid.
62. Holman, *Woodbine Willie*, 99.
63. Ibid., 46.
64. Studdert-Kennedy, *Dog-Collar Democracy*, 76.

qualities of ordinary people."[65] This led Tawney to a fundamental political premise, which Geoffrey Studdert Kennedy ignored: real social change involved a clear-eyed view of the structural relations of interest and power between classes.[66]

Studdert Kennedy's most explicit engagement with political issues came in *Democracy and the Dog Collar*, which appeared in 1921. Even the admiring Holman said that it "lacks dynamism."[67] Studdert Kennedy seemed confused about class, arguing that while the church does not "recognise class distinction in any form," it is also the case that the "upper classes" are "upper partly through essential superiority of brain power and ability."[68] On the question of how this superiority was achieved in the first place, he offered no insight.

Holman's assertion that "Father Geoffrey" and Tawney had similar beliefs comes under more strain when the following assertion, which appeared in *Democracy*, is considered: "There is no lie more utterly devoid of truth than the lie of the equality of man."[69] It is impossible to imagine Tawney writing such a sentence, although it was a sentiment to which Studdert Kennedy gave repeated expression. Similarly, although Studdert Kennedy was sympathetic to the plight of the working class, he was suspicious of trade unions and thought that strikes were a form of class warfare. How could workers improve their lot without recourse to industrial action? Well, they must rely on the essential righteousness of their cause and "the appeal which it has made to the conscience of men."[70] On what to do if, for example, the consciences of the hard-faced men who owned the coal mines were not moved, he was silent.

In this respect, Studdert Kennedy is more than a little reminiscent of Charles Dickens. In his celebrated essay on Dickens, George Orwell wrote that: "The truth is that Dickens's criticism of society is almost exclusively moral. . . . He attacks the law, parliamentary government . . . without ever clearly suggesting what he would put in their places."[71] Again, Dickens's "whole 'message' is one that at first glance looks like an enormous platitude: If men would behave decently the world would be decent. . . . Hence that

---

65. Ibid., 79–80.

66. Ibid., 79.

67. Holman, *Woodbine Willie*, 104.

68. Studdert Kennedy, *Democracy*, 26 and 198.

69. Ibid., 198.

70. Ibid., 53.

71. George Orwell, *Decline*, 83.

recurrent Dickens figure, the good rich man."[72] In *Oliver Twist*, Dickens takes on poverty, child labour, crime, and urban squalor, but he cannot get beyond the idea that the world needs not structural change, but rather more Mr. Brownlows. Similarly, Holman observed that "although Father Geoffrey wants politicians to tackle social injustices, he never explains in detail what he means by this."[73]

During the last years of his life, Studdert Kennedy gave unstinting commitment to the Industrial Christian Fellowship (ICF). He was as passionate and eloquent as ever, but it is worth noting Neville's judgment that in the ICF, the old Christian Social Union (CSU) principles foundered: "its current ran into the sand of shop-floor evangelism when it took on the guise of the Industrial Christian Fellowship and recruited Woodbine Willie as its missioner."[74] At first sight this is harsh, but the ICF focused on "fellowship" to such a degree that the brutal reality of the conflicts of the time were underestimated. Holman wrote of Studdert Kennedy's limited influence during the ICF years: "he was not on close terms with politicians of any party or with trade unionists. When governments announced legislation intended to help the unemployed and poor, Studdert Kennedy did not write about or publicly discuss it in detail. If he had nurtured friendships with political figures, he would have developed a better understanding of social policy. If he had related more closely to trade union leaders, he might have gained deeper insights into their strategies and why they sometimes resorted to strikes, which he tended to condemn."[75]

It is no surprise that people flocked to hear Studdert Kennedy preach and found inspiration in his example. There was, however, as Holman indicated, a certain unreality in his message, which was utterly sincere, but detached from the concrete conditions of inter-war Britain. As Matthew Grimley has observed, Henson was more realistic in thinking that "class conflict was so serious and endemic a threat that it could not be countered by conciliatory talk of social fellowship."[76] In such circumstances, whatever

72. Ibid., 84.

73. Holman, *Woodbine Willie*, 106.

74. Neville, *Radical Churchman*, 295. Those who consider the inoffensiveness of the ICF to be in question might contemplate the way in which it was approved of by the *Spectator*, no less (10 April 1926, 5): "One would have expected . . . an active enthusiasm for a society which would have it within its power, if its doctrines were sufficiently spread about, to guarantee that no industrial or Labour movement in this country should be anti-religious. . . . In general the I. C. F. stands only for the doctrine that Christianity should concern itself with the conditions of industrial life. That is not Socialism" (http://archive.spectator.co.uk/article/10th-april-1926/5/the-industrial-christian-fellowship).

75. Holman, *Woodbine Willie*, 164.

76. Grimley, *Citizenship*, 7.

its virtues, the ICF could make no effective challenge to what Selby termed the "class captivity" of the church. Gerald Studdert-Kennedy rightly described the CSU tradition as "a complex of affiliations" fed by a variety of theological perspectives; while it had its "reformist vitality" in the form of the ICF, it "evolved into . . . uneventful respectability."[77] Thus, David Edwards could speak of Geoffrey Studdert Kennedy as "ultimately non-political,"[78] and Gerald Studdert-Kennedy thought his uncle's social radicalism was a "myth."[79]

The latter point is strengthened when the influence of W. H. Mallock on Studdert Kennedy's thought is taken into account.[80] Mallock was a right-wing intellectual who feared democracy and socialism in equal measure, and supposed that "the rule of the few over the many . . . is a practical necessity in all democracies."[81] For Mallock, the key fallacy of the democratic age was that the majority would benefit from egalitarian social policies.[82] Although, according to Gerald Studdert-Kennedy, there is only one direct reference to Mallock in Studdert Kennedy's works,[83] Studdert Kennedy breathes the same spirit, as when he wrote: "First let us recognise this great fact, that if men are to unite in order to work there must be discipline. . . . That is, there must be in every co-operative effort those who command and those who obey."[84] Studdert Kennedy's expression of the view that a serious re-distribution of wealth would be both impractical and wholly undesirable also derive very straightforwardly from Mallock.[85]

What of Tawney? Goldman argued that Tawney's "language and expression" are "unfamiliar" because we no longer have the words to "express a personal and moral commitment in our politics." We have a utilitarian vocabulary "where once Tawney could inspire commitment and spiritual transcendence." If this seems pessimistic, he continues: "There can be no prophets without a prophetic language. . . . Our political discourse has lost the capacity to instil belief and become a matter of routine; without the words to inspire and uplift we are unable to imagine a different future."[86]

77. Studdert-Kennedy, *Dog-Collar Democracy*, 4–5.

78. Edwards, "'Woodbine Willie,'" 11.

79. Studdert-Kennedy, *Dog-Collar Democracy*, 14.

80. Ibid., 96–104.

81. Ibid., 103.

82. Cowling, *Religion*, 298. See 297–304 for a summary of Mallock's views.

83. Studdert-Kennedy, *Dog-Collar Democracy*, 97; cf. Studdert Kennedy, *Lies!* 42.

84. Studdert Kennedy, *Lies!* 50–51.

85. As demonstrated in Studdert-Kennedy, *Dog-Collar Democracy*, 98–99.

86. Goldman, *Life of R. H. Tawney*, 314.

Furthermore, the world that Tawney knew is lost to us, and we confront new challenges, "so it would be easy enough to argue that Tawney has no obvious relevance today."[87] This is too pessimistic. Reflecting on Tawney's place in the English radical tradition, Stefan Collini put him alongside those who "foregrounded the ethically corrosive power of the financial imperatives at the heart of market societies. Faced with the social destruction wrought by unchecked 'market forces' in recent decades, it is hard to see how anyone could regard the concerns of this tradition as altogether passé."[88] This idea is worth some examination.

Conclusion

Recently, my sister posted on social media a photograph of our maternal grandfather, Private Alfred James Whorton, which I had never previously seen. It was taken in 1916, somewhere on the Somme. He is smiling and looks absurdly young. In the uniform of the Staffordshire regiment, he sits astride what appears to me a frighteningly large horse. It seems a long way from the Rose Hill Methodist Chapel in Dudley where his worldview was formed. Thinking back over forty years, I can remember his wartime anecdotes clearly and there remains a sense of real regret that I didn't write things down or record them. My first thought on seeing the photograph was that I am as far away in time from the battle of the Somme as he was from the battle of Waterloo. In what sense does that world relate to mine? Edward Hicks died in 1919, Studdert Kennedy a decade later, and while Tawney lived on until 1962, we can only guess what he would have made of the last half century. Nonetheless, they remain in their different ways, sources of inspiration.

The Italian writer Primo Levi, who survived Auschwitz, observed that most people do things so as to talk about them later, while there are some rare people who simply live in their deeds.[89] Studdert Kennedy was no social thinker, but he lived in his deeds. P. T. R. Kirk said of his friend that "his life was of one piece."[90] The depth of that apparently simple tribute should not be missed as it is actually very hard to unify one's principles with one's attitudes and actions. On the occasions when I preside at the eucharist in St. George's Chapel at Worcester Cathedral, it is impossible to be unmindful of the presence of that simple but profound memorial to Studdert Kennedy on

87. Ibid., 317.

88. Collini, *Common Writing*, 192.

89. Angier, *Double Bond*, 137–41.

90. Kirk, "I. C. F. Crusader," 167.

the south wall of the chapel (see figure 7). It is a permanent challenge to live with generosity and authenticity.

In their different ways, Hicks and Tawney believed that faith must be expressed practically through collective provision for health, education, and the welfare needs of the most vulnerable. Hicks was a Liberal who "did not adopt any theoretical views of a socialist kind about an ideal society,"[91] while Tawney was a democratic socialist who may have had too much faith in public ownership as a solution to poverty and inequality.[92] They were, after all, men of their time. Dell, for example, suggests that there was a Puritan element in the socialism of Tawney and others of his era, such as Clement Attlee, which would simply not resonate in the consumer culture that developed in the latter part of the twentieth century.[93] What remains important, however, is not Hicks's and Tawney's particular views, but their profound belief that the church must always challenge untrammelled materialism and individualism. Both were prepared to support unpopular causes, and neither thought that taxation and re-distributive spending would improve society if there were not also a moral change in how people interacted.

Where can that spirit now be found in the church? A good example would be the work of Peter Selby. In *An Idol Unmasked: A Faith Perspective on Money*, he raises some profound questions about the role that money plays in the modern world. At one point, he reflects on what two popular advertising slogans tell us about how we live now. Access credit cards were marketed with the slogan that "Access takes the waiting out of wanting." Selby observes that "the significance of that offer cannot be overstated," as it marked the end of a culture of saving, prudence, and prioritising, in favour of a culture of immediate gratification and debt.[94]

The symbol of the National Lottery is two crossed fingers and the slogan "It could be you." The slogan itself is worthy, as it could be a call to community service or unselfish action. Then Selby observes:

> But put the two crossed fingers logo alongside that slogan and the meaning is quite different. What "could be you" now is the status of multi-millionaire; the right numbers that would win that night might be yours; somebody is going to have their life transformed—and "it could be you." The attitude suggested by

91. Neville, *Radical Churchman*, 311.

92. It is worth noting that as early as 1925, Tawney appreciated the danger of national industries becoming over-centralised and producer rather than consumer orientated. The "leaden inertia" of public ownership was to dominate political discourse during the Thatcher years. See Goldman, *Life of R. H. Tawney*, 310.

93. Dell, *Strange Eventful History*, 15–16.

94. Selby, *Idol*, 77.

the possibility of this reward derives much of its power from the portrayal of those with massive pay bonuses, enjoying a lifestyle that is way beyond the imagining of most who set off for work in the morning and bring home an ordinary day's wage. But thanks to the lottery "it could be you." It is money that might produce for you the major life transformation you seek—not something so unrewarding as a call to service.[95]

Selby is concerned that money has become an idol because it has the idol's power to transform human desire in a way that is injurious to true community. It led him to a concern about such things as the introduction of a National Lottery, a concern which was as popular as was Hicks's opposition to the liquor trade in Edwardian Britain. Nonetheless, it is not difficult to see that Studdert Kennedy, Hicks, and Tawney would have shared Selby's concerns about the ethics of the financial system and the triumph of market values. The key difference between Selby and his predecessors lies in the fact that they saw British society as essentially Christian and could appeal to shared cultural values rooted in a widespread level of biblical literacy. This is now no longer possible.

Callum Brown has argued forcefully that during the 1960s, British society secularised rapidly.[96] He later refined his view, but it remains a fair generalisation that the marginalisation of traditional forms of Christianity accelerated towards the end of that decade.[97] Christianity moved to the edge of society as fewer and fewer people practised religion and important public policies ceased to be rooted in what were understood as biblical values. In this respect, something like the decriminalisation of homosexuality can be seen as a significant cultural marker. Brown probably overstated his original case, and McLeod was nearer the mark when he called the sixties a "hinge decade" between the relative certainties of the earlier post-war era and the startling challenges of both the permissive society and the Thatcherite reaction to it.[98] It is clear that whatever view is taken of the long-running debate about secularisation, the Church of England found itself in an increasingly *plural* situation. As McLeod points out, there had been "a social order in which, regardless of individual belief, Christian language, rites, moral teachings, and personnel were part of the taken-for-granted environment."[99] By the end of the sixties, this was gone.

---

95. Ibid., 78.
96. Brown, *Death of Christian Britain*, 187.
97. Brown, *Religion and Society*.
98. McLeod, *Religious Crisis*, 264.
99. Ibid., 265.

By contrast, in contemporary Britain, there is a whole variety of religious and ideological options available, ranging from atheism to Zen, with a good deal in between. Berger, Berger, and Kellner put it thus: when "pluralism develops the individual is forced to take cognizance of others who do not believe what he believes and whose life is dominated by different, sometimes contradictory beliefs[;] . . . pluralism weakens the hold of religion in society and on the individual."[100] Reflecting on the religious impact of conflict on British soldiers in two world wars, Michael Snape observes that there was a widespread concern that "industrialized warfare" would have a "secularizing influence" on them, but actually "there is no indication of a widespread drift towards atheism."[101] The soldiers in both world wars were overwhelmingly working class and their general indifference to organised religion certainly did not take this form. In the longer run, however, this was not necessarily good news for the mainstream churches, as pluralism rather than atheist secularism became the key marker of British religiosity. Thus, in their recent study of the religious situation, Brown and Woodhead neatly identify a key indicator of pluralisation as the "proliferating possibilities of identity."[102] This free market in religious and spiritual options has become a problem for all traditionally structured churches. Thus, Brown and Woodhead call their story one of "an England which has changed too much, and of a national church which has changed too little."[103] In this context, therefore, the social witness of the Church of England can no longer be premised on the assumption of a shared Christian vocabulary of the common good.[104]

100. Berger et al., *Homeless Mind*, 75–76.

101. Snape, *God and the British Soldier*, 245.

102. Brown and Woodhead, *That Was the Church*, 213.

103. Ibid., 212.

104. In this respect, it is intriguing that Selby ends his book with a reflection from the governor of the Bank of England, Mark Carney, rather than a theologian. At a conference on "Inclusive Capitalism," Carney observed that there are good reasons why people care about distributive justice, social equity, and inter-generational equality. He cites three crucial reasons: "First, there is growing evidence that relative equality is good for growth. At a minimum, few would disagree that a society that provides opportunity to all of its citizens is more likely to thrive than one which favours an elite. . . . Second, research suggests that inequality is one of the most important determinants of relative happiness and that a sense of community . . . is a critical determinant of well-being. Third, they appeal to a fundamental sense of justice. Who behind a Rawlsian veil of ignorance—not knowing their future talents and circumstances—wouldn't want to maximise the welfare of the least well off?" (Selby, *Idol*, 133–34). Carney's final point may need a little explanation. John Rawls's *A Theory of Justice* was published in 1971, and it transformed the global debate about political philosophy with its passionate but coolly detailed advocacy of distributive justice. At its core is a simple thought-experiment. Suppose that you had to devise a society in which you would then have to live. Suppose

Selby is right to argue that the boundary "between secular and religious commentary is more fluid than we often suppose,"[105] and therefore the church's social witness must be expressed through dialogue with all those who care about human flourishing, rather than through issuing demands for a return to a Christian society. Instead of lamenting the plurality of postmodern conditions in a mood of false nostalgia, the church should embrace the possibilities of its new role. Studdert Kennedy and his peers should inspire us, but we cannot return to their world.

---

also that you are behind a "veil of ignorance" about your future state. You may be clever, you may not; you may be male or female, fit or disabled; you may be part of the majority community or an ethnic minority. Given this, argued Rawls, would it not be rational for you so to order society that, whatever your circumstances, you had reasonable access to the things that enable human flourishing such as healthcare, education, housing and welfare provision? In the light of this, argued Rawls, there should be a presumption of equality, and only those inequalities were justified which assisted the least well-off. In other words, the surgeon may justifiably earn a great deal more than the shop-worker if, and only if, the surgeon's work enables the life chances of the least well-off.

105. Ibid., 134.

8

"The Pity of War"
The First World War and Humanitarianism[1]

David R. W. Bryer

HUMANITARIANISM—EXTENDING KINDNESS AND SYMPATHY to all human beings—is a theme that is found in all faiths. While, historically, it has been an evolving concept, universality and impartiality have been common to its development. In Europe, from at least the time of the Enlightenment in the late seventeenth century, the equal valuing of all human beings has been combined with a call for social reform (the movements to abolish torture and slavery being prime examples), and the word "humanitarianism" has been widely employed to contrast with philanthropy or charity which carries out benevolent acts without seeking those political changes that make the philanthropy necessary. The Brazilian archbishop and liberation theologian Hélder Câmara made the distinction effectively when he remarked: "When I give food to the poor, they call me a saint. When I ask why the poor have no food, they call me a communist."[2]

Geoffrey Studdert Kennedy began the First World War in support of British involvement, and, like many other clergy, encouraged men to volunteer. He became a chaplain in late 1915 and joined the troops in France. His

---

1. "The pity of war" is a phrase used by Wilfred Owen in his preface to *Poems*, vii.

2. Hélder Pessoa Câmara (1909–99) was archbishop of Olinda and Recife in Brazil, and fearless in standing up for the poor during the military dictatorship of 1964–85. See Câmara, *Essential Writings*, 11.

earliest writings, notably *Rough Talks of a Padre*, suggest an immersion in military life and a keenness to connect gospel principles with the standard reasons for the pursuit of the war. In particular, Studdert Kennedy argued that British soldiers were fighting to end German "aggression" and, effectively, to end militarism, ushering in a more lasting peace. They fought for freedom, honour, and peace, and, in a word, for "Christ."[3]

Studdert Kennedy's attitude to war began to change, largely as a result of his face-to-face encounter with human suffering and the outcome of human violence. Away from his preaching engagements, his pastoral ministry took him to aid stations and to the injured and dying. Indeed, he was awarded the Military Cross for tending to the wounded under fire after the attack on the Messines Ridge. It was real encounter, rather than dispassionate, objective theorising that led him to shift his understanding both of war and of the nature of God. A dead German soldier, a sergeant in hospital who asked searching questions, the chaos and consequences of deadly warfare, led him to challenge his earlier assumptions.[4]

He was, of course, a priest and, perhaps inevitably, his internal wrestling with his situation found expression in his theology. After the war, preaching for peace and against the wasteful horror of armed conflict, he argued that the only way for human beings to emerge from violence was through a deeper faith in Christ who suffered on the cross. Indeed, although respectful and admiring of those who sought to make the world a better and more peaceful place through medicine, science, and education, he saw "humanity," rather than Christ, as the creed of such people. Humanitarians lacked religion: "They have the Christian ethic, they need the Christian religion. It is only as religion that humanitarianism can become a vital force transforming character and making men anew. And that is the great need of all humanitarians."[5]

This chapter will outline a history of humanitarianism before, during, and after the First World War, demonstrating how the war helped to focus the movements that had preceded it, and how it shaped future developments. It will show that the organisations that we now take for granted rarely began within mainstream Christian churches—indeed, official religion played a marginal part in some of the world's most compassionate activity within the theatre of war—and that significant humanitarian contributions were often started by the endeavours of small numbers of committed individuals,

3. Studdert Kennedy, *Rough Talks*, 66.

4. See further, Bell, "Collusion to Condemnation."

5. Studdert Kennedy, *Food*, 92. My thanks to the editors for these insights into Studdert Kennedy's views.

whose faith and social connections enabled great enterprise. Those who were involved believed that change could be brought into effect primarily through human agency, exerting pressure on governments; for governments could develop, and attempt to enforce, international humanitarian law that limited the effects of armed conflict by protecting persons who were not or were no longer participating in hostilities, and by restricting the means of warfare available to combatants. Such campaigning was intertwined with practical action by governments and non-governmental organisations (NGOs) to reduce the suffering caused by war.

Looking back at the First World War and the growth of international humanitarian law, the creation of humanitarian wings in governments and religious bodies, and the steady increase in NGOs, one might imagine that their development was assured; well-organised responses to the growing horror of war and its aftermath. The reality is rather different. In 1914, very few envisaged the scale or challenge of the war ahead, let alone the accompanying genocide of the Armenians or the political turmoil and mass movement of people that followed the war. It was perhaps because of this that during the war years, neither humanitarian constraints through legal change nor action through new organisations really developed. In an atmosphere of intense patriotism and moral certainty, appeals to humanitarian principles of impartiality were rare and, when made, little appreciated. The greater power of government and the armed forces also left little room for voluntarism. For the four years of war there was a feeling of muddling through, using the tools developed in the half-century before, but with no time or will to look further.[6] It is significant that Bruno Cabanes dates humanitarianism as beginning properly at the end of the war.[7] Nonetheless, it was the experience of what had and had not worked during the war that led to major moves forward in the years beyond 1918, as part of a flood of repulsion at war and a determined effort, at least by some, to find new ways of managing the problems of the world.

6. Cf. Peter Howson's use of the expression "muddling through" for the history of British army chaplaincy during the course of the war, in his book of that very title.

7. Cabanes argues (*Great War*, 4) that humanitarianism became more organised around transnational networks, more secular, and, increasingly, more reliant on emerging professional groups, such as physicists, engineers, and social workers, alongside traditional volunteers and missionaries.

Humanitarianism before the First World War

The decades before 1914 show the significance of the influence and impact of individuals in the history of humanitarianism. The haphazard humanitarian activities of the First World War were made possible because of the actions of one man, walking across a battlefield more than fifty years earlier. On the evening of 24 June 1859, a Swiss businessman, Henry Dunant, arrived in Solferino, a small town in the Lombard plain, in search of Napoleon III.[8] He had come to find help for his agricultural schemes in Algeria. The French emperor, fighting alongside his ally, Victor Emmanuel II, the king of Sardinia, in support of Italian independence, had spent the day leading his troops against an Austrian army led by a youthful Emperor Franz Josef. Three hundred thousand men had fought and now at least twenty thousand were lying wounded on the battlefield. Dunant never met Napoleon and his agricultural schemes collapsed in due course, but it was his horror at what he saw, heard, and smelt that evening that led directly to the foundation of the Red Cross and the beginnings of what would become, over the next century, international humanitarian law.

For the next few days, he organised teams of local women to take food and water to the wounded, he sent off to Brescia for bandages and "comforts" including cigars, and he then dragooned passing travellers including four English tourists and Philippe Suchard, the chocolate manufacturer, to dress wounds and write farewell letters. After a week, Dunant headed home, but the horrors of Solferino would not leave him and in 1862, he published *A Memory of Solferino*. This was not just an account of what he had seen, but also included a proposal for setting up societies of volunteers who would help the wounded in war and draw up some international principles for the relief of the wounded. His ideas were sympathetically received by others of the Protestant elite in Geneva, including General Dufour,[9] probably the most respected man in the city, and the lawyer Gustave Moynier.[10] Two others joined them, and by February 1863, they had formed an International Committee for Relief to the Wounded. The background of these Red

8. For a full account of the work of Dunant (1828–1910), and the foundation of the Red Cross, see Moorehead, *Dunant's Dream*.

9. Guillaume-Henri Dufour (1787–1875) prevented the break-up of the Swiss Confederation in 1847, leading the army which defeated the breakaway cantons in less than a month and with fewer than one hundred casualties. Already a humanitarian, he prevented any further harm coming to the wounded.

10. Gustave Moynier (1826–1910) came from an old banking family in Geneva. He was a major figure in building the Red Cross and was its president from 1864 until 1910, though sadly the cause of Dunant's expulsion from the organisation in 1867 and of the prevention of Dunant's return.

Cross founders is typical of many significant players in the humanitarian movement thereafter: prosperous enough to have the time to develop their organisations, respected for their solid bourgeois ancestry, and motivated by an ethic coming from their practising Christianity, but not representative of any particular denomination.

By October of the same year, this small organisation was ready to host an international conference in Geneva.[11] Dunant had spent the summer drumming up support. The kings of Saxony, Denmark, Belgium, and Portugal sent letters of support, while the Russians proposed the inclusion of prisoners of war in the discussion. Despite the lack of enthusiasm on the part of the British delegate, who thought that the army could deal with such matters itself, the conference was nevertheless a remarkable success and ended with agreement to set up committees in a number of countries which would recruit and train voluntary medical personnel to assist army medics where they existed. Such volunteers were to be seen as neutral and wear a distinctive emblem: a red cross. The International Committee in Geneva was designated the hub of the network and would be the keeper of the articles of humanitarian conduct which the conference had agreed.[12]

Dunant's initiative may have had the single biggest long-term effect on humanitarianism, but it was by no means unique. There were other examples of significant changes brought about by the efforts of individuals. Preparations for the Geneva conference coincided with the climax of the American Civil War. On 1 January 1863, President Lincoln (1809–65) had promulgated the Proclamation of Emancipation, declaring that all persons held as slaves within the rebellious states would, henceforward, be free.[13] Jefferson Davis, president of the Confederate states, insisted that this violated the customary rules of warfare and he announced that the south would treat black Union soldiers as criminals, not as soldiers, subject to execution and re-enslavement upon capture. Lincoln replied on 24 April with what became called the Lieber Code, named after its author, the German-American legal scholar and political philosopher Franz Lieber.[14]

---

11. Moorehead, *Dunant's Dream*, 20–21.

12. The basic structure of national societies (linked, after the First World War, through a second Geneva Secretariat [now the IFRC] and the ICRC, an International Committee of the Red Cross) has, with modifications, remained until today.

13. http://avalon.law.yale.edu/19th_century/emancipa.asp.

14. Franz Lieber (c.1798–1872) was a man of many parts: born in Berlin, he falsified his age to fight at Waterloo, where he was wounded, fought in the Greek War of Independence, was imprisoned in Germany for opposing the Prussian monarchy, went to Boston to run a gymnasium, and became a professor of history and political science first in South Carolina and then at Columbia University.

It dictated how soldiers should conduct themselves in wartime. The main sections concerned martial law, military jurisdiction, and the treatment of spies, deserters, and prisoners of war; and the document insisted upon the humane, ethical treatment of populations in occupied areas. It was the first codified law that expressly forbade killing prisoners of war, except in such cases when the survival of the unit that held these prisoners was threatened. It forbade the use of poisons and the use of torture to extract confessions, it described the rights and duties of prisoners of war and of capturing forces, and it specifically defended the lawfulness of emancipation under the laws of war—insisting that those same laws prohibited discrimination on the basis of colour among combatants.[15]

While a German-born professor had inspired a president to alter the conventions of military conduct in wartime, a middle-aged civil servant, Clara Barton, led a voluntary response to the treatment of the wounded.[16] The American armies proved quite incapable of looking after their own wounded, let alone those of the other side. Badly wounded men were left not only with their wounds and subsequent gangrene untreated, but they did not even get food and water. As Dunant found at Solferino and Florence Nightingale in the Crimea, the government thought that voluntary help would be a distraction;[17] yet Barton managed to change opinion. A "Sanitary Commission" was set up and began to mitigate the situation with voluntary stretcher-bearers, supplies, nurses, and field hospitals. By the time the Geneva Conference was taking place, her movement was in full swing, though it was some time before the European and American initiatives recognised and collaborated with each other.

Back in Geneva, Moynier and Dunant had been busy, the former preparing a draft treaty to be discussed by national delegations and Dunant urging leaders to set up societies to work with the wounded in war. They

15. Lieber, ed., *Instructions for the Government*. See especially articles 57 and 58 regarding colour (17).

16. Clara Barton (1821–1912) started life as a schoolteacher, and went on to work in the federal patent office, the first woman to work at that level at a salary equivalent to a man's. Although opposition to women in government work led to her being eased out of the civil service, she was more than ready for a new challenge when the Civil War began.

17. Florence Nightingale (1820–1910), credited with changing not only army hospitals, but nursing more widely, was, despite her own endeavours, also in fact suspicious of any humanitarian action in wartime beyond the army medical services themselves. Indeed, in a letter to Sir Thomas Longmore, she declared that she could "conceive of circumstances of force majeure in war where the more people are killed the better." War was better if it was quick and not prolonged by well-meaning assistance (Moorehead, *Dunant's Dream*, 47–48).

also, for the first time, sent delegates to observe military conduct during the Schleswig-Holstein War between Denmark and Prussia/Austria in the spring of 1864.[18] By 8 August 1864, a "Diplomatic Conference" opened in Geneva's Hotel de Ville. Twenty-six delegates from sixteen countries attended. Within two weeks, they had agreed "the Geneva Convention for the Amelioration of the Condition of the Wounded and Sick in Armed Forces in the Field," with important clauses guaranteeing neutrality for medical installations and personnel, and noting the Red Cross as the universal emblem of such.[19] Twelve countries ratified the treaty including France and Prussia, though it took some years before the British or Americans did so. It was this convention that was to be the base of the first of the Geneva Conventions that make up international humanitarian law today.

Over the next fifty years, the local societies grew in number and size. By the opening of the Russo-Japanese War in 1904, the largest Red Cross was in Japan with a million members. From being a purely European venture, the movement spread until members were found from China and Thailand to the USA and Brazil. Individual societies moved into new areas and increased their peacetime activities; the Americans, in particular, became increasingly expert in providing assistance after natural disasters, for example, after the earthquakes in San Francisco in 1906 and Messina, Sicily, in 1908. Societies also began to intervene far from home, such as in the Russian famine of 1891 and the aftermath of the Armenian massacres of 1895.

The International Committee of the Red Cross (ICRC), meanwhile, had to cope with the growing problems thrown up by war, such as the Franco-Prussian War, the Anglo-Boer wars, the Russo-Japanese War, various Balkan conflicts, and the siege of Paris. The red cross emblem was misused and exploited by armies, politicians, and businessmen or, in the case of the 1878 war in Bosnia, regarded as a purely Christian symbol.[20] The two key problems were first, that the only form of enforcement was by persuasion and negotiation, and second, that the conventions only concerned combatants. Thus, for example, the Anglo-Boer wars were beyond the reach of the ICRC. The British did not regard their engagement as covered by the

18. The Schleswig-Holstein question, which bedevilled Danish-German relations for many years, reportedly led Palmerston to remark: "Only three people have ever really understood the Schleswig-Holstein business—the Prince Consort, who is dead—a German professor, who has gone mad—and I, who have forgotten all about it" (Strachey, *Queen Victoria*, 182).

19. The text of the Convention is included in Dunant, *Memory of Solferino*, at 137–46. See 142–46.

20. This led to the addition of the Red Crescent in Muslim countries (a precedent that produced new problems a century later, so that now there is also a "Red Crystal").

conventions. The greatest sufferers were civilian women and children: forty thousand of them (half of them children) died in the so-called "concentration camps," with the Red Cross left as helpless bystanders.

While the Geneva Convention dealt with the treatment of combatant victims in war, governments were beginning to look at ways of limiting war itself. The leader of this movement was Tsar Alexander II, liberator of the serfs and something of a reformer.[21] In the Brussels Conference of 1874, some progress was made, beginning with the definition of a soldier as a man in uniform obeying the laws of war. In 1899, the tsar's grandson, Nicholas II, summoned a further conference in the Hague, attended by twenty-six governments. Although this First Hague Conference failed to limit or reduce armaments as the tsar had hoped, they did pass three important conventions and three declarations. The conventions covered the peaceful settlement of disputes and the creation of the Permanent Court of Arbitration, the laws and customs of war (endorsing the Geneva Convention, but also forbidding the use of poisons, the killing of soldiers who had surrendered, the bombarding of undefended towns, collective punishment, etc.), and, lastly, the application of the Geneva Convention at sea. The three declarations were against the launching of projectiles from balloons and the like, against the use of projectiles to spread poison gas, and against expanding bullets. The conventions were ratified by all the participants, and the declarations by all except the USA and, in the case of projectiles from the air, also the British.[22]

Thus, by the outbreak of war in August 1914, there existed the limited framework of a humanitarian agenda because of the efforts of individuals, small groups, and governments. The Geneva Convention and the two Hague Conventions offered frail constraints on total war, while the thirty-eight Red Cross societies, and some religious organisations, notably some Catholic nursing sisterhoods, the Salvation Army, the Quakers, and, in the British Empire, the Order of St. John of Jerusalem and the St. John Ambulance Brigade, gave some limited extra support to the hugely overstretched medical resources of armies.[23]

21. Alexander II (1818–81) was tsar of Russia from 1855 until his assassination. Known as "the Liberator" for his emancipation of the serfs in 1861, he was a rare reformer among Russian rulers, also ending capital punishment, encouraging education, and devolving some power to local authorities.

22. A second Hague conference, called in 1907 by the American president Theodore Roosevelt (1858–1919), made minor changes mainly around naval warfare, and forbade the waging of war without explicit warning. As with the first Hague Conference, it failed to limit armaments.

23. Founded in 1865, the Salvation Army first became involved in relief work after the Galveston Hurricane in 1900, the deadliest natural disaster ever to hit the USA, and the San Francisco earthquake in 1906.

Humanitarianism during the First World War

No nineteenth-century humanitarian could possibly have foreseen the scale of this new war. Caroline Moorehead graphically describes the challenge: "a war that would draw in twenty-eight countries, see an average of 20,000 people die every day for the fifty-one months of conflict, and challenge fundamentally, repeatedly and with considerable brutality the very basis of the Geneva Convention, the Committee and the Red Cross movement."[24] Few envisaged the killing power of new weapons, the diseases of trench warfare (tetanus, typhoid, and gangrene), the effects of high explosive shelling on men kept too long in trenches, and the fear and injuries caused by different kinds of poison gas. During the course of the war, it was, once again, through the initiatives of private individuals and volunteers that, building on existing foundations, the work of humanitarians was taken forward.

Despite "pious noises of agreement" regarding the Geneva Convention in the first months of the war, violations, reprisals, and retaliations soon took over, and the Hague Conventions were radically breached.[25] The war, indeed, began with the invasion of Belgium without the necessary explicit warning, and poison gas was used. In January 1915, the German army launched a chlorine gas attack in Poland, then in April near Ypres. By July, poison shells were being fired, and, by September, the British began to use gas at the battle of Loos (unsuccessfully as the wind was blowing towards the British trenches). From then on, both sides developed ever more lethal chemical weapons. Vera Brittain wrote, "I wish those people who write so glibly about this being a holy war, and the orators who talk so much about going on no matter how long the war lasts and what it may mean, could see a case—to say nothing of ten cases of mustard gas in its early stages—could see the poor things all burnt and blistered, with blind eyes—sometimes temporarily, sometimes permanently—all sticky and stuck together and always fighting for breath, with voices a whisper, saying that their throats are closing and they know they are going to choke."[26] By the end of the war, the Allies were mounting more gas attacks than the Germans.[27]

24. Moorehead, *Dunant's Dream*, 177.

25. Ibid., 201.

26. Brittain, *Testament of Youth*, 395. Vera Brittain (1893–1970) was a nurse and writer. See further, her entry in the *ODNB*.

27. The horror of gas led to the 1925 Geneva Protocol, a much more detailed prohibition of biological and chemical weapons which, though not ratified by Japan and the USA, and despite violation by Italy in Ethiopia, was nevertheless largely observed in the Second World War—the huge exception being the holocaust. Since then, the only major exceptions have been the use by Iraq in the war with Iran (1980–88) and against the Kurds (1988), and, more recently, in Syria (from 2013).

Another unforeseen issue was the sheer number of prisoners of war (POWs). The 1907 Hague Convention had agreed the principle of exchanging information about POWs. But nobody had expected that by September 1914, there would already be several hundred thousand prisoners, mainly French, but also Belgian, British, and German. At this time, the ICRC may have had influence and been seen as the protectors of the Convention; but the reality in Geneva was nine unpaid members of the committee, a small secretariat, and a handful of Swiss men ready to serve as delegates. Within weeks, the nephew of Gustave Moynier, Gustave Ador, who had succeeded his uncle as president of the ICRC in 1910, had recruited hundreds of volunteers, taken over one of Geneva's museums as a workplace, and established the International Agency for Aid and Information on Prisoners of War. Over the next four years, they processed seven million names, each meticulously filed on cards. At first, they merely matched requests for information from families with information coming in from governments. In time, they began proactively to trace those who were missing, seeking information from those who might have had contact with them. A sub-office was established by the Danish Red Cross to deal with Russian prisoners in Germany and vice versa. In due course, they moved to include enemy aliens held in the warring countries: 20,000 Germans and Austrians in the UK, and smaller numbers of French and Belgians in Germany.

Beyond combatants and prisoners of war, there were also growing numbers of civilians displaced by the conflict, on a scale not known in Europe since at least the Thirty Years' War (1618–48). Civilians were not covered by any convention (a situation not remedied until 1949), but, gradually, the ICRC included them in its work anyway, though tracing refugees and displaced people proved far more difficult than tracing POWs. Despite the difficulties already associated with tracing, the International Committee also began to work on the repatriation first of interned doctors and nurses, and then the seriously wounded.

Of course, most prisoners remained interned throughout the war and, although, again, the ICRC had never been assigned such a role, it began to send delegates to inspect places of internment and ensure that supplies reached those interned. These delegates were the forerunners of the ICRC delegates who for the next century were to carry out some of the most dangerous missions in wartime all over the world, passionately declaring their neutrality, endlessly patient, endlessly determined to reach those they were there to help. During the First World War, there were never more than forty-one of these delegates, but they worked tirelessly, crisscrossing Europe, inspecting conditions, and checking the amount of food, clothing, and supplies that each prisoner received. The work became more difficult as stories began to come in of brutal treatment, usually isolated cases by individual commanders, but each story had to be painstakingly followed up. However, it soon became clear that there was one country—Russia—where conditions really were appalling. Prisoners of war and several hundred thousand enemy aliens had been moved east and left to fend for themselves. The most unfortunate were sent off, as later generations would be, to build railways in the far north. Of 70,000 sent to build the Murmansk railway, a third died. The Geneva delegates, supported by the Scandinavian and American Red Cross societies, did what they could and, in some camps, conditions did improve, partly because of outside help, but also because of the self-help efforts of the internees.[28]

Although the Convention itself had no built-in means of monitoring or enforcing, all through the war the ICRC documented breaches: for example, failure to observe the Red Cross emblem on hospitals, the imprisonment of medical staff, the use of exploding bullets, the shooting of nurses, the bombing and torpedoing of hospital ships, and firing on shipwrecked sailors after their ship had been torpedoed. All breaches were meticulously examined, and protests made. The ICRC's scrupulously maintained neutrality was its chief defence against accusations of bias.

Just as the ICRC more than fulfilled its mandate looking after POWs and trying to ensure that the Geneva Convention was observed, equally impressive was the work of the national Red Cross societies which, increasingly, took on the work of caring for the wounded and sick members of the armed forces. As in earlier wars, the default position of army medical services was at first to reject or marginalise the volunteer bodies, but their own inability to cope as the war went on made the role of the Red Cross more and more crucial, both on the home front and near to the fighting. In Britain, the number of trained Red Cross volunteers was hugely supplemented by the creation of Voluntary Aid Detachments: volunteers, mainly women, trained as auxiliaries by the Red Cross and the Order of St. John, who, as the war staggered on, found themselves doing ever more crucial work. By the end of the war, some 100,000 volunteers had joined up, including such future famous writers as Agatha Christie, Vera Brittain, and Freya Stark, all of whom were to give a less official account of their wartime experiences.[29] Given how utterly male the ICRC had been—the first woman joined the Committee only in 1918—it is remarkable how the societies, often run by royal or aristocratic women, gave huge openings to women from all sections

28. Moorehead, *Dunant's Dream*, 195.

29. Christie, *Autobiography*; Brittain, *Testament of Youth*; Stark, *Traveller's Prelude*.

of society, opening doors that could never be completely closed after the war.

The large numbers of volunteers who joined existing organisations did not deter individuals from starting and forming their own efforts to alleviate the sufferings of war. From at least the mid-nineteenth century, it had been common at times of humanitarian crisis for relief funds to be set up, and food, money, and clothes distributed particularly on behalf of Christian communities in the Ottoman Empire, sometimes by sympathisers far away, sometimes close at hand. Such relief was bound to be haphazard, reliant on small numbers of people making dangerous journeys and then finding (usually foreign) doctors, nurses, or missionaries whom they felt that they could trust with their gifts. Similar enterprises—less official than the Red Cross, started by passionate and committed individuals, funded by popular subscription, willing to work across borders, and with the capacity to do the work themselves—continued in the First World War.[30] One of the first of these forerunners of the modern international NGO was the Friends War Victims Relief Committee (FWVRC), which proved to be a universal and long-lasting organisation set up by British Quakers in response to the destruction wrought by the Franco-Prussian War. Members not only provided emergency relief, but helped to plough fields and sow seeds. Although its activity decreased as matters improved, the FWVRC was revived in 1876 and again in 1912 to help in the Balkans. In 1914, it was re-founded yet again and Ruth Fry was appointed secretary, a post that she held until 1923. Bernard Canter described her as "a sort of generalissimo-cum-quartermaster general . . . responsible for a vast programme of supplies, administration, personnel management, public relations, fund-raising, leadership and inspiration."[31] From 1915 until after the armistice, the FWVRC worked in the Netherlands in camps set up for Belgian refugees and other civilians. In France, the FWVRC took charge of hospitals and convalescent homes and provided district nursing care as well. As in the Franco-Prussian War, the FWVRC helped to bring in harvests that would otherwise have been lost.

A similar organisation began in 1915 in New York. The American Committee for Syrian and Armenian Relief, soon to be called the Near East Foundation, was founded in response to the massive humanitarian crisis precipitated by the war in the Ottoman Empire and, more specifically, the

---

30. For example, the pianist, composer and later prime minister of Poland, Jan Paderewski, in 1915 set up, with the Polish writer Henryk Sienkiewicz, the Polish Victims Relief Fund. Edward Elgar gave his support by writing and performing *Polonia* for a fundraising concert at the Queen's Hall that summer.

31. Obituary in the *Friend*, 4 May 1962, quoted in Storr, *Excluded from the Record*, 138. Fry (1878–1962) came from a leading Quaker family.

plight of Armenians and Assyrians, of whom over a million and a half died as a result of deportation, forced marches, starvation, and execution. During the next fifteen years, the organisation raised over $100 million and gradually expanded its work from immediate emergency relief to the promotion of longer-term sustainable development, pioneering many of the strategies employed by the world's leading development organisations today.

In Châlon-sur-Marnes, fifteen miles from the front line, Quakers Hilda Clark and Edith Pye, who, a quarter of a century later, would provide the catalyst for the beginning of Oxfam, set up an urgently needed maternity hospital in the wing of an old people's home, while in Samoëns in Haute Savoie, they set up a convalescent home for refugees.[32] The Friends Ambulance Unit was set up in 1914 by another Quaker, Philip Noel-Baker.[33] The unit was to work alongside, but, as far as possible, separately from, the (inadequate) military ambulance capacity. While Quaker-founded and funded, it always included many non-Quakers; in particular, after conscription began in 1916, the Friends Ambulance Unit was a place for conscientious objectors to carry out useful alternative service to joining the armed forces. In 1917, with the entry of the United States into the war, the FWVRC was joined by members of the newly-founded American Friends Service Committee. Together, they took responsibility for the reconstruction of a 200-square-mile area of Lorraine, near Verdun. In Serbia, they rebuilt two villages, an orphanage, a hospital, and two dispensaries. Margaret McFie, a Scottish doctor, built the first school for the blind in Yugoslavia, while

32. Edith Pye (1876–1965) trained as a nurse and midwife, and became a Quaker in 1908. One of very few women to be made a Chevalier of the Légion d'Honneur for her work in the First World War, she then moved to Vienna to organise the feeding of starving children in 1920–21. In 1929, she was made president of what became the Royal College of Midwives, a position that she held for twenty years, during which time she oversaw the use of anaesthetics by midwives in home births. As vice-chair of the Friends German Emergency Committee, she also continued to be actively involved with relief work. In 1937, she helped in the evacuation of thousands of Basque children from war-torn Spain to England, and in 1939–40 worked with Spanish refugees on the Franco-Spanish border, catching the last boat from Bordeaux to Britain in 1940. In the Second World War, she became secretary and chief organiser of the Famine Relief Committee chaired by another great humanitarian, George Bell, bishop of Chichester, with a view to getting food and medical supplies to starving civilians in occupied Europe, especially Belgium and Greece. In this role, she set out to encourage support groups in cities throughout Britain. Two of these committees for famine relief continued after the war, on a small scale in Huddersfield (Hudfam), and on a growing scale in Oxford (Oxfam). After the war, she devoted herself to the League of Nations and the cause of peace. She met Hilda Clark (1881–1955) in London and they became life-long companions. See Pye's entry in the *ODNB*.

33. Philip Noel-Baker (1889–1982) became a politician and won the Nobel Peace Prize forty-five years later for his work in disarmament. See his entry in the *ODNB*.

another Scottish doctor, Katherine McPhail, opened a children's hospital. After the war, the American and British Quakers sent some 1,700 volunteers to Germany and Austria who, with up to 40,000 German volunteers, took on responsibility for feeding half a million German children daily until 1921.[34]

Another private Quaker-inspired American initiative was the Commission for Relief in Belgium (CRB), founded by Herbert Hoover, then an engineer based in London, who had already organised the repatriation of 200,000 Americans at the outset of war.[35] He initially struggled to persuade the British government to allow the blockade to be broken to deliver food.[36] With agreement grudgingly given to go ahead, he managed to move five million tons of food from North and South America to occupied countries in Europe, building up a volunteer force of fifty thousand to manage such an operation ever more professionally. Brilliantly run and effective though the CRB was, its motives were not only humanitarian. The future president was quite open in his recognition of the political and economic benefits that such a huge operation would create for the US economy then and in the future. "The result of this war will be that America will be rich, prosperous, wealthy, and will have made untold millions of this wealth out of the woe and swelter of Europe."[37] At the time and given the needs, the multiple aims seem not to have been a problem, but such confusion over aims by humanitarian organisations was to lead to far more tensions and criticism at the end of the twentieth century and the beginning of the twenty-first.

Humanitarianism after the First World War

As with the years preceding the war, and the four years of the war itself, the immediate post-war period saw the causes of humanitarianism driven on by passionate individuals and organised volunteers. The situation that faced them was severe. The armistice in November 1918 led to a long period of tortuous negotiations over the fate of the defeated countries, only ending, as far as Germany and Austria were concerned, in June 1919 with the signing of the Treaty of Versailles. The decisions over the Ottoman Empire

34. This was known as "Quäkerspeisung" or "Quaker feeding": http://www.quakersintheworld.org/quakers-in-action/302.

35. Herbert Hoover (1874–1964) was raised as a Quaker, and trained as a mining engineer. He became well-known for his extremely effective humanitarian work during and after the First World War. In the 1920s, he served as secretary of commerce in the administrations of Presidents Harding and Coolidge. In 1929, despite having no electoral experience, he was elected president.

36. Oxfam faced the same struggle during the Second World War.

37. Cabanes, *Great War*, 208.

took even longer. While the politicians argued, the economic blockade of Germany and Austria continued, with dire consequences for the most vulnerable—especially children. A report by Frédéric Ferrière of the ICRC described children starving on the streets of Vienna, seven-year-olds having the physique of three-year-olds; in Germany, it was estimated that eight hundred a day were dying of starvation.[38] In France and Britain, the press and governments were universally unsympathetic; Woodrow Wilson, the only leader who was working for a peace that would be not merely punitive but restorative, was, from November 1918, hampered by a Republican-dominated senate and a Republican-controlled House, which opposed most of his proposals (and would, in due course, prevent the United States from joining the League of Nations).

Despite the blockade, a number of individuals committed to the relief of suffering found a way of getting through. Coming from a well-to-do conservative Anglican background, Eglantyne Jebb was, in many respects, an English equivalent to the Geneva founders of the Red Cross. She "was never one for boundaries except in the overstepping of them," and, as for religion, "the more organised it was, the less it appealed to her. . . . Her rather mystical brand of Christianity emphasised not only human equality under God's law, but the actual spiritual unity of people."[39] In 1904, her sister Dorothy Jebb had married Charles Buxton, a liberal politician and philanthropist who, the year before, had founded the Macedonian Relief Committee with his brother Noel.[40] During the war, the Buxtons worked tirelessly to reduce xenophobia and, from 1916, to urge a negotiated peace.[41] Dorothy, perhaps surprisingly, persuaded the prime minister, David Lloyd George, to allow her to import twenty-five newspapers, weekly, from neutral and enemy

38. Frédéric Ferrière (1848–1924) was a doctor and long-term member, delegate, and then vice-president of the ICRC. His setting up of a wing to help civilian refugees, outside the original mandate of the Committee, both hugely extended and also hugely increased the popularity of the Red Cross movement.

39. Mulley, *Woman Who Saved the Children*, 273–74. Eglantyne Jebb (1876–1928) was co-founder of Save the Children.

40. Dorothy Jebb (1881–1963) was active with her husband Charles in the Liberal Party until 1917 when they joined both the Labour Party and the Society of Friends. She co-founded Save the Children with her sister. In the 1930s, increasingly concerned by the treatment of Christians in Germany, she went to see Hermann Göring. Despite Charles's belief in appeasement, she became convinced that only war would solve the Nazi threat. See her entry in the *ODNB*.

41. Supporters of this venture included Thomas Hardy, Bertrand Russell, George Bernard Shaw, and Gilbert Murray (1866–1957)—who would later be a major player in establishing the League of Nations and, who, in 1942, was a founder of Oxfam.

countries and to publish a digest of news, more balanced than anything else available in Britain, in the *Cambridge Review*.

In 1917, Eglantyne, a semi-invalid, joined the team of translators for the *Cambridge Review* and, through this work, learned of Romanians without fuel, dying of cold, and of Belgian, Austrian, and Polish children and old people dying of starvation. By the end of the war, the economic blockade was causing a humanitarian crisis on an unprecedented scale and largely affecting the most vulnerable. When it was clear that the victorious governments intended to keep the blockade in place, at least until a peace settlement was agreed, the two sisters joined with other friends in January 1919 to set up a "Fight the Famine" Council, with the aims of ending the blockade and securing an international loan to stimulate European economy. Thirteen bishops and several deans, along with Asquith, William Beveridge, and many others, supported the cause, and even Winston Churchill, now secretary of state for war, stepped out of line to say that "the blockade was repugnant to the British Nation."[42] By April, Eglantyne was so appalled by the worsening situation and lack of action that she decided that lobbying was not enough and that she must create an organisation able to provide immediate relief. She garnered publicity when arrested in Trafalgar Square for distributing leaflets showing starving Austrian children. Four days after her trial, she and Dorothy launched the Save the Children Fund at a huge public meeting in the Albert Hall. This was to be the first British charity to move from being a one-off relief fund into a permanent international organisation, not only providing emergency relief, but also promoting sustainable development. Not that the creation of the Save the Children Fund led to a flood of similar organisations: indeed, the International Rescue Committee was created in Germany only in 1931, taking its current shape in the United States in 1933. Oxfam was born from a Quaker initiative in England in 1942, but the vast majority of modern international NGOs were developed after the Second World War.

This post-war period also saw the growth of the *idea* of humanitarianism, a realisation that response to the human suffering brought by war had to be trans-national, more professional in its organisation, and more clearly related to internationally agreed norms and rules. The unprecedented catastrophe of the First World War, to quote Cabanes, "did more than create disaster. It fostered deep and long-term pacifist feeling among a substantial population, and it made the protection of all the war's victims, civilians and soldiers alike, an absolute necessity—a project that drew to it a surprisingly

---

42. Mulley, *Woman Who Saved the Children*, 229.

large and talented group of activists and their supporters."[43] Attitudes were changing. Geoffrey Studdert Kennedy offers a good example of someone moving from robust welcome for the war and positive expectations of what it would achieve to a conviction that war in general was an unmitigated evil. What is surprising, given the drive and time that he threw into industrial relations after 1918, is that he seems not to have gone beyond a denunciation of war into practical forms of mitigation. He preached earnestly against war, but his energies lay in preaching, rather than pragmatic transformation.

Ultimately, of course, even the best efforts of individuals and small organisations was not enough; lasting and significant changes to the waging of war could only be brought about by international will. The most hopeful sign of this was the creation of the League of Nations, founded on 10 January 1920 as a result of the Paris Peace Conference that ended the First World War. It was the first international organisation with a principal mission to maintain world peace. Its primary goals, as stated in its covenant, included preventing wars through collective security and disarmament, and settling international disputes through negotiation and arbitration. In its early years, it achieved a good deal, only failing when countries withdrew to push their own aggressive agenda. Other important moves in the post-war years for advancing international humanitarian law included a Red Cross conference in 1921, which agreed principles for helping both sides in a civil war and giving the ICRC a clear right to intervene if a nation's own society were unable or unwilling; Eglantyne Jebb's persuasion of the League of Nations in 1924 to adopt her Declaration of the Rights of the Child, which led in 1989 to the UN Convention on the Rights of the Child (ratified by every country in the world except Somalia, South Sudan, and the USA); and the expansion of the Hague Conventions in the Geneva Protocol of 1925, forbidding all forms of chemical and biological warfare.

It took another thirty years for such developments in the professionalisation of humanitarian assistance and the assertion of humanitarian rights through legal instruments to lead to the creation of the UN High Commission for Refugees (UNHCR) and the four Geneva Conventions, promulgated in 1949. This was due to the events of the late 1920s and 1930s, the isolationist agenda of the USA, the global economic depression, the rise of fascism, and the collapse of the League of Nations. Without the energy for humanitarianism witnessed in the period from 1918 to 1924, the later developments would, undoubtedly, have been much harder to achieve.

---

43. Cabanes, *Great War*, 1.

Conclusion

What is remarkable is that throughout the whole period addressed by this essay, the idea of humanitarianism and its practical consequences was constantly refreshed and rebuilt by inspired and brave individuals speaking truth to power and building support by effective action. Among this collection of people there are some common features. First, those noted in this essay were nurtured in the Christian faith and that environment played a part in their motivation, but they were not explicit about it and neither did they proselytise. Genevan Protestants, Quakers, Anglican women, and Roman Catholics acted from what might be seen as a highly-developed Christ-like compassion for fellow human beings, but this was not the overt or given reason for why they acted as they did. Second, and related to this, they were motivated primarily by what they saw or heard. They did not start with a principle—of pacifism, or an objective desire to limit casualties—they began with a human response to the suffering caused by war. It was the sight and smell of the battlefield that led Henry Dunant to gather his volunteers; Hilda Clark and Edith Pye set up a maternity hospital and a home for refugees because that was what was needed. Third, they were, undoubtedly, well-connected individuals. Dunant walked to Solferino because he sought an audience with the emperor and imagined that he would be received. Dorothy Jebb had the ear of Lloyd George. The individuals concerned were part of larger webs of people ready not only to provide support, but also able to offer significant influence. Fourth, they were able to marry passion with organisation. Clara Barton drew on her civil service training; Herbert Hoover was an engineer with logistical talent. Concern for the well-being of others was not enough; vision, commitment, and structure played an important role.

Institutions, such as governments and churches, played some part, but often reluctantly and usually only under pressure. Apart from Catholic orders and Quakers, religious humanitarian organisations for the benefit of those outside their own community only began to appear in the 1940s and 1950s. Unlike the humanitarians discussed, churches and governments were not (and are not) single-issue organisations, but rather held together a diversity of views and opinions concerning the conduct of war and the treatment of participants. It was, therefore, only the passion and commitment of dogged, well-connected individuals that could drive forward a new agenda, forcing national governments to take seriously the victims of war—both combatants and non-combatants—and the suffering endured by many in its aftermath. Although only governments could make laws, it took non-government agencies to push them towards a more humanitarian focus.

The greater questions of whether war can be justified and whether its horrors can be limited have not been resolved in the century since the First World War. International wars may now be rare, but civil wars continue apace. In 2015 alone, there were thirteen wars with an overall death toll of more than half a million; most of these violated many or all of the international conventions; some were so violent that even the ICRC found difficulty in assisting. War, as Studdert Kennedy noted, is ever-present and the human instinct for it has not yet subsided.[44] Like Henry Dunant, Florence Nightingale, Clara Barton, Ruth Fry, Eglantyne Jebb, Edith Pye, and Gilbert Murray, perhaps we can only continue to build, in the words of the Polish philosopher Leszek Kołakowski, "an obstinate will to erode by inches the conditions which produce avoidable suffering, oppression, hunger, wars, racial and national hatred, insatiable greed and vindictive envy."[45]

44. Studdert Kennedy, *Hardest Part*, 31.
45. As quoted in Healey, *Time of My Life*, 472.

9

"The Glorious Dead"?

Images of Glory in First World War Memorials and the Life of Antony of Egypt

Alvyn L. Pettersen

The First World War memorials of 1919 and 1922 in Worcester

IN AUGUST 1919, in time for an historic peace march, when ten thousand troops and women war-workers of the city and county of Worcester marched through Worcester, a cenotaph was erected on the north side of Worcester Cathedral. At the first Armistice Day ceremony before the cenotaph that November, "the colours were flown, all eyes turned right, plain clothes men saluted, and the male portion of the public reverendly uncovered their heads before the simple and impressive memorial to the glorious dead. . . . [A]round the monument sat the widows and dependents of those whose sacrifice the Cenotaph commemorated."[1] The cenotaph itself, though a temporary structure, formed of a light framework attached to scaffolding poles, and covered with large asbestos and cement sheets, was impressive (see figure 9). A similar photograph, in the supplement for *Berrow's Worcester Journal* of 30 August 1919, shows the cenotaph, a wreath upon the Union flag draping its top; another huge wreath hung high on its vertical front; the

1. Account of the ceremony in November 1919 quoted in the *Worcestershire Echo*, 9 June 1922 (scrapbook cutting, Worcester Cathedral Library, Muniments A405 [6], 69).

legend, in block capitals, "The Glorious Dead," was inscribed below (the same legend appeared the previous month on the temporary—and then the permanent—cenotaph in Whitehall, London); and, on its base, in the very centre of numerous other wreaths, one lay prominently with the word "Firm," the regimental motto of the Worcestershires. Two soldiers stood watch, to left and to right, arms reversed. In contemporary newspapers, it was referred to both as "a simple and impressive memorial to the glorious dead" and as a memorial to the "sacrifice" made by the many buried elsewhere. The *Worcestershire Echo* drew particular attention to the "sacrifice," highlighting that, "literally, Cenotaph means 'empty tomb,' and is the name given to a monument erected to one who is buried elsewhere."[2]

Figure 9: The temporary cenotaph erected outside Worcester
Cathedral in 1919

2. Ibid.

Not far from the cenotaph stood the Boer War memorial. Its inscription spoke of the county's grateful memory of the men of Worcestershire who, between 1899 and 1902, gave their lives for their country in South Africa. It is topped with a statue of a soldier, urging upwards and forwards, rifle with bayonet fixed. Overshadowing him is a winged Victory, her hair garlanded, her right arm cradling lilies, her left hand resting on a sheathed sword, another victory garland decorating its hilt. The triumphant Boer War memorial's proximity to the cenotaph only reinforced the glory of the First World War's dead. For it would have been difficult not to read the latter in the light of the former.

Figure 10: The Boer War memorial
outside Worcester Cathedral

Figure 11: The Boer War memorial outside
Worcester Cathedral (detail)

Over the next couple of years, the people of the city and county of Worcester regularly attended the cenotaph. Another photograph in *Berrow's Worcester Journal* of 4 October 1919 shows a Welsh choir singing round the monument. One of the choir holds a floral tribute, which, we may assume, was later laid at the cenotaph's base. The audience is large, and of all ages. Pilgrimages—and that is the word, with its hagiographical overtones, that is used in the reports—were made to it each armistice anniversary. Gradually, but not surprisingly, for those whose kin and friends were buried far away, the cenotaph became a place of not only collective but also personal memorial. "There has not been one single moment," the *Worcestershire Echo* reported, "when it has been without a few simple tributes laid at its foot in memory of some fallen son of Worcester."[3]

Compared with these scenes from his home town, the address by the Reverend Geoffrey Studdert Kennedy at the Central Hall, Westminster, on the night of Armistice Day 1921, was the more startling.[4] For then, before a large crowd, he argued that future generations would be saved from the horrors, degradation, and poverty of any future war not "because of any victory won by the sword but because we have passed within the threshold of 'Heartbreak House,' and there have wept bitterly over a victory which on positive results has proved barren."[5] The address caused such a reaction that Studdert Kennedy, back at Worcester and preaching at evensong in the cathedral on 11 December, felt obliged to comment further. He acknowledged that his address at Westminster had caused significant pain. Nevertheless, he believed that the theme of that address, though containing, to use his words, "a very bitter truth," yet needed to be voiced. For "truth, however bitter, was always kinder than any sugar-covered lie."[6] As reported in the *Worcestershire Echo* under the title, "A Barren Victory: Mr. Studdert Kennedy and Futility of War: A Lesson from the Glorious Dead," he spoke of the futility of war. At a critical point in the war, he argued, he had "allowed himself to be taken away from his distinguishable Christian work of keeping alive in the minds and hearts, the constructive force of human nature, a spirit of humanity and kindness, of Christian chivalry and forgiveness, and allowed himself to be sent out upon a campaign of war propaganda."[7] Nothing then, he confessed, had mattered to him but victory; and so his message to his men had been that they should "fight on at any cost and . . . give us complete and utter victory which would bring our enemies down to their knees and make them not only plead for terms, but for mercy."[8] With no one being able to say "nay" to Britain, Britain, now supreme in power, would be able to establish a world founded on a new order of freedom, honour and peace.

---

3. Ibid.

4. For the address and the stir that it caused, see Studdert-Kennedy, *Dog-Collar Democracy*, 61, Todman, *Great War*, 132, and Bell, "Collusion to Condemnation," 161–62.

5. As reported by the *Worcestershire Echo*, 12 December 1921, in its account of Studdert Kennedy's sermon in Worcester the previous day (scrapbook cutting, Worcester Cathedral Library, Muniments A405 [6], 43).

6. Ibid.

7. Ibid. He was undoubtedly referring to his work in 1916–17 for the National Mission of Repentance and Hope.

8. Ibid.

That was then, Studdert Kennedy argued. Now, however, what he had then believed and preached he no longer believed and so could no longer preach. Force and slaughter might deliver freedom in the sense of staying the enemy from a country's shores and bringing to a halt the undermining of a people's rights and proper pride. However, that freedom was but a base freedom. For freedom, he now realised, meant much more than that. It meant the abolition of militarism, "a faith that had its roots deep down in every nation of the world, including," he added significantly, "our own"; and that, he continued, required moral disarmament, which, in turn, would lead to material disarmament, both of which would come about, if and when "the futility, the barrenness of any victory in war [was] recognised by the whole world."[9]

Studdert Kennedy then returned to the "very bitter truth" of which he had spoken in his speech of armistice night. Those who had "made the great sacrifice and [had given up] their sons," he asked to make one more sacrifice, by giving up "the belief in victory, and . . . [looking] at their dead as victims rather than victors, glorious and beautiful victims," victims not entirely dissimilar from the victim of Good Friday, the awful crime against whom had been "rendered splendid by sacrifice and love of Him upon whom it was committed."[10] If that further sacrifice was made, requested by Studdert Kennedy of those who had already sacrificed their own sons, they would hear and might then heed the dead's cry that "nothing can be got out of victory by war by anybody, any time, any where";[11] and so, realising war's futility, might find hope. "How," Studdert Kennedy concluded by asking, "is history going to be taught to . . . children? . . . Are they going to be taught of it as Britain's supreme glory or as the country's lasting and dreadful shame? An enormous lot for the future depends upon that."[12]

Studdert Kennedy clearly did not seek to deny the inscription upon Worcester's cenotaph. He did, however, wish to re-interpret how "the glorious dead" should be understood. The dead were victims, victims of militarism, but not mere victims of militarism. They were *glorious* victims of militarism. For they had given their all to defeat militarism, in order that, in militarism's place, moral disarmament, with its accompanying boons, might be established, everywhere and for the sake of all others. Interestingly, the glory of the dead here was not wrapped in a national flag, as the cenotaph had been. It could not have been so wrapped. For militarism, according to

9. Ibid.
10. Ibid.
11. Ibid.
12. Ibid.

the Studdert Kennedy of 1921 (though not of the early years of the war), was rooted deeply even in Britain, and so Britain, like the other nations of the world, needed to mend its ways, and learn, as all others needed to learn, to live truly gloriously, through meeting even the most awful act with sacrifice and love. The glory of the dead rightly could be wrapped only in sacrificial love.

Nor did Studdert Kennedy think that true glory was limited to those who enlisted and fought. That same evening, after his impassioned sermon from the pulpit of Worcester Cathedral, he went on to a mission service held under the auspices of the Free Church Council in a crowded public hall in the city, where he adamantly denied that "soldiers were glorious" while "the workers are not."[13] For Studdert Kennedy, as has been noted, glory came of sacrifice and love. Hence, he held that it was universally true that a life lived for another's sake was a life lived gloriously; and so, he insisted, "all honest work done for the service of [humanity] whether making boots, or cleaning sewers is glorious."[14] The paradigm of such glory was, as Studdert Kennedy insisted on the same occasion, the "gentle, meek and kindly Figure that could do no one any harm."[15]

Worcester's cenotaph had always been seen as temporary, and its replacement in 1922 by a permanent memorial, based on the White Cross in Hereford, was in no way the result of Studdert Kennedy's addresses of the year before.[16] Unveiled on the fourth anniversary of Armistice Day, the permanent memorial, so the *Worcestershire Echo* reported, "put the seal on [Worcestershire's] gratitude to her valiant sons who made the great sacrifice."[17] The *Worcestershire Echo's* language was a little richer than that of the inscription on the monument itself, which read, "The County to her sons who gave their lives in the Great War 1914–1918." The addition by the *Worcestershire Echo* of the adjective "valiant," and its replacement of "gave their lives" with "made the great sacrifice" reflected the sentiments of the lord lieutenant of Worcestershire, Lord Coventry, in his speech on the occasion of the new memorial's unveiling.[18]

13. Ibid.

14. Ibid.

15. Ibid.

16. The White Cross is a standing cross at the junction of five roads in the west of Hereford, with an original hexagonal base and pedestal, dating from the third quarter of the fourteenth century.

17. *Worcestershire Echo*, 10 November 1922 (scrapbook cutting, Worcester Cathedral Library, Muniments A405 [6], 88).

18. George William Coventry (1838–1930) was the ninth earl of Coventry. As lord lieutenant of Worcestershire (1891–1923), he was a leading figure in the county's war

Figure 12: The county war memorial outside Worcester Cathedral

Large crowds had assembled. Troops, led to the new memorial's location by their regimental colours, stood around the memorial, forming
three sides of a hollow square. Local units which had played their part in
the Great War also attended. At each corner of the monument, surrounded
by a screen of green and white canvas, stood the colours of the Worcestershire regiment, and on the steps of it, at each corner, "a representative of

effort. He was, for example, an honorary colonel of the 3rd and 4th battalions of the
Worcestershire Regiment, and president of the Worcestershire Volunteer Regiment.

the county's fighting men."[19] Lord Coventry arrived at 10.45 am, took the general salute, inspected the troops, and then positioned himself at the memorial's foot. The service, which led up to the memorial's unveiling, began with words from the bishop of Worcester: "Let us remember before God the brave and the true who laid down their lives to defend us, and have departed into the resurrection of eternal life, especially the men of the Worcestershire regiment and of the county and city of Worcester, to whom this memorial has been dedicated."[20] Two minutes' silence followed. The four soldiers at the memorial's four corners leant on reversed arms, and the sea of still faces stood motionless. The silence ended, the dean, William Moore Ede, led the people in prayer, beginning with the words from the Gospel according to John, "I am the resurrection and the life, saith the Lord. He that believeth in me, though he were dead, yet shall he live."[21] The troops then presented arms, and Lord Coventry unveiled the memorial. His words were reported in the *Worcestershire Echo*: "In the faith of Jesus Christ I unveil this memorial erected by the people of Worcestershire, in memory of the officers, non-commissioned officers, and men of the City and County of Worcester and of the Worcestershire Regiment who laid down their lives in the Great War."[22]

The language of Lord Coventry's speech is not entirely dissimilar from the bishop's. That said, it is noteworthy that the bishop spoke of the "brave and true who laid down their lives to defend us," while Lord Coventry referred to "officers, non-commissioned officers and men . . . of the Worcestershire Regiment who laid down their lives in the Great War." The differences might seem rather insignificant were it not for the tone of Lord Coventry's ensuing address. Lord Coventry, speaking in his role as the lord lieutenant, referred to "the men . . . who gave their lives for their King and Country in the Great War." He spoke of "the gallant 10,941 officers and men," "their heroic deeds," soldiers playing "a glorious part in all the heavy fighting," and there being, "by 1918 . . . not a battalion of the Regiment which had not seen heavy fighting, suffered many casualties, and helped to add fresh lustre to the splendid record already won by [the] County Regiment."[23] He mentioned the Yeomanry who "won undying fame by their gallant charge

19. Ibid.

20. Ibid. The bishop was Ernest Pearce (1865–1930), who was vicar of Christ Church, Greyfriars (1895–1912); treasurer (1912–16), archdeacon (1916–18), and subdean (1918–19) of Westminster; and bishop of Worcester from 1919 until his death. See further, his entry in the *ODNB*.

21. John 11:25 (Authorised Version).

22. *Worcestershire Echo*, 10 November 1922 (scrapbook cutting, Worcester Cathedral Library, Muniments A405 [6], 88).

23. Ibid.

in the battle of Gaza." With pride, he stated that "more than one gallant Worcestershire man [had] won the Victoria Cross." In conclusion, he "then, with great emphasis and emotion, recited the whole of Kipling's solemn requiem, 'Lest we forget.'"[24]

Both the bishop of Worcester and the lord lieutenant spoke of a loss, but for a good cause, the former "to defend us," his fellow Worcestershire men, women, many then widowed, and children, some now orphaned, the latter "for their King and Country." The lord lieutenant's speech sounds bellicose, certainly in comparison with the bishop's, whose words were more humanitarian and more obviously couched in theological and pastoral terms. Yet, even for all that, there does seem to be some change of emphasis in tone regarding the 1922 memorial, compared with the 1919 cenotaph. The cenotaph gave way to a memorial surmounted with an unadorned cross, a change made despite a strong appeal by a Mr. F. A. W. Simes at a meeting of the County Memorial Committee that the county memorial should take the form of a cenotaph. The inscription on the cenotaph, "The Glorious Dead," gave way to one that spoke of the county's "sons who gave their lives in the Great War 1914–1918." Further, the new memorial was not so immediately contiguous with the Boer War memorial. This is perhaps more significant than may initially be thought. For the memorial's position reframed the context in which the new memorial could be interpreted. Indeed, it was within this new context that the *Worcestershire Echo* had reflected upon the two-minute silence. "The throng," the *Worcestershire Echo* reported, "stood motionless and the only sound was the fluttering of falling leaves, and the slight sigh of the wind about the masonry of the Cathedral, which made so fitting a background for the picture."[25] This change of emphasis in tone between that of the cenotaph and the county war memorial perhaps is also noticeable in Lord Coventry's recitation of the solemn requiem, "Lest we forget." For it afforded its hearers the possibility of viewing their nation's power as "beneath [the] awful hand . . . [of] the Lord God of Hosts," the troops' sacrifice over against God's "ancient sacrifice," and any triumphalistic pomp as but "one with Nineveh and Tyre" when judged by the "Judge of the Nations."[26]

The unveiling of the new county memorial involved great military presence, repeated reference to the dead as "gallant," and a listing of the very many campaigns and battles in which Worcestershire soldiers had heroically

24. Ibid.

25. Ibid.

26. Rudyard Kipling, "Recessional," in Quiller-Couch, ed., *Oxford Book of English Verse*, 1044–45.

taken part. Yet the lord lieutenant, and especially the dean, did offer people the possibility of reframing any remembrance, particularly through the latter's reference to Jesus as the resurrection and the life, through whom, though dead, all may yet live. At the very least, the bishop's reference to God permitted people not only to moderate any brash understanding of military glory but also to see any human glory as finding its origins in the all-glorious and only truly-glorious God, with the corollary that human glory needed to be understood as contingent, and to be owned with humility.

The First World War memorial in Magdeburg Cathedral

In her book on foreigners and foreignness, *Strangers to Ourselves*, the philosopher Julia Kristeva reflected on the role that an alien may play in national life. Her thinking is that people can never become fully appreciative of their own nationality if they ignore their encounter with the stranger, with him or her who is alien to them, and for whom they are foreign. For the stranger is for them a "mirror" and they are a "mirror" for the stranger, a mirror in which they can learn to see their own strangeness and strangers theirs. Curiously, but truly, the stranger plays the role of reminding them of their own strangeness. This stranger faces them with the fact that everything that they consider familiar also has another side; and the stranger faces them with the truth that what they do and think and believe can be different from what it is, even that it can be improved. In short, for Kristeva, the stranger may be a catalyst to critical reflection upon a people's own culture and to the growth in maturity consequent upon being shown its own cultural limitations and strangeness.

By extension, it would seem reasonable to suggest that a reader may better understand a book by allowing it to be read in the light of another book, a book "strange" to it. Indeed, this appears to be what the nineteenth-century Regius professor of Greek in the University of Oxford, Benjamin Jowett, did when writing his contribution to *Essays and Reviews*.[27] For Jowett, an expert on Thucydides, argued in his essay that it was appropriate to interpret the Bible like any other book, or, more particularly, like any other *ancient* book, and that when interpreted like any other ancient book, the reader would find that the Bible is unlike any other ancient book. To paraphrase Kristeva, the strangeness of, for example, Thucydides's writings would remind the reader of the strangeness of the Bible, highlighting its

---

27. Jowett, "Interpretation of Scripture." For *Essays and Reviews*, see Chapman, "*Essays and Reviews*," and Inman, *Making of Modern English Theology*, 97–109.

very particularity. Perhaps, we, in our turn, may adopt a similar process. If we view the cenotaph and the war memorial in Worcester in the light of both Ernst Barlach's war memorial in Worcester Cathedral's twin cathedral in Magdeburg, in Germany, and the fourth-century *Life of Antony*, we may find ourselves better understanding the Worcester memorials, and how they speak of the glorious dead. The Barlach memorial is chosen because it dates from roughly the same time as the Worcester memorials, and because it is the creation of and a monument to, not a victorious, but a defeated people. The *Life of Antony*, meanwhile, is selected because it contains a theological reflection on the apostle Paul's statement, "I die daily,"[28] and the related theme of the triumph of the Saviour in and through the one who is willing to sacrifice all for the truth. That the ideas of "glory" associated with Barlach's memorial and present in the *Life of Antony*, a monk who was willing even to be martyred in his stand against what he saw as the heresy of the Arians, are strangers to, but not entirely distinct from, the ideas of glory attached to Worcester's cenotaph and war memorial, allows the former ideas to be catalysts for critical reflection on the latter.

In 1918, Germany had been defeated. Some 1.8 million Germans, almost twice the number of those killed fighting for the whole British Empire, had been killed or died of their wounds. From beyond, those Germans who survived the war were repeatedly accused of starting the war and were faced with demands for reparation. From within, the same Germans were challenged by destabilising riots, attempted coups, and the divisive assertion that the German army had not been defeated, simply betrayed by its own politicians. It was within this context that, in 1929, the year in which Studdert Kennedy died, Ernst Barlach carved his controversial memorial to the German dead.[29] Carved from three oak trees, trees traditionally used by Germany's rulers as emblems of survival and rebirth, the memorial was installed in Magdeburg Cathedral.

The cathedral, the parish churches, and the city, towns, and villages of Worcestershire have, like their counterparts across Britain, long had their memorials to remember both the lost and the high price of victory. Both prior to 1914, and after 1918, Germany did have something equivalent. Witness, for example, the gilded Victory, right hand holding aloft a triumphal wreath, standing on a two-hundred-feet-tall column in Berlin's Tiergarten,

---

28. 1 Corinthians 11:1.

29. Ernst Barlach (1870–1938) was a German expressionist sculptor, printmaker, and writer. Initially supportive of the First World War, he reacted against it, and his works were deemed "degenerate" by the Nazis. See further, Jackson Groves, ed., *Ernst Barlach*, Paret, *Artist Against the Third Reich*, and, most recently in German, Laudan, *Ernst Barlach*.

and erected in 1864 to celebrate Prussia's nineteenth-century victory over Denmark and the ensuing victories over Austria and France; or Georg Kolbe's 1934–35 warrior memorial in Stralsund, which depicts two, strong, handsome, naked male figures, the right hand of each resting on the hilt of a shared sword, both standing high and erect on a plinth bearing the legend, "1914–1918 Ihr seid nicht umsonst gefallen," "You did not fall in vain."

Figure 13: The First World War memorial in Magdeburg Cathedral

Figure 14: The First World War memorial in Magdeburg Cathedral (detail)

Barlach's memorial was, however, very different. Initially, Barlach was an enthusiastic supporter of the First World War. Indeed, in 1915, in his mid-forties, he enlisted. For he thought that in and through the war, a new and better society would evolve. Experience at the Front, however, caused him radically to change his mind. Invalided out in 1916, he became a very vocal advocate of pacifism. It was not only his experience as a participant in the war but also the experience of non-participants that prompted this change in attitude. One of his great friends was Käthe Kollwitz, a fellow artist.[30] When the war began, Kollwitz's younger son, Peter, was in Norway, hiking. He returned home to Berlin on 6 August 1914, eager to volunteer. He was, however, not able to do so without his father's permission, for he was not yet twenty-one years old. His father initially refused his son's request; but his mother persuaded her husband to change his mind. Permission was given, and Peter enlisted. On 12 October 1914, Peter

30. Käthe Kollwitz (1867–1945) was a German artist noted for the realism of her work, and also associated with the expressionist movement. The first woman elected to the Prussian Academy of Arts, her work was removed from museums by the Nazis. See further, Kollwitz, ed., *Diary and Letters*; Klemperer, *Passion of a German Artist*; and, most recently in German, Schymura, *Käthe Kollwitz*.

left Berlin for Belgium. A mere ten days later, he was killed. In the Berlin household, guilt and grief combined. It coloured Kollwitz's art. It changed her antipathy to the German state's callow militarism into an implacable hostility to war. And it strengthened Barlach's sense that neither heroism nor war nor death were to be glorified.

Central to the work is a gravestone cross. It is plain, except for the date of the war. The manner in which the date is recorded is, however, not the more usual hyphenated 1914–1918, but a list of the years: 1914, 1915, 1916, 1917, 1918. The longevity of the war is thus emphasised, which only adds to the sense of pain and resignation etched in the faces of the member of the German home guard, too old to be fighting, and of the inexperienced Prussian soldier, a mere boy, too young to be acquainted with the horrors of killing. The choice of these two age-groups cannot be entirely coincidental. For these were the two age-groups to which, especially in the final days of the war, the German government appealed as it desperately sought new recruits. The eyes of both men are closed, their mouths set in a line of sadness. Behind the cross, hands resting lightly on the crossbeam, a wounded soldier stands, his head covered, not with a helmet, as in the case of the German and Prussian, but with a bandage. His eyes are the only eyes that are open. They are, however, blank, unfocused. Directly below him, at the foot of the cross, is the hunched, gaunt figure of a soldier, half-disinterred, right hand over left. Half-hidden by his steel helmet is a face, or rather, a skull, echoing the skulls that in many medieval paintings litter the ground at the foot of Christ's cross. To his right are thin, tightly clasped hands, supporting a face shrouded by a cloak. The woman's grief is palpable, her loss inconsolable. To his left, a bare-headed old man, a soldier judging from the gas mask hanging loosely and ineffectively on his chest, with long-fingered hands holds his head in shock. The woman and the old man are scarcely alive; both are the victims of each and every stage of the terror of warfare, which dehumanises and strips away any dignity.

Barlach's memorial was controversial. In 1934, after the Nazis assumed power, the church council of the cathedral parish petitioned for its removal. Initially, it was put in storage in the Nationalgalerie in Berlin. Following Barlach's death in October 1938, it was then taken to his studio in Güstrow. Only in 1955 was it returned to its original place in Magdeburg Cathedral.

The monument contains no suggestion that the injured and the dead suffered and lost their lives for a just or worthwhile cause. Rather, it portrays need, despair, and death, and not in an abstract way. Each is depicted as an individual. Each is reflected in its particularity. There is no escaping the need and despair and death, no possibility of looking away from them, of belittling them. For the suffering figures stand, distinct in their individual pain and grief. Yet their pain and grief are not treated individualistically. The young suffer with the old, women with men, civilians with soldiers. Theirs are a deeply personal pain and death. Yet theirs is also a shared suffering, united by a common, vulnerable humanity, and bound together by the cross, the inscription of each year of the war recalling the length of their shared suffering. The cross itself further suggests one who suffered for all. There is therefore no lauding the hero. There is no glorifying death and war, which is also the case in Barlach's memorials in Güstrow, Hamburg, and Kiel.[31] Equally, however, there is no sense of an ultimate victory for suffering and death. They are taken very seriously, and, among other things, point to how blindly people walk into war; they suggest that there has been more than enough dying, as Käthe Kollwitz—of whom observers cannot but think as they ponder the monument's devastated woman and the so young soldier—reflected during the final years of the war; and they allude to the one who suffered and died for all, in order that suffering and death might not have the final word. Like his war memorials in Güstrow, Hamburg, and Kiel, Barlach's memorial in Magdeburg reflects on pain, death, and grief, although not without some cry of hope *de profundis*.

Viewed from the perspective of the Barlach memorial, the Worcester cenotaph and the county war memorial are open to critique, especially in their portrayal of both the "glory" of the "glorious dead" and of hope. The glory of Worcestershire's fallen is, unsurprisingly, understood as that of the fallen victors. The cenotaph, as is captured in the photographs of the time, is richly adorned with victors' garlands. Studdert Kennedy acknowledged that he had asked men to fight on at any cost, so that no one in the world would be able to say to them "nay." Lord Coventry's address at the unveiling of the county war memorial, an address reported in the *Worcestershire Echo* as "gallant," spoke of the fallen's "heroic deeds." The picture is of heroic glory. There are certainly moments when the reports in the *Worcestershire Echo* modify or reflect upon the cost at which that glory was won. There are references both to there not being a time when the cenotaph was without a few simple tributes laid at its foot, in memory of some fallen son of Worcestershire, and to widows and dependents of those whose sacrifice the cenotaph commemorated. In the report on the county war memorial's unveiling, there is mention of, alongside the floral tributes "of proud sorrow," "the simple bunches of flowers and wreaths made from the blossom of

---

31. For these memorials, see Jackson Groves, ed., *Ernst Barlach*, 104–11.

cottage gardens, . . . in some cases . . . carried by children so small that they could have but little remembrance of the lost father or brother."[32] The pathos in the report is evident. There is also a description of the silence kept as the county's war memorial was unveiled: "the only sound was the fluttering of falling leaves, and the slight sigh of the wind,"[33] a trope common in newspapers of the time, which here movingly suggests something of the passing of fleeting lives and the sorrow and sighing of those left behind. All that said, the general picture is yet of heroic glory.

Not even the cross atop the county war memorial, a cross that might invite the viewer to understand a soldier's sacrifice in the context of a life given for all, greatly qualified the glory's heroism. For the legend at the foot of the memorial, "The County to her sons who gave their lives in the Great War 1914–1918," still allows the lives too easily to be understood as given in imitation of Christ's self-sacrifice, with little sense of any distinction between the soldier's and Christ's sacrifice, and so granting little permission for any critique of the motive and manner of the soldier's sacrifice. When compared with another Worcester memorial to the dead, the county memorial's association of the soldier's and Christ's sacrifices, and so its inability to critique the motive and manner of the soldier's sacrifice, are more obvious. That other memorial was erected outside Studdert Kennedy's Worcester church, St. Paul's in the Blockhouse.[34] Its Portland stone base was heavily inscribed on three sides with the names of the parish's 140 fallen. Above the names was the legend, "To the Glory of God[:] in loving memory of the men of this parish who gave their lives for us in the Great War 1914–1918." Above that legend, high and lifted up, is the figure of Christ, head not bowed but raised, arms not heavy with suffering. "[I] could not bring [myself] to have a Calvary made," Studdert Kennedy said in his address when he dedicated the memorial, "where Christ looked broken and dead."[35] This Christ, he continued, portrayed the victory of good over evil; this Christ, "not beaten, broken or defeated," was the one in whom all who gave their lives will triumph; this Christ was the one in whom all for whom the many gave their lives will triumph, having "pledged to fight against the common enemies of [humanity] and die to the end unbroken and unbeaten."[36]

32. *Worcestershire Echo*, 10 November 1922 (scrapbook cutting, Worcester Cathedral Library, Muniments A405 [6], 88).

33. Ibid.

34. See figure 6.

35. As reported in *Berrow's Worcester Journal*, 16 April 1921, 7.

36. Ibid.

Nor can this memorial easily have escaped the notice of those who planned and erected the county memorial. For this memorial was planned by Studdert Kennedy, a not insignificant Worcester resident. It was created by a highly regarded Worcester woodcarver and sculptor, George Sprague. It was sited, at most, ten minutes' walk from where the county memorial was to be sited. It was unveiled and dedicated on 12 April 1921, only nineteen months before the unveiling of the county memorial. It is therefore difficult to suppose that those who designed and dedicated the county memorial were unaware of the earlier memorial at St. Paul's. When compared with the memorial at St. Paul's in the Blockhouse, the county memorial seems to make little or no use of the christological significance of the cross atop its memorial, and leaves those standing before it with a sense that the glory of the fallen commemorated there was predominantly an heroic glory, won by each as a result of a readiness to fight and not to count the cost.

The Barlach memorial also particularly points to the cost of war, in terms especially of numbers and the manner of fighting. Lord Coventry made reference to "the names of the gallant 10,941 officers and men whose names are recorded in the Vellum Books of Remembrance inside the Cathedral."[37] These many books of remembrance, and their list upon list of names, still in Worcester Cathedral, do underline the number of soldiers involved. What, however, is not so visible there, but is visible in the Barlach memorial, is the number of *civilian* casualties. The shrouded woman's head and the hands tightly gripped in grief speak eloquently of the innumerable families bereaved and of the mothers distraught. The *Worcestershire Echo* does tell of widows; but its descriptions tend to point the reader not to the widows themselves, but to their dead spouses. Barlach's memorial, meanwhile, points very directly to the widow in her suffering and grief. Indeed, there is, in the Barlach memorial, a poignant sense that *all* humanity suffered in 1914–18, not just those who fought on land and sea and in the air. Further, the man in Barlach's memorial whose gas mask has either slipped or been torn from his face speaks of the manner of fighting, highlighting the very inglorious nature of war through the inglorious use of gas, which is indiscriminately blown where the wind wills, but which, unlike the Johannine Spirit that blows where it wills, is death-giving.[38] From the perspective of Barlach's memorial, the glory of "the glorious dead" was won at very great cost, and by the use of gas, that most indiscriminate of weapons. Altogether, Barlach's memorial, with its sense of wasted lives, a sense especially

---

37. *Worcestershire Echo*, 10 November 1922 (scrapbook cutting, Worcester Cathedral Library, Muniments A405 [6], 88).

38. Cf. John 3:8.

portrayed in the already skeletonised soldier, his helmet shrouding empty eye-sockets and fleshless face, questions, if not challenges, Worcester's sense of lives lost: lost, yes, but gloriously given in noble struggle.

Another theme in which Barlach's memorial critiques Worcester's is that of hope. Barlach's older, living soldier and the wounded soldier respectively hold and rest a hand on the cross. The presence of the cross suggests that the two soldiers are not without hope. They do not despair. They have a hope, but a hope that, the cross's inscribed years of fighting suggest, is not a brash, complacent, "come what may" hope. Their hope is the psalmist's hope, which cries *de profundis*.[39] For their hope is born in the depths of the enormity of evil that was the First World War, an evil that traumatised the old soldier and the young, the civilian and the enlisted. In the face of such, as John Macquarrie suggested, any hope that is an unqualified optimism is misplaced, even appearing blasphemous or atheistic in its arrogant supposition that a mere creature may redeem and save itself in this cruelly and absurdly broken world.[40] In comparison with Barlach's memorial, the Worcester cenotaph and the county war memorial appear not to give sufficient theological weight either to the evil to which war brings people or to the need of more than a fellow creature to rescue other fellow creatures from evil's thrall. The cenotaph and the memorial were and are not brashly optimistic; but they were and are confident, perhaps more trusting in themselves and in those whom they remember than may theologically be reasonable, even given that Worcester's and Magdeburg's memorials emerged respectively from a victorious and a defeated people. Even the tone and the words of the bishop of Worcester which opened the service that marked the unveiling of the county's war memorial, remembering "before God the brave and the true who laid down their lives to defend us, and have departed into the resurrection of eternal life,"[41] are tested by the eloquently silent group gathered around Barlach's heavy oak cross.

"Glory" in the Life of Antony of Egypt

Not long after the death of the monk Antony in 356, a request was made, in all probability to Athanasius, the bishop of Alexandria, for information about Antony's life, and especially about Antony's early life, his introduction

---

39. Cf. Psalm 130:1.

40. Cf. Macquarrie, *Humility of God*, 13.

41. *Worcestershire Echo*, 10 November 1922 (scrapbook cutting, Worcester Cathedral Library, Muniments A405 [6], 88).

and progress in *askesis* or discipline, and the manner of his dying.[42] Athanasius acquiesced and, at some time during his third exile from Alexandria, wrote the *Life of Antony*.[43] What is important for these reflections on "the glorious dead" is the *Life's* reflection on the apostle Paul's statement, "I die daily," and the related theme of the triumph of the Saviour in and through the one who is willing to sacrifice all for the truth.

Early in the *Life*, Antony's biographer tells of Antony's "resolve" and of "his great faith and . . . [his] constant prayers."[44] In the face of sexual temptations, he reports Antony's "prayers and fasting, . . . [his] thinking about the Christ and [his] considering the excellence won through him"; and, in the face of thoughts of "the softness of pleasure," he writes of Antony's "ponder[ing] the threat of the fire of judgment and the worm's work."[45] Antony's part in resisting temptations clearly is significant; but Antony is not, however, depicted as the sole combatant against evil. For as his biographer continued, "working with Antony was the Lord, who bore flesh for us."[46] It was the Lord, incarnate in humanity's tempted flesh, who "gave [Antony's] body the victory over the devil" and enabled Antony to make his own the apostle Paul's words, "it is not I, but the grace of God which is in me."[47] No wonder, then, that the biographer, writing of a very early triumph by Antony over the devil, reframed Antony's "first contest against the devil" as "in Antony the success of the Savior."[48]

The need for *askesis* did not, however, end with that early triumph, as if that one, early victory meant that the devil was now fully and finally vanquished. Aware from his reading of the Scriptures that the devil was a lover of sin and that his treacheries were numerous, Antony, his biographer reported, "did not then become careless or arrogant," attitudes that in themselves were part of the devil's arsenal, but "more and more . . . mortified [his] body and kept it under subjection," words that echo the apostle Paul's "I punish my body and enslave it,"[49] "so that he would not, after conquering

---

42. Athanasius, *Life of Antony*, Prologue. All references to texts by Athanasius are by section rather than page number.

43. The usual dating is 357. For a discussion of date and authorship, see Hertling, *Antonius*; Quasten, *Patrology*, 39; Barnard, "Date of S. Athanasius' *Vita Antonii*"; and Brennan, "Dating Athanasius' *Vita Antonii*."

44. Athanasius, *Life of Antony*, 5.

45. Ibid.

46. Ibid.

47. Ibid.; 1 Corinthians 15:10.

48. Athanasius, *Life of Antony*, 7.

49. 1 Corinthians 9:27.

some challenges, trip up in others."[50] For Antony's biographer, not only Antony's first victory over the devil was "in Antony the success of the Savior," but so too was the second, and the third, and the fourth, and *every* victory.

In the light of this emphasis upon it not being Antony but the grace of God within Antony that won victories over the devil, Antony's biographer stressed the apostle Paul's "I die daily." Antony is portrayed as understanding death not simply as something that will happen once, and some time in the future, but as something that will happen in the future *and* that colours and shapes the whole extent of present life. Indeed, for Antony, death is both the natural end-point of a mortal life and the natural culmination of that far more prosaic process of daily dying, a daily dying to be understood not simply in terms of the natural diminution of physical processes.

Advising those young in the faith and in the early stages of their monastic lives, Antony said, "the desire for . . . [any] sordid pleasure, we shall not merely control—rather, we shall turn from it as something transitory, forever doing battle and looking toward the day of judgment. For the . . . fear and dread of the torments [of the end time] always destroys pleasure's smooth allure, and rouses the declining soul."[51] Death, with its ensuing judgment, *is* a catalyst for holy living. Yet Antony was not content to leave the matter so. For him, death was the natural culmination of, not only mortal life, but also that far more prosaic process of daily dying. So Antony also said to those young monks, "in order that we not become negligent, it is good to carefully consider the Apostle's statement: *I die daily*."[52] For if we so live, as people dying daily, we will not commit sin.

In short, Antony was seeking to prompt young monks, on rising daily, not to suppose that they would live till evening, and, on preparing for sleep, to consider that in the morning they may not awaken. For, as he is reported as telling his colleagues, "if we so live as people dying daily . . . as people who anticipate dying each day we shall be free of possessions, and we shall forgive all things to all people."[53]

Given, then, both that the monk is daily to die to himself, and that God's grace is always active in and through the monk, his identity is seen increasingly as Christ's, and his deeds increasingly as those normally reserved for God incarnate. Antony's powers of discernment, wisdom (emphasised in and through the references to him being an "unlettered man" who yet

50. Athanasius, *Life of Antony*, 7.

51. Ibid., 19.

52. Ibid., quoting 1 Corinthians 11:1.

53. Ibid.

speaks sagely),[54] his exorcisms, his standing for the truth, whatever the cost, and his acting as a spiritual adviser and unbiased judge are all portrayed as God-given powers, and each of them is portrayed as God's power operating unhindered in and through the monk Antony. Understandably, the concluding paragraph of the *Life* therefore commended its being read "to the other [monks] so that they may learn what the life of the monks ought to be, and so that they may believe that our Lord and Savior Jesus Christ glorifies those who glorify him."[55]

So, having come utterly to rely on, indeed, having identified himself wholly with, his divine Saviour, Antony worked good things for others, even as the Christ worked good things for him. In a sense, Antony became other people's "saviour." He became their "Christ." For the Saviour, the Christ, so operated in and through him and for the sake of all others. Yet, only "in a sense" did he become other people's "Christ." For while the monk became a "Christ" for all others, he never became *the* Christ. While Antony was being "deified" (a favourite verb of his biographer), Antony did not become God.

Behind this portrayal of victorious discipline in the face of evil is a rejection of an Arian understanding of salvation effected by *fiat*, a process that reduced an individual's life to "a dreary succession of sins and absolutions."[56] There is rather an acceptance, which tallies with Antony's explicit criticism of the Arians in Alexandria, of both the Nicene belief that "the Word coexisted with the Father always,"[57] and an understanding of human nature as being receptive, according to which "sinlessness is receiving grace rather than deliberately doing good . . . [and] the object of asceticism [is] to subdue one's will and allow the Logos to take over the self."[58] Any glory therefore associated with salvation and any ensuing victorious discipline in the face of evil belong to God, the One who alone can secure salvation and did so by becoming marred and marring humanity.

This time, setting the "strangeness" of this fourth-century *Life* alongside the early twentieth-century war memorials of Worcester and Studdert Kennedy's sermon of 1921, further questions are raised by the former of the latter two. In his sermon following his misunderstood address delivered on the night of Armistice Day 1921, Studdert Kennedy declared that "material disarmament is in itself perfectly useless until moral disarmament

54. Cf. ibid., 1.

55. Ibid., 94.

56. Williams, *Wound of Knowledge*, 48.

57. Athanasius, *Life of Antony*, 69. Cf. Athanasius, *Orationes Contra Arianos*, 1.9, for a similar response to the theology of Arius and his followers.

58. Young, "Reconsideration," 114.

precedes it."[59] For, as he added, honour and peace could not be brought about by force. The *Life* would suggest not only that Studdert Kennedy was correct insofar as he went, but also that he did not go far enough. For the *Life* would suggest that moral disarmament and peace will only be realised if God is integrally involved. For there to be an enduring, vivifying peace, there is, both the *Life* and the Nicene theological framework in which the *Life* is set would suggest, need of not just an amendment of life, born of forgiveness of the past and an imitation of the Prince of Peace's working, but also the acceptance that even the bloody, broken bodies of 1914–18 were assumed by the immortal God, that they might be made whole. Grace needs to be internalised. As Athanasius would have said, creatures cannot redeem themselves, and godly forgiveness and instruction alone leave lives but a constant repetition of sin, forgiveness, and amendment of life.[60] Indeed, as Athanasius would further have said, God alone saves, as is witnessed in that God became human that humans might be deified.[61]

Secondly, in the *Life* generally and particularly in its concluding paragraph addressed to those who would wish to progress in the monastic life, there is acknowledgment that the "Lord and Savior Jesus Christ glorifies those who glorify him."[62] It is in a monk's glorifying Christ in and through his obedience to Christ that Christ glorifies a monk. In terms of the evangelist Matthew's thinking, the monk will be glorious insofar as he lets his light so shine that others may see his good works and glorify his Father in heaven.[63] Accordingly, Antony asked philosophers marvelling at exorcisms attributed to him, "Why do you marvel at this? It is not we who do it, but Christ, who does these things through those who believe in him."[64]

The Worcester cenotaph boldly proclaimed "the glorious dead." Lord Coventry's address, on the occasion of the unveiling of the county war memorial, spoke of gallant men, heroic deeds, and Worcestershire men who were awarded the Victoria Cross; he spoke of such in the context of lives given for king and country. The focus of the cenotaph and Lord Coventry was on brave men, and on glory arising from service of a nation. Certainly

59. *Worcestershire Echo*, 12 December 1921 (scrapbook cutting, Worcester Cathedral Library, Muniments A405 [6], 43).

60. Cf. Athanasius, *Orationes Contra Arianos*, 2.22, 26, 67–70.

61. Cf. Athanasius, *De Incarnatione*, 54.

62. Athanasius, *Life of Antony*, 94.

63. Cf. Matthew 5:16.

64. Athanasius, *Life of Antony*, 80. Cf. 84, where Antony is described as healing "without issuing commandments, but by praying and calling on the name of Christ, so [that it might be] clear to all that it was not he who did this but the Lord bringing his benevolence to effect through Antony."

Antony did serve others. His virtues were indeed celebrated. Even Greek philosophers called him a "man of God."[65] Antony's glory, however, was not understood to have been earned, but received as a gift from God, a gift that continually suggested that not Antony but the One who had glorified Antony was the one truly to be glorified. "Glory" in the *Life* is *theo*centric, and it challenges the more anthropocentric understanding of the "glory" of "the glorious dead."

Conclusion

In retrospect, those a century later reflecting upon "the glorious dead" may wish to heed a number of themes. Evil is so pernicious, especially in and through its seductive attractiveness. In this way and that, it insinuates itself into the lives of individuals and societies. It breaks families, begets orphans, and sets people against people. It dehumanises, breaking creaturely inter-dependence, hindering love of neighbour, and hoping to instil in people carelessness or arrogance, believing that, having on one occasion defeated evil, they have finally conquered evil. It tempts people to allow the means to justify the end. It seeks to turn hope into either arrogant optimism or suffo-cating pessimism, both atheistic in their denial that God became incarnate so that even in death there is the hope of life.

Those who contend against such evil, in an honourable way, and with the aim of winning not only the war but also the peace, even if they die in the process, are indeed glorious. They are, however, glorious in a *derived* sense, all true glory being that which proceeds from God. Indeed, any glory that is thought of as self-existent, which a people draw down and attribute to any of its members, is a glory that fits, not a monotheistic, but a polytheistic theology.[66] The glory, then, of those who truly contend against evil comes from, is the gift of, the only glorious One; and their glory is manifest in and through their participation in the mission of the one God, to whom alone is due all majesty and might, all power and glory. These, in and through the one God, are the truly glorious ones. As the monk Antony remarked, the "Lord and Savior Jesus Christ glorifies those who glorify him."[67]

---

65. Ibid., 70.
66. Cf. Barth, *Dogmatics in Outline*, 35–41.
67. Athanasius, *Life of Antony*, 94.

PART III

Conclusion

10

English Theology in the First World War and Its Aftermath[1]

Mark D. Chapman

SHORTLY AFTER THE OUTBREAK of the First World War, there was a popular suspicion of all things "made in Germany." An advertisement in October 1914 for Wolsey woollen underwear claimed, for instance: "To every Briton worth the name the day of German underwear is past. Wolsey, with its British honesty of manufacture, of material, and of value, waits to take its place. For German Underwear—branded or otherwise—has hardly ever shown its buyers other than a spurious advantage; its 'cheapness' has seldom meant true economy."[2] What I will show in this chapter is that for many churchmen, it was not just shoddy underwear that had to be replaced by a better and perhaps less itchy home-grown product. Much theology, too, was highly suspect because of its "Made in Germany" origin. Indeed, the war provided an excellent opportunity for expelling what many, especially from Anglo-Catholic quarters, regarded as the pernicious influence of liberal theology, which had made such inroads into the leading theology faculties

---

1. I have discussed the ideas presented in this chapter at much greater length in *Theology at War*. On British theological opinions in the First World War, see Bailey, "British Protestant Theologians." From an evangelical perspective, see also Hoover, *God, Germany, and Britain*. See also Wilkinson, *Church of England* and Marrin, *Last Crusade*.

2. *Guardian*, 8 October 1914, 1156.

at Oxford and Cambridge. It consequently served to change the character
of English theology.

Theology at the outbreak of war

Around the outbreak of war, the archbishop of Canterbury, Randall Davidson, was busy in a meeting at Lambeth Palace where three East African
Anglican bishops had been summoned to discuss the crisis in the Anglican Communion following the missionary conference that had been held
in Kikuyu in British East Africa in June 1913.[3] The problem was that the
Anglican bishops William Peel of Mombasa and John Willis of Uganda,
both supported by the evangelical Church Missionary Society, had committed themselves to a temporary scheme for the Federation of Missionary
Societies, and had invited non-Anglicans to share in communion. This had
deeply upset the staunchly Anglo-Catholic bishop of Zanzibar, Frank Weston. In a series of letters and pamphlets, he accused his fellow bishops of
heresy,[4] since they had "contravened" what he thought was "the fundamental principle of Church order."[5] From his missionary perspective, Weston
condemned the liberal direction that the Church of England had been taking in the previous few years, particularly during the discussions over the
controversial collection, *Foundations*, produced by members of the Oxford
Theology Faculty under B. H. Streeter's editorship in 1912. Weston felt that
Kikuyu was simply one more example of what he regarded as the infection
of the church with a liberal theology that stemmed from Germany. From
his base in the predominantly Muslim British colony of Zanzibar, Weston
claimed that "the power of Islam will be broken not by a debating society but by the living, speaking church of the infallible Word Incarnate."[6]
With typical hyperbole, Charles Gore, bishop of Oxford, a former bishop of
Worcester and leader of the Anglo-Catholics on the bench of bishops, had
commented at the end of 1913: "I doubt if the cohesion of the Church of
England was ever more seriously threatened than it is now."[7]

The most important representative of theological liberalism by the
outbreak of war was Weston's teacher, William Sanday (1843–1920), Lady

---

3. Bell, *Randall Davidson*, 690–708, esp. 702–3. See Davidson, *Kikuyu*, 6, and
Chapman, "Kikuyu."

4. Weston, *Ecclesia Anglicana*, 19–20. On Weston, see Chapman, *Bishops, Saints
and Politics*, 199–222.

5. Weston, *Case Against Kikuyu*, 33.

6. Weston, *Ecclesia Anglicana*, 14.

7. *Times*, 29 December 1913, 3.

Margaret professor of divinity at the University of Oxford, and for a long time one of the chief mediators of German theology into England.[8] For much of his career, he had been a cautious high churchman with a reputation as "a scrupulously fair man" who, "in order to make sure he was doing full justice to his opponents, . . . read everything that he could lay his hands on,"[9] as exemplified in his work on the life of Christ.[10] He kept up a correspondence with many German theologians, including Ernst von Dobschütz (1870–1934) and Friedrich Loofs (1858–1928). Over the years, however, Sanday gradually moved into the liberal camp and by 1911 had made clear his distrust of what the historical method might yield.[11] This drove him into a position of what he called "relativity."[12] He privately announced his conversion to the "Modernist cause" in 1912,[13] a year that also saw him siding with Streeter and *Foundations*. His reputation for moderation, which had outlasted his mediating theology, could be dangerous in alliance with the new theology. Shortly before the outbreak of war, Sanday was engaged in vigorous controversy with his diocesan bishop, Charles Gore, part of which focused on Gore's disdain for German theology.[14] Among English theologians, however, Sanday was not unique in his high regard for German scholarship. Also important were his friends, the polymathic Essex rector Henry Latimer Jackson (1851–1926) and Francis Crawford Burkitt (1864–1935), Norrisian professor of divinity in Cambridge.

Given this background, it comes as little surprise that it did not take long for churchmen and theologians to make the connection between German militarism and liberal tendencies in theology. In a sermon published shortly after the outbreak of the First World War, James Wilson, canon librarian of Worcester, preached in the cathedral against Teutonic ethics.[15] For Wilson, a particular form of German ethics, labelled "Teutonism,"

8. On Sanday, see my books *Bishops, Saints and Politics*, 149–76; and *Coming Crisis*, 58–80. On the debates immediately before the First World War, see Clements, *Lovers of Discord*, 49–106; Langford, *In Search of Foundations*, 114–42; and Stephenson, *Rise and Decline*, 99–103.

9. Henson, *Retrospect*, 2:50.

10. Sanday, *Outlines* and *Life of Christ*.

11. Sanday, "Apocalyptic Element," 109.

12. He first stated this in *Life of Christ*, 199. It later became the guiding principle of his theology. See, for instance, Sanday, "Continuity"; and Sanday and Williams, *Form and Content*.

13. At a meeting of the Theological Dinner in 1912: see Prestige, *Life of Charles Gore*, 347.

14. See Gore, *Basis of Anglican Fellowship*, 8–10, and Sanday, *Bishop Gore's Challenge*, 29.

15. *Guardian*, 17 September 1914, 1078–79. For Wilson, see above, 87, n. 98.

posed a threat to the moral life of the Western nations. This was an ethics associated with the aggressive militarism that had taken hold of German foreign policy and even swathes of its intellectual life in the years leading up to the war. Wilson asked: "What is it that has united the Anglo-Saxon and Celt and Slav, yes, and India and Japan, against the Teuton?" His answer was simple. Western ethics united peoples across the empire and rested on something far deeper than a narrow nationalism. Far "below all our superficial differences," he claimed, there was a principle that served to unite "Nationalist and Ulsterman" in Ireland, "in South Africa Boer and Briton, in India Mussulman and Hindu, and in England united us all." This uniting principle was based on an appeal "to something far deeper than the innate love of fighting, than motives of self-interest, than ordinary patriotism. . . . Ultimately it arises from the presence in the soul of man of another and a higher conception of God and His purpose and working than that of the Teuton." A week later, once the news of further German atrocities, including the "battering and burning of Rheims Cathedral," had begun to reach the press, it had become clear to the leader-writer of the *Guardian*, the leading Church of England paper of the time, that a Germany that "glories in calculated scoundrelism" was clearly "outside the pale of civilisation." The war was consequently a "spiritual conflict . . . between brutal materialism and the noblest ideals of humanity."[16]

Shortly after the outbreak of war, a number of German theologians sought to influence British and American public opinion. A group of twenty-nine theologians and churchmen, including Karl Barth's teacher, Wilhelm Herrmann of Marburg, produced the well-known "Address of the German Theologians to the Evangelical Christians Abroad" on 4 September.[17] They pleaded that the war should be confined to Europe lest the gains in the mission field should be put at risk on account of a dispute between the great Christian missionary powers. The real fear, they claimed, came from what they called "Asiatic barbarism."[18] Even "heathen Japan" was now involved in the war "under the pretext of an alliance." When the native peoples saw white fighting white and "flourishing Mission-fields . . . being trampled

---

16. *Guardian*, 24 September 1914, 1100. See also Oakeley, "German Thought," and Bontrager, "Imagined Crusade." On Teutonism, see also G. K. Chesterton, "The Serbs in History: Harnack and Teutonism, Again," *Illustrated London News*, 10 October 1914, in Chesterton, *Collected Works*, 30:175–76.

17. "An die evangelischen Christen im Ausland," *Die Eiche* 3 (1915) 49–53; it was published in English as an appendix—"Address of the German Theologians to the Evangelical Christians Abroad"—in *To the Christian Scholars*, 19–23. See the *Guardian*, 1 October 1914, 1118. For details of the various manifestos and counter-manifestos, see Bailey, "Gott mit uns," esp. 479–87.

18. *To the Christian Scholars*, 20.

in ruin," the "great hour of the missionary enterprise" was consequently at risk.[19]

This appeal elicited a reply from a group of forty-two churchmen, led by the archbishops of Canterbury, York, and Armagh, but also including Free Church leaders, which sought to address some of what were regarded as its false claims.[20] There were a number of prominent theologians among the signatories, including Henry Scott Holland, Regius professor of divinity in Oxford, Sanday, and H. B. Swete, his counterpart in Cambridge, as well as Eugene Stock, former secretary of the Church Missionary Society.[21] The tone was conciliatory but firm, upholding the rightness of the British cause: while uniting "whole-heartedly with our German brethren in deploring the disastrous consequences of the war, and in particular its effect on diverting the energies and resources of the Christian nations from the great constructive tasks to which they were providentially called on behalf of the peoples of Asia and Africa," we "have taken our stand for international good faith, for the safeguarding of small nationalities, and for the essential conditions of brotherhood among the nations of the world."[22]

A second response to the German appeal was produced by a group of predominantly Anglican Oxford academics who, while recognising the "enormous output of the German universities in every department of scholarship,"[23] dealt more directly with the Asian threat against "Teutonism" and Protestantism.[24] Not unreasonably, it pointed out that Germany's ally, Turkey, was "religiously just as much an Asiatic power as Japan" and that the British Empire was a cohesive force in the fight against might where non-Christians "can only rejoice if these Christian principles find an echo in the breast of non-Christian peoples."[25] Germans, they held, could no longer claim to be defending culture on the basis of the "sinister deeds" that they had perpetrated, which included burning the library at Louvain University and bombarding Rheims Cathedral.[26] Shortly afterwards, Sanday wrote one of the first reasoned responses from the English academic community. Throughout the war, he attempted to keep abreast of German opinion and to

19. Ibid., 21.

20. *Guardian*, 1 October 1914, 1118. See also 8 October 1914, 1129.

21. *Guardian*, 1 October 1914, 1110. See Bell, *Randall Davidson*, 740–44.

22. At least one theologian refused to sign. Burkitt provoked a response from the archbishop of Canterbury, Randall Davidson. See Davidson to Burkitt, 18 September 1914, Burkitt Papers, Cambridge University Library, Ms. Add. 7658 B256.

23. *To the Christian Scholars*, 14.

24. Ibid., 8–10.

25. Ibid., 13.

26. Ibid., 15.

retain some degree of objectivity about events by trying as best he could to maintain links with his German friends. The first of Sanday's four wartime booklets, *The Deeper Causes of War*, published in 1914, is remarkably eirenic. He understood his duty to be to "weigh calmly and try to understand."[27] He regarded most Germans as "quiet, peace-loving people,"[28] in contrast to what he saw as the uncompromising perversion of the German character by Prussian militarism.

German militarism and liberal theology

The theme of German militarism continued to dominate the church press in the autumn of 1914. George Frodsham, a canon of Gloucester Cathedral and former bishop of North Queensland, for instance, preached on the ethics of war, focusing on the sorts of claims that had been made by Count Friedrich Adolf Julius von Bernhardi, best-selling author of *Deutschland und der Nächste Krieg*.[29] Bernhardi, he claimed, had mistaken Bonapartism for Christianity, disguising "the Corsican in the robes of Christ." In a letter written shortly afterwards, he continued in the same vein, this time making explicit links with liberal theology: at its heart, the war was "a deadly conflict between Christian and pagan ideals—between Christ and anti-Christ—contesting for empire over the souls of men. . . . The real question is, are we on the side of Christ, whom we know, not as a philosophical 'term of value,' but as the incarnate Revealer of the mind of God? This is the supreme issue of the war."[30]

Similarly, an anonymous review of W. O. E. Oesterley's book, *The Books of the Apocrypha*, published in the *Guardian* on 15 October 1914, made the link between German militarism and theology very clear: "If in Josephus's case this 'shining armour' of the warrior may have 'concealed a Rabbi,' we are tempted to ask whether the philosopher's cloak of the modern German theological professor is always innocent of covering the 'shining armour' or other less attractive features of Prussian militarism? Will the present great war which is likely to result in a very wide transmutation of German values, lead us also to a revised estimate of German scholarship, and more especially of German theological scholarship?" Although the reviewer felt that it would be "a ridiculous spirit of Jingoism, utterly foreign to the prevailing temper of Britain today, if one were to object to critical and

27. Sanday, *Deeper Causes*, 10.

28. Ibid., 5.

29. *Guardian*, 8 October 1914, 1147–48; Bernhardi, *Germany and the Next War*.

30. *Guardian*, 19 November 1914, 1271.

historical 'results' or to theological opinions simply on the grounds that they are 'Made in Germany'," he nevertheless felt that the "conduct of the war, interpreted by the writings of the Bernhardi school, has taught us more of Germany's ways and temper than we knew before." He went on to suggest in tentative but nevertheless clear terms that "it would not be altogether unfair to cast some of the blame of those unspeakable deeds which have branded modern Prussianism as savagely pagan on the extreme left of German theological scholarship. . . . Has German theological scholarship after all any of the characteristic traits of Prussian militarism?" He concluded on a christological note: "Does the theological leader suffer from any of that lack of the finer feelings of humanity—sympathy, love, mercy, and judgment, even of sympathetic imagination—which is so conspicuous a trait of the contemporary Teutonic war-leader?"[31]

Explicit links between Prussianism and liberal theology were made by Edward Lyttelton, headmaster of Eton and well-known cricketer, in a university sermon preached at Oxford in October 1914, where he spoke of "The Danger of Critical Christianity." The real threat, he felt, was that "the Christian Creed loses its mystery; and, while ceasing to challenge doubts, it ultimately fails to arrest attention. Its history is first to become inoffensive, then negligible, then contemptible." After Napoleon's defeat of Germany in 1806, the nation had been prone to a kind of heresy, coming to the belief that "a strong army would bring them something more tangible, more desirable, than was to be expected from the corporate worship of the Most High God or the reverent acceptance of the mystery of His Revelation." He concluded by asking his congregation: "Why was the [German] national mind so receptive of the overtures of the God of this world? And the answer is that the great antidote which might have been securely lodged in their thoughts was not there. It was diluted with rationalism; the salt had lost its savour, and the corruption worked unhindered. And it is for us now to put the same question. Are we, too, not drugging ourselves with the same poison?"[32]

Something similar was suggested by Charles Wood, Lord Halifax (1839–1934), the lay leader of the Anglo-Catholics, at a meeting of the English Church Union held on 25 November 1914.[33] After observing that the war was a sign that "culture and civilisation apart from Christianity were doomed to destruction," he went on: "If German Professors and theologians could be so hopelessly wrong about events in our own cognisance, they were likely to be equally wrong about those weightier matters dealing

---

31. *Guardian,* 15 October 1914, 1171.

32. *Guardian,* 22 October 1914, 1213; cf. Matthew 5:13.

33. *Guardian,* 26 November 1914, 1313.

with religious criticism especially associated with their names. . . . For us, as for Russia, the war was a holy war." For such men as Lyttelton and Halifax, the holy war was proving a useful weapon in the attacks on liberals, who could be accused of Germanophilia. This charge was not without substance: on 1 August, for instance, the day after Russian mobilisation, nine British academics, including the well-known Anglican liberals Burkitt and Latimer Jackson, along with Frederick John Foakes-Jackson, dean of Jesus College, Cambridge, wrote to the *Manchester Guardian*, claiming that war against Germany would be a "sin against civilization."[34]

Further accusations were made the following year after the publication in the spring of 1915 of the archbishop of Canterbury's report on the Kikuyu controversy. In a response, which bore the telling title *Missionary Principles and the Primate on Kikuyu: Three Addresses with Some Observations on the Present German Movement in the Church of England*, the Anglo-Catholic controversialist Leighton Pullan (1865–1940), fellow and chaplain of St. John's College, Oxford, explicitly used German aggression as a way of attacking liberal theology. He had long identified degenerate German culture and liberal theology. In a short book on the history of New Testament criticism published in 1907, for instance, he described the "new religion" of "liberal Protestantism" or "Modern Protestantism," which was "no longer content to remain in the study and the university lecture room," but had spread throughout Germany through organised lectures, both among the "cultured and the working classes."[35] According to Pullan, "we are face to face with a non-Christian religion,"[36] which was partly responsible for the moral breakdown of German society: "Protestantism is honeycombed with rationalism, and the sense of moral obligation is weaker where the sense of intellectual submission to divine truth is weaker."[37] The war was simply confirming the worst fears of the English conservatives.

In his Kikuyu booklet, Pullan spoke of the need to purge the church of the German heresy, which had revealed its true colours in the morally degenerate invasion of Belgium: "Up to the very brink of the war," he claimed, "the reverence which was paid in this country to a certain class of German professors went beyond all reasonable bounds." This had served to encourage "among many of our clergy, and some of our laity, a temper which was unpatriotic and even anti-Christian" and was even "asphyxiating vocations to the ministry." Just as "second-hand versions of second-rate German

---

34. *Manchester Guardian*, 1 August 1914, 9.
35. Pullan, *New Testament Criticism*, 30.
36. Ibid., 32.
37. Ibid., 34.

divinity flooded the country," he went on, so "in our universities Germany, and not the most religious part of Germany, was coming to be regarded as the Englishman's 'spiritual home.'"[38] He continued with a rhetorical flourish:

> For such English people as these, when Berlin had spoken, a cause was finished. We cannot prudently overlook the fact that when the Bishop of Winchester and the Bishop of Oxford showed their resolve to maintain within the limits of their jurisdiction the teaching of the New Testament, writers of such different talents as Mrs. Humphrey Ward and Dr. Sanday appealed to the Protestant universities of Germany.
>
> The German movement is still being actively organised and the Creed steadily assailed by clergymen and laymen who call themselves "Modern Churchmen" or "Liberal Churchmen." Some appear to hold a lower view of Christ than that taken by a reverent Moslem. . . . Others act in agreement with Dr. Sanday's advice, and abstain from "a bleak and unqualified denial." . . . It is enough for them to repeat the words of evangelists and saints, and then to suggest "restatements" drawn from Harnack, Loofs and Schweitzer.[39]

Pullan was deeply critical of men such as Sanday who appealed "to the opinions of the Protestant Universities of Europe," as they mediated German theology to England.[40] The "Prussianizing of theology in Great Britain" was affecting the way in which the creeds were being increasingly questioned.[41] He concluded with a passionate plea for a return to the Great Commission rather than the morally dubious Christ of a Germanising liberal theology: "We shall either keep the Gospel of Galilee and carry it to the heathen, or we shall adopt the Gospel of Berlin."[42]

Another example of this identity of Germanism and liberal theology is that of Arthur Champneys (1854–1924), who wrote a pamphlet in 1915 with the bold title *"Criticism" as Made in Germany and Common Sense*. "The line of thought and the arguments used against miracles, the sapping of at least the outworks of belief in the Incarnation or the Resurrection (as well as the practical denial of our Lord's real deity)," he wrote, "for the most part unquestionably hail from Germany."[43] He linked a critical

---

38. Pullan, *Missionary Principles*, iii.

39. Ibid., iv.

40. Ibid., 27.

41. Ibid., 10.

42. Ibid., 30.

43. Champneys, *"Criticism,"* 18.

attitude towards Christianity and what he considered the lies promulgated
by the German government: "The clergy and the professors and learned
men, with the rarest exceptions, are as the rest in accepting and repeating
current falsehoods. And though all this has been accentuated by the War
it is an older story than that."[44] Champneys concluded his pamphlet with a
broadside against the English liberal churchmen: "As in Germany pastors
of the Lutheran communion and their teachers claim—and are allowed—to
deny and undermine the received tenets of Christianity, whether as regards
to the person of Christ or the historical facts of the Gospels, so a like history
or licence is claimed by their disciples—that very small minority of the
clergy—in England. . . . But it is perhaps natural that, in the process of
'peaceful penetration,' German ethics should come to the aid of German
theological speculations."[45]

Other voices

Despite such conservative critics and the prevailing hostile mood of the
time, some theologians tried to distinguish between the more enlightened
strain of German thought and the excesses of Prussian militarism. In a
pamphlet of 1915, W. B. Selbie, principal of the Congregationalist Mansfield
College, Oxford, reflected on the tendencies expressed by conservatives:
"Already advantage is being taken of the present crisis by those whose fear
of German theology is greater than their knowledge of it. They argue that
British theology has been over-germanized, and that, now that our eyes are
opened to the true character of the German spirit, we had better have done
with this obsession once and for all."[46] Selbie felt that critical theology posed
no great threat, believing that even though it might originate in Germany, it
"belongs to Christendom." He concluded with a bold plea for reconciliation
with more enlightened thinkers.[47] Similarly in Cambridge, Foakes-Jackson,
in the first university sermon preached after the outbreak of war on 8 October 1914, was equally worried lest the war should "serve as a sufficient
pretext for a reaction against all modernism in religious thought and for the
encouragement of the application of methods of scholarship to Christian
problems."[48]

44. Ibid., 23.

45. Ibid., 27–28.

46. Selbie, *War and Theology*, 3.

47. Ibid., 4.

48. *Cambridge Review*, 14 October 1914, cited in Wakefield, "Biographical Introduction," 42.

Several theologians sought to keep up their contacts with their German friends as the war progressed, even if in the end their efforts proved futile. Sanday's second pamphlet, *The Meaning of the War for Germany and Great Britain: An Attempt at Synthesis*, was read in Germany by (among others) Martin Rade and Adolf Jülicher.[49] The tone of the pamphlet was patriotic: "I was never so proud of my nation as I was in the first week of the war." Nevertheless, unlike many of his contemporaries, he was prepared to listen to the German case and was sensitive to the matter of fairness to the enemy, never failing to point to the positive aspects of German culture: it was "a noble nation for a time gone wrong."[50] War with Germany was a last resort brought on by "severe pressure of honourable obligations" to resist "Napoleonic tendencies."[51] Sanday concluded his pamphlet on an optimistic note: "I do not doubt for a moment that in the end Germany will see her mistake. . . . We shall hail the penitent's return. Some day the clouds of war will roll away like an evil dream."[52]

As the war progressed, even though Sanday grew increasingly pessimistic, he continued in his efforts to understand the enemy and to place his trust in reconciliation, even during its most desperate days. For instance, in an answer to Conan Doyle's letter to the *Times* of 18 October 1915, which called for French aviators to "make raid upon Karlsruhe and Stuttgart,"[53] he responded on the following day with the question: "What good can it do our innocent dead to know that there are innocent dead in Germany?"[54] He published a third pamphlet in the summer of 1916, entitled *In View of the End: A Retrospect and a Prospect*. Kenneth Mozley (1883–1946), dean of Pembroke College, Cambridge, who was one of the most conciliatory of the English theologians, wrote to Sanday after reading *In View of the End*: "I think there were more faults in our English attitude towards Germany, than you admit. But still, the war was made in Germany. . . . Though Germany appears to us to have sinned very badly, I do not think we should try to punish her. She might make recompense in some of her destructive doings but

49. Gustav Adolf Bienemann, Anglican chaplain at Neuchatel in Switzerland, distributed the pamphlet in Switzerland, and passed on copies to Arthur Titius and Gustav Jahn (Bienemann to Sanday, 15 April 1915, Sanday Papers, Bodleian Library, Oxford [Bod.], Eng. misc. d.122 [I] no. 139).

50. Sanday, *Meaning of the War*, 66.

51. Ibid., 104.

52. Ibid., 122–23.

53. Conan Doyle to the *Times*, 18 October 1915, 9.

54. Sanday to the *Times*, 19 October 1915, 10.

that is a different thing."[55] A few weeks later, Mozley called for a negotiated peace.[56]

Sanday published a fourth pamphlet for the "Evangelical Information Committee" in 1917, entitled *When Should the War End?*, which was translated into German, but which seems to have made little impact.[57] Writing to the *Times* on 20 September 1917, he lamented the failure of his pamphlets to overturn Junker militarism in Germany as displayed in the escalation of the submarine war. Seeing his four pamphlets as progressive efforts to "get at the real truth about the war—not merely the truth as seen through patriotic spectacles," he asked himself whether in the light of war crimes there was anything he should retract. "I do not feel called upon to retract what is perhaps only a cruder statement of what I should say today, though essentially along the same lines with it. . . . I was writing then before the days of 'unrestricted submarine activity' and the like. There are things since that I could not so easily forgive."[58] By 1917, Sanday's approach had become increasingly rare: the situation had moved so fast during the war that there were very few who managed to retain a positive view of the enemy. His lecture to the British Academy on "International Scholarship after the War," given in May 1918, with its call for restoration of academic links after the war, provoked an extreme reaction from some of his opponents, most notably the physiologist C. S. Sherrington of the University of Oxford.

The aftermath of war

It comes as little surprise that, in the years after the armistice in November 1918, there were very few who were prepared to defend German theology in England. The general mood was well expressed by Hensley Henson, at the time bishop of Hereford, in a perceptive letter to Burkitt of 3 December 1918: "the Clergy are well to the front in 'voicing' the popular sentiment, and giving the cry for vengeance the decorous aspect of a cry for justice. I wish the clergy could be silenced. They are invariably disgusting when they bustle to the front in these times of excitement in the self-selected rôle of the Lord's prophets. . . . The end of the War has released into voluble expression

55. Mozley to Sanday, 23 November 1916, Sanday Papers, Bod. Eng. misc. d.124 (II) no. 506.

56. Mozley to Sanday, 2 December 1916, Sanday Papers, Bod. Eng. misc. d.124 (II) no. 511.

57. Sanday, *When Should the War End?* It was translated as "Wie soll der Krieg endigen?" in the Swiss journal, *Wissen und Leben* 11 (1917) 9–16.

58. Sanday to the *Times*, 20 September 1917, 5.

all the old partisan passions both here and in America. We have learned nothing, and forgotten nothing, though the world is breaking up, and revolution marches."[59] The public mood did not change significantly in the years that followed: Anglo-German theological relations were never restored to their pre-war heights. Indeed, it took a number of years before the first German theologian was able to visit England, and even then the Universities of Oxford and Cambridge refused a platform. Personal relationships were never properly restored. Burkitt wrote to Ernst von Dobschütz on 7 July 1922:

> There was too much "England ist der Feind" in Germany during the War for us over here to forget.
>
> You don't seem yet to realise what a difference the War has made, a War which we believe was caused not by the ex-Kaiser, but by the will of the German people. We think now of Germany as a nation that does not care what it does to those that stand in its way—witness always Belgium!—but a nation that at the same time complains whenever anyone else interferes with its desires.
>
> We all consider Germany has been let off very lightly and are amazed to see the old arrogant spirit still so active.
>
> That is the general impression here: I am not arguing about the rights and wrongs of it. In my opinion the time has not yet come to discuss these things calmly. Discussion of the kind that you and some other Germans seem anxious to start would convince no one and only lead to a loss of temper.
>
> I venture to think we must forget before we can agree.[60]

Even though forgetting ultimately proved impossible, there was a slight thaw in relations between English and German theologians during the 1920s, which in part emerged from the nascent ecumenical movement. This was best exemplified by the meeting in Canterbury in April 1927 of thirteen relatively young scholars from Britain and Germany organised by George Bell, dean of Canterbury, who had been Davidson's chaplain through the First World War, and Adolf Deissmann of Berlin (who did not attend), on the theme of "the nature of the Kingdom of God and its relation to human society."[61] The conference was reported at length in the journal *Theology*,

59. Henson to Burkitt, 3 December 1918, Burkitt Papers, Cambridge University Library, Ms. Add. 7658 B433.

60. Burkitt to von Dobschütz, 7 July 1922, Burkitt Papers, Cambridge University Library, Ms. Add. 7658 A10.

61. Robertson, *Unshakeable Friend*, 8–23, and Chandler, *George Bell*, 29–30. For Bell, see also Chandler, ed., *Church and Humanity*.

which had become the leading popular theological journal.[62] Among the contributors were Sir Edwyn Hoskyns, dean of Corpus Christi College, Cambridge; A. E. J. Rawlinson, later bishop of Derby; E. G. Selwyn, editor of *Theology*; C. H. Dodd, the Congregationalist New Testament scholar; Gerhard Kittel of Tübingen; and the Luther scholar, Paul Althaus of Erlangen. This was followed by a second conference on the theme of Christology in August 1928, held in the Wartburg, near Eisenach, which also included scholars from Sweden and Denmark.[63] The papers of both conferences were published as *Mysterium Christi* in 1930.[64] A third conference, "Corpus Christi," which tackled the theme of the church, was held at the Bishop's Palace in Chichester in 1931, where Bell had been appointed bishop and where Otto Dibelius shared the chair.[65] While the meetings themselves reveal a commitment to reconciliation and joint endeavour, they also reveal the distinct differences between the theological traditions of the two countries as well as differences between the scholars within Germany and Britain. There was certainly little sense, as there had been before the First World War, of the supremacy of German learning. Perhaps equally important was the lack of representation, at least on the German side, of those who might have been regarded as liberals. Indeed, Kittel and Althaus became supporters of National Socialism.

In Germany and Switzerland following the First World War, there was a marked change in direction in theology, especially from younger theologians: many became critical of liberal scholarship, frequently using some striking levels of rhetoric. This was most obviously displayed by Karl Barth, whose *Römerbrief* (*Epistle to the Romans*) of 1919 became something of a manifesto for a new form of dialectical theology that offered a radical critique of the perceived breakdown of society in the First World War. While Barth and his friends and colleagues who established the journal *Zwischen den Zeiten* (*Between the Times*) helped to change the direction of theology in Germany, their writings were little known in England.[66] Hoskyns, who had been working on Barth since the mid-1920s and helped to introduce many Cambridge undergraduates to a form of biblical theology,[67] published his translation of the *Römerbrief* as late as 1933. In his preface, he

---

62. *Theology* 14 (1927) 247–95.

63. *Theology* 17 (1928) 182–86.

64. Bell and Deissmann, eds., *Mysterium Christi*.

65. *Theology* 22 (1931) 301–46.

66. See Morgan, *Barth Reception*, esp. 100–23, and Roberts, *Theology on Its Way?* 95–154. More generally, see Gorringe, *Karl Barth*, 73–116.

67. Morgan, *Barth Reception*, 116.

admitted that many of the book's allusions and references to movements of thought would simply not be understood in England.[68] He later noted in a "letter from England" to Barth, dated Tuesday in Holy Week, 1936: "We are separated by the very real barrier of a different language, a different political tradition, a different quality of piety and impiety, a different structure even of theological and untheological heritage."[69] Those efforts to overcome such differences between the two theological and political cultures, which seemed to promise so much in the days before 1914, did not survive the devastation of the First World War.

Conclusion

Four things emerge from this brief survey of English theology through and after the First World War. First, there were close connections between the rhetoric of war and the party polemics of the Church of England: particularly in the early years of the war, the bankruptcy of German culture and its militarism were equated with the "heresy" of liberal theology by a number of conservative Anglo-Catholics. Secondly, more liberal theologians were forced to distance themselves from their former German friends, partly out of fear of being seen as Germanophiles or heretics or both. What all this also shows is that Karl Barth was not unique in his condemnation of the state of German theology in 1914: far lesser theologians from a completely different context were making what to some might seem to be equally implausible connections between Prussian militarism and liberal theology. This meant that there was an irreversible distancing between the two countries, which manifested itself after the war in the loss of most serious reception of German theological scholarship for a long time: the efforts in the 1920s came to very little, and in the 1930s, there were very different forces at work in the German churches that required a quite different response.

Thirdly, theological liberalism in its pre-war form was forever tainted by its association with a "made in Germany" slogan, which meant that in the 1920s, English liberalism with rare exceptions became increasingly associated with a more distinctively home-grown version, finding expression in the Modern Churchmen's Union of the 1920s, which lost many of its earlier connections to German theology.[70] The final key effect of the First World War on theology, at least in the Church of England, was in ensur-

68. Barth, *Epistle to the Romans*, xi. On the translation, see Roberts, *Theology on Its Way?* 110–11.

69. Hoskyns, *Cambridge Sermons*, 218–19.

70. See Morgan, *Barth Reception*, 100–110.

ing the widespread acceptance of Anglo-Catholicism. Something that had hitherto been regarded as a little suspect and unpatriotic, especially in its support of things Roman, had through the war become increasingly regarded as patriotic. By the 1920s, it had become the dominant party in the Church of England. Liberals in general were on the back foot and German-inspired liberals had virtually disappeared altogether. With the rise of Anglo-Catholicism, that form of English theology which was most unlike the Protestantism of Germany was on the ascendant. Indeed, it is noteworthy that the 450th anniversary of Luther's birth in 1933 was not marked at all in the Anglican press. Three years earlier, Archbishop Lang had refused an invitation to send representatives to Germany to mark the 400th anniversary of the Augsburg Confession, since, he held, this might "seem to identify the Church of England with [the] Evangelical Church at home or on the Continent."[71] It is consequently not unreasonable to claim that the First World War played a significant part in distancing the Church of England from its Protestant inheritance.

71. Lang to Bell, 5 March 1930, cited in Chandler, Introduction to *Brethren in Adversity*, 9.

11

On Integration, Balance, and Fullness

Michael W. Brierley and Georgina A. Byrne

> But the old man would not so, but slew his son,
> And half the seed of Europe, one by one.[1]

WILFRED OWEN'S POEM "THE Parable of the Old Man and the Young" is a remarkably poignant testimony to the tragedy of the First World War. The biblical story of the willingness of Abraham to sacrifice his son Isaac in obedience to divine command is tragic enough for commentators. Owen provides the chilling, dramatic twist that in the First World War, the old man ignored the angel's call to stay the knife, which he heeded in the account in Genesis, and carried out the sacrifice; and indeed, the sacrifice of not just one son, but "half the seed of Europe," each of them an individual.[2]

The First World War was a tragedy on an unprecedented scale. At least fifteen million people lost their lives, "one by one." That is not to say that loss of life did not take place on a greater scale during the course of the twentieth century: in the Second World War, which included the horrors of the holocaust and atomic bombs, the number of those who died was over

---

1. Owen, *Poems of Wilfred Owen*, 151; cf. Genesis 22:1–14.

2. For the vastness of the tragedy and yet at the same time its composition of particular individual stories, see (Andrew) Studdert-Kennedy, "Somme."

three times as many.[3] But because in the latter, the effects of mechanised and atomic warfare were already known or anticipated, and because a large part of the destruction was calculated and deliberate, the word "evil" tends to be associated with the Second World War, and "tragedy" with the First. "Tragedy" can have an unforeseen, unintentional, or accidental quality, a set of circumstances that could easily have been otherwise, "the terrible dilemmas, ironies, unforeseen consequences, intolerable burdens and intractable situations in which people find themselves";[4] it has less of the sinister or premeditated quality of "evil." It is therefore a category that tends to be used for a war that took the world by surprise—a war into which soldiers were initially sent without helmets, in which live bodies were pitched against artillery, and in which cavalry charged against machine guns. Combatants in 1914 expected to be home by Christmas. Digging trenches and living in them for four years was unenvisaged.

Integration

Theology is the study of God, and of everything else in relation to God.[5] That is not to make any pre-judgment about whether God and everything else are separate from each other, identical to each other, or somehow subsist within each other (forms of classical theism, pantheism, and panentheism respectively); it is simply to establish theology as the task that studies God, and how that which is not God is related to God. Straightaway, then, theology identifies two "poles," "sides," or "dimensions" to reality—God and that which is not God—and this polarity runs through theological discourse: "the church and the world," "the sacred and the secular," "religion and society," and so on. It is no coincidence that the theologian Paul Tillich talked of the principal theological task as "correlation"; that the favoured term of Scottish theologian John Macquarrie was "dialectical theism"; and that process theologians speak of "dipolarity." Before his early death in 2014, John Hughes was beginning to work out what he called an "integralist" approach to theology, seeing theology, and in particular the Anglican tradition, as an attempt to integrate the things of God with the contingencies of creaturely existence.[6] Theology seeks to bring the two sets of poles together. It uses the language of faith—God, Christ, incarnation, redemption—in its search for the meaning of the rest of life; it brings the spiritual to bear on other

---

3. Pinker, *Better Angels*, 235.

4. Ford, "Tragedy," 239; cf. Williams, *Tragic Imagination*, 6, 30–54, and 97–98.

5. A definition deriving from Aquinas: see Becker, *Fundamental Theology*, 72.

6. See Hughes, *Graced Life*.

levels of reality. In this way, theological responses to the First World War attempt to uncover meaning in an experience of extreme global loss; they seek to facilitate the emergence of God in the context of enormous tragedy, doing on a vast scale what theology endeavours to do with tragedy on a smaller scale: integrate it into a meaningful whole. In visual terms, theological responses to the war strive to transform the scars of war into an overall and ongoing beauty, just as the marks of Christ's crucifixion were integrated into his resurrection body.[7] Our concern in this book is the integration of tragedy with Life, in the sense of divine Life, life in all its fullness.[8]

The First World War itself was anything but an "integrating" force. Mark Chapman, in his examination of theology in the period during and immediately after the war, shows how, far from integrating British and German thought, the war undid the integration that had been happening before it began, and increased the divide between the nations' theologians into the next decade. Yet the essays in this volume also demonstrate the ability of humans to work in the other direction, and illustrate the activity of "integration" during the war in a number of different spheres. One sphere is that of "place," the subject of the essay by John Inge, who considers "home" as a place where negative human experiences can be integrated with positive ones. So Inge observes how Geoffrey Studdert Kennedy, in his home of Worcester—a slum parish of considerable deprivation—and on the Western Front, integrated the suffering of these places with a legendary pastoral ministry. Inge relates this to Studdert Kennedy's notion of a God who is "at home" with suffering, a God into whom suffering is integrated by means of the cross. On a national scale, Inge considers how countries can develop "homes" by transforming areas in which tragedies have taken place, into places of beauty. Examples include those locations on the former Western Front where cemeteries have been carefully plotted, and are devotedly cared for, amid landscapes that have been rebuilt or returned to agricultural use: here, the places where bodies have been buried and continue to be remembered are integrated with "business as usual," not in a jarring way, but in a way that enables each aspect of the place to "respect" the other. The sites themselves induce a tranquillity that aids and contributes to their restorative work. While there are differences between British and German war memorials, and indeed, subtle differences between British memorials of the First and Second World Wars (the former most commonly took the form of stone monuments with lists of names, while the latter, though often imitating the former, also took the form of memorial parks and halls, perhaps indicating

7. Luke 24:36–40; John 20:19–20, 26–27.
8. Cf. John 10:10.

the greater effect of that war on civilian communities), memorials nonetheless represent attempts to create spaces in which the painful past can be integrated meaningfully with the present. Even "arbitrary" places, in the sense of places that have not been the scene of traumatic action, can exercise this integrative function, as shown by the National Memorial Arboretum at Alrewas in Staffordshire. Inge also looks at triumphalist monuments, and the successful integration of the more recent painful past within the structure of a traditional victory monument in Munich. Moving on to consider the continent of Europe as a whole, Inge suggests that Auschwitz can be a place of "integration," where the unspeakable acts that took place there can be recalled in ways that ensure that they are never repeated.

Places or "homes" that successfully integrate the painful past with the pleasant, can assume a "sacramental" role.[9] The discipline of theology understands a sacrament to be a particular visible place or occasion in which God is operating "invisibly" or internally. So the classic sacraments of the church are baptism and the eucharist, in which the love of God is enacted through immersion in water, and the sharing of bread and wine. But God is by no means limited to these particular occasions. Rather, "the sacraments" are indicative of a general "sacramental principle," that anyone and anything has the capacity to become a vehicle for the divine life. The particular occasions themselves are signifiers, "intensifications," "loci," or "foci" of this principle, establishing the principle as something that can be applied more widely. In this way, "homes" that integrate the positive and negative experiences of life are sacramental, as they point to the possibility of such integration elsewhere. They are particular points where the principle is known, in order that its benefits may be shared more broadly.

Inge's principle of "homes" for individuals, nations, and continents, can be applied to the world as a whole. One place that could act as the "home" of the world, a place where tragedy has the potential to be constructively integrated with ongoing life, is the Holy Land. It is, of course, currently very much a contested space, with its history of tragedy and (for Christians) the ultimate tragedy of Calvary. Yet it has the *potential* to be a place of healing, of successful integration of that which is worst in life with that which is best. In this context, the appellation of "Holy Land" is peculiarly apposite, for that particular land has the latent capacity to signify that which is "holy" for the rest of the world. The "sacramental principle" of Christian theology suggests that we need particular places of material exchange between the divine and the creaturely, that we need particular sacraments, precisely in

9. For the sacramental understanding of place, see further, Inge, *Christian Theology of Place*, 59–90.

order to demonstrate that anyone and anything has the capacity to become infused with divinity, a site of "integration" or exchange with God. The theologian David Brown argues that this amounts to a re-sacralisation of creation, a much more thorough engagement by theology with the range of human experience, which, in past centuries, would have been seen as mediating the divine.[10] So the places that witnessed, or even elicited, destructive power in the First World War can become the places that exercise a healing or redemptive power today. The integration is incomplete, this side of the eschaton—"here we have no lasting city"[11]—but our "homes" become a sign and foretaste of that city, insofar as we transform their wounds into "glorious scars."[12]

The essays in this volume point to another way in which tragedy is integrated with "Life," and that is in the images and metaphors that are used to describe the divine. The chapter by Michael Brierley indicates how, in the trenches, Geoffrey Studdert Kennedy found the Christian (indeed, biblical) image of Christ on a throne to be insufficiently marked by the tragedy of the cross to resonate with troops in their suffering. In the oft-quoted words of Dietrich Bonhoeffer, written, significantly, from his prison cell, "only the suffering God can help."[13] Studdert Kennedy began to see a crucifix in every situation of suffering, from the bodies of dead soldiers to over-crowded houses in his parish. Brierley points to the difficulty of integrating suffering and glory within a single symbol, and both he and Alvyn Pettersen draw attention to the crucifix that Studdert Kennedy devised as the war memorial for his own parish of St. Paul (see figure 6), in which Christ, on the cross, holds his head high, to indicate his ultimate unbrokenness—the fact that, in the resurrection, he was unbeaten. Brierley draws out of Studdert Kennedy's corpus a further image, at which Studdert Kennedy's writing only hinted, but which was embodied by Studdert Kennedy's own military service: the biblical image of the shepherd constantly seeking the lost sheep, until every last one of the flock has been found; this translates, on the battlefield, into the image of the chaplain or stretcher-bearer, ever proceeding into No Man's Land in order to rescue the wounded. Such images portray God's glory in terms of persistence, a "never ceasing" to redeem what is wounded or lost. Those who question whether such a suffering God would be able to over-

---

10. Brown, *God and Enchantment of Place*, 5–36. Brown suggests that the marginalisation of religion in society is due to a lack of such engagement by the church and its theologians, rather than an inevitable consequence of modernity.

11. Hebrews 13:14.

12. From the hymn "Lo, he comes with clouds descending" by Charles Wesley (1707–88); cf. Ford, "Tragedy," 234.

13. Bonhoeffer, *Letters and Papers*, 361.

come evil, whether that might leave the triumph of the divine denuded or in doubt, underestimate the strength, glory, and triumph of "never ceasing." Therein lies divine power, and divine infinitude: not infinite in coercion, but infinite in accompaniment. "For the love of God is broader than the measure of [our] mind, and the heart of the Eternal is most wonderfully kind; but we make his love too narrow with false limits of our own, and we magnify his strictness with a zeal he will not own."[14] Those who find a suffering God emasculated, Brierley would argue, do not know the power of (to use Sam Wells's terminology) "being with."

The intriguing point to note is the consonance of this doctrine of God with the style of Studdert Kennedy's own pastoral ministry. The overwhelming impression of Studdert Kennedy is of a man who sought to "be with" those who were suffering, whether the poor of his parishes, the troops to whom he was attached in war, or the women at home who waited anxiously for their loved ones' safe return. Studdert Kennedy's desire to serve alongside the men, rather than in safety behind the line, indeed the paramount importance that he attached to doing so, is a representation and embodiment of his own model of God. It is probably an unprofitable question to ask whether Studdert Kennedy's ministry derived from his doctrine of God, or whether his doctrine of God derived from his pastoral ministry: the two are likely to have exercised a symbiotic relationship, each reinforcing the other.

This leads on to the important observation that in the process of integration, in bringing theology and human experience together, they are each affected by the other. Thus, the integration of theology and tragedy needs to pay attention to the physical, emotional, psychological, and spiritual contexts in which theology is expressed for a full and critical integration to be achieved. Those who have experienced tragedy in their lives have often been more susceptible to interpreting God in tragic terms; Studdert Kennedy is not the only theologian to have come up with the doctrine of passibility in the context of suffering. Other First World War chaplains expressed the same idea, adding fresh impetus to a notion that, under the influence of German idealism, had begun to be expressed in Britain at the end of the nineteenth century. Similarly, the expressions of passibilism by Kazoh Kitamori and Jürgen Moltmann in the later twentieth century had roots in their experiences of the Second World War. Simple equations must, of course, be avoided. It is not the case that everyone's experience of the First World War was negative;[15] nor is it the case that suffering leads inexorably to passibi-

14. From the hymn "There's a wideness in God's mercy" by Frederick Faber (1814–63). Cf. Baker, *Foolishness*, 134.

15. For some, the First World War was a positive experience: men who would otherwise have had very little opportunity to travel "saw the world" or the war "made"

lism. It is interesting to speculate on the possible causes of the resurgence of impassibilism in Western theology in the opening years of the twenty-first century—a counter-reaction to the passibilist impulse? a renewed interest in Aquinas? The point is that theology is conditioned by experience, as well as itself impinging on that experience.

Peter Atkinson, in his contribution to this volume, points to the "melancholic" nature of Studdert Kennedy's poetry and character, in comparison with the "joy" of Geoffrey Dearmer. If "we do not know" "quite why the thorn was in [Studdert Kennedy's] flesh,"[16] the apparent suicide of his brother Robert, when Geoffrey was fourteen, is a very suggestive gloss on that melancholy.[17] Studdert Kennedy seems to have been drawn to the cross, just as (and perhaps because) he was drawn to the tragedy of human suffering. He was brought up in a parish of deprivation, and chose to minister amid the slums of Worcester, just as he chose to serve as an army chaplain and chose to make his way to the Front to be nearer to his men. Those were his choices and they demonstrate his great sympathy for his fellow human beings. This temperament might also explain why, as Mark Dorsett has noted, he was better able to offer compassion to the soldiers and the slum-dwellers than he was to think through the greater social changes that might improve their lives. He found it more natural to "suffer with," as Christ did, than to press for the transformation of society and offer realistic hope for the future.

Yet the Christian story is not exclusively told through the imagery of the cross and Christians are not necessarily as drawn to it as Studdert Kennedy was. It is inevitable that Christians find themselves drawn towards aspects of theology and faith that suit their temperament. Jesus the healer or teacher might be preferable imagery to someone inclined to humanitarianism; Jesus the radical preacher of the kingdom to someone who longs for social justice. From such images, theologies may be worked out and lives touched by fresh insights. None of these attractions is exclusive or superior to the others and, within the context of the liturgical cycle, each is given prominence. Yet it may go some way to explaining why some aspects of the faith attract us more than others, when we know that every part of the life, death, and resurrection of Christ is significant. It may also explain why, to some, Studdert Kennedy's writing is gloomy or melancholic, whereas for others he still speaks so eloquently of the human condition and the compassion of God.

---

them in other ways.

16. Edwards, "'Woodbine Willie,'" 11.

17. It is strange, however, that this is not mentioned by Kenneth Mozley (in "Home Life"), who of all people would most likely have known of such an effect.

This consonance between doctrine and psychological constitution opens up the possibility that integration might become too close, that the things of the world might be so identified with the things of God as to lose distinction and the imperative for self-critique. How far, for example, should integration be effected between the sacrifices of those who were killed in the First World War, and the sacrifice of Christ? Alvyn Pettersen's essay demonstrates how easily war memorials drew connections between these two types of sacrifice, such as the county memorials erected in Worcester temporarily in 1919 and more permanently in 1922, which respectively described the deaths of those commemorated as "glorious" and as "given lives." While, as Pettersen shows, Studdert Kennedy's attitude was more nuanced, Studdert

Kennedy was still keen to imagine a crucifix by every corpse. The classic depiction of this pictorially is James Clark's painting, *The Great Sacrifice*, which precisely shows the cross of Christ appearing beside (even arising from) a killed soldier, and which, significantly, became one of the most popular pieces of British art during the course of the war.[18] In hymnody, the same sentiment is expressed in John Arkwright's "O valiant hearts," which parallels the "lesser Calvaries" of the First World War dead, who responded to "God's message" and proved their "knightly virtues," with the martyrdom of Christ who "passed the self-same way."[19] Like Christ, soldiers may not have wished to die, but they were willing, for their

Figure 15: *The Great Sacrifice* by James Clark

18. See Wilkinson, *Church of England*, 191–92. A piece of art more congenial to Pettersen's position would be *The Place of Meeting* by the Anglo-Catholic artist Thomas Noyes-Lewis (1862–1946), reproduced in Wilkinson, *Church of England*, ii, and Beaken, *Church of England*, ii (cf. 154). While an assessment of the picture might not be uncritical, Christ's sacrifice is nonetheless focal, and any "glory" for the departed seems to be derived from that.

19. Sir John Arkwright (1872–1954) was the Conservative MP for Hereford from 1900 to 1912.

"cause," to place themselves in a position that potentially involved their deaths. The popularity of Arkwright's hymn (even at remembrance services today) and the sentiments of memorials reveal a strong, implicit, popular urge to "integrate" the tragedy of the war with Christian belief, people's deep desire to ally their lost loved ones with the death that lies at the heart of the established faith.

Against this urge, Pettersen sounds a note of caution, lest the integration be made too readily or simplistically. The fact is that most soldiers of the First World War did not "give their lives": they had them taken away from them against their will. The "cause" for which they were fighting was more complex than that of the Second World War; the clearer dichotomy between "good" and "evil" in the latter has retrospectively rendered the First World War a more ambiguous enterprise.[20] At the beginning of the war, the violation of Belgium and the need to protect "small nations" dominated discourse about the reasons for fighting; but this reasoning did not hold the same position in public consciousness four years later. Most soldiers, if asked why they were fighting, would have talked less about the state, and more about not wishing to let down their friends. Again, links can be drawn with Christian teaching—"Greater love hath no man than this, that a man lay down his life for his friends"[21]—but such links operate within the larger context of, and are to some extent compromised by, the overarching British cause, with its moral ambiguities of empire, supremacy, and influence. Pettersen would hold that in associating soldierly sacrifice and Christ's sacrifice, allowance needs to be made for the latter to critique the former. "O valiant hearts" may appeal to popular sentiment, but it lacks any element of critique. It has been misled by romanticism. Similarly, the language of "heroes," which is often used of those who bear arms for Britain today (replacing the language of service to God, king, or country that was familiar in the first half of the twentieth century), does not readily allow critique of the fact that arms are borne, nor of the reasons for bearing them.

Balance

The necessity for "critique" in the process of integration between faith and worldly experience can be described in other ways. One biblical motif for

20. For the "character values" which the world wars have assumed, see Beaken, *Church of England*, 239–41.

21. John 15:13 (Authorised Version). The moving setting of these words by the English composer John Ireland (1879–1962), written in 1912, both presaged, and was popularised by, the war.

the same imperative is that of "refinement" or purgation, using the image of a fire that burns off the dross of the entity which is subjected to it.[22] The advantage of this image is its suggestion that the negativity lies in accretions, that the entity is good in itself.[23] Another biblical theme involves the removal of excess. This theme is most powerfully expressed in the Song of Mary in Luke's Gospel, often referred to as the Magnificat, in which God is said to bring down the mighty from their seat and exalt the humble and meek, filling the hungry with good things, and sending the rich empty away.[24] This reversal of roles, in which what is wrong is sheared away and what is right is brought to the fore, is essentially a balancing act: that which is true, honourable, just, pure, pleasing, and commendable, is accepted;[25] and that which is not, is rejected. Thus, the process of integration that this conclusion seeks to explore might be articulated in terms of affirmation and challenge, corresponding to the divine "yes" and "no" to every creaturely situation, featured in the correlational (one might say integrational) theology of Paul Tillich: "yes" to that which is of God, and "no" to that which is not. The process of "integration" involves—to use the words of the American journalist Finley Peter Dunne (1867–1936), coined in the context of journalism, but since applied to politics, poetry, and art in general, as well as the church—comforting the disturbed and disturbing the comfortable. The Christian life is, in this sense, one of balance.[26]

So in these essays, the sharpest critique of Geoffrey Studdert Kennedy comes from Mark Dorsett, in his suggestion that by emphasising religious transformation, Studdert Kennedy was effectively socially conservative, and insufficiently willing to challenge and criticise the political structures that needed to change for the sake of the poor; that beyond the extreme circumstance of armed conflict, Studdert Kennedy was less inclined to propose concrete measures that would bring about reform. Dorsett argues that Studdert Kennedy, while longing for people to behave more generously towards one another, ultimately preferred the social status quo. In a famous anecdote, for example, Studdert Kennedy was content to give away a family bed to a needy parishioner, but does not appear to have questioned why such a generous gift was necessary.[27] Dorsett locates this social deficiency—

22. See, for example, Malachi 3:1–4.

23. Cf. Genesis 1:31.

24. Luke 1:46–55, at 52–53.

25. Philippians 4:8.

26. This is part of the meaning of a popular passage, Ecclesiastes 3:1–8, which otherwise seems to state the obvious.

27. Moore Ede, "His Life in Worcester," 92.

what he calls the "Brownlow fallacy," after the kindly character in Dickens's *Oliver Twist* who represents charity rather than structural change—not only in Studdert Kennedy, but also in the Church of England at large. A contemporary example might be the way in which church groups have established and staffed foodbanks. In doing so, Christians have engaged in the sort of social action (feeding the hungry) commended by Christ, and, in many circumstances, have been part of the crucial voluntary network of support for people experiencing financial hardship and lack of food. While this activity undoubtedly soothes and comforts those in difficulty, it could be argued that foodbanks have done little to challenge or alleviate the root cause of the problem: namely, that changes to the benefit system coupled with the present economic environment have thrown rising numbers of people into poverty. The church's assistance with such projects could thus be portrayed as a pietistic dealing with the mere symptoms of poverty, rather than a way of treating poverty's causes.

Dorsett is not the first writer to accuse the Church of England of acting as though "niceness" will solve all social ills, a disposition that is susceptible to interpretation by the outside world as either "hand-wringing" or sentimentality; nor is he the first to wonder whether the Industrial Christian Fellowship for which Studdert Kennedy worked after the war was the best forum for the deployment of his manifest talents. The church had, and still has, a role as an intermediate (or even integralist) institution, creating values that the market and the state themselves cannot create, especially given the demise of other intermediate institutions. However, this shaping of hearts and minds, which most characterised the ministry of Studdert Kennedy, should not come at the expense of the church's overt contribution to the political fray. It is a matter of balance (and sometimes the tension that balance involves) between offering compassion to all who suffer and challenging the context in which that suffering occurs; a question of how the church, and especially the established church, which espouses a gospel of good news to the poor, also lives out the Magnificat in practice. Churches need to offer relief to the needy neighbour, as well as be prophetic in their criticism of social and political structures that keep the neighbour needy in the first place. The church, deeply embedded in the warp and weft of passing culture, needs to be truly critical when it raises its voice.

It is perhaps an indication and indictment of the socially conservative nature of the church in the early twentieth century that, as the essays by David Bryer and Georgina Byrne show, the strongest voices for the humanitarian and reforming concerns that, a century later, are more taken for granted, came from the fringes of the church and not its core. Byrne shows how Maude Royden was free to speak her mind because she wasn't a licensed preacher; she may not have felt able to be so openly pacifist if she had been ordained.[28] Bryer's contribution shows how individuals, well-off, well-networked, and mostly without formal endorsement by church authorities, were shocked by the humanitarian needs that they encountered, challenged the assumptions behind them, and determinedly sought to transform them. This is a significant story of the First World War, because by the time of the Second World War, and largely because of the initiatives emerging from the First, the mainstream churches had organised themselves in such a way as to be able corporately to contribute to humanitarian needs. It is another example of the tragedy of the First World War, its nature and scale taking participants by surprise. In the second half of the twentieth century, the church established a good track record of translating its values into the realms of education and healthcare (a particular example being the hospice movement pioneered by Dame Cicely Saunders)—what the sociologist of religion Robin Gill calls the "transposition" of Christian views so that they underpin society[29]—and Dorsett rightly identifies the contemporary challenge for the church of endeavouring to transmit values within the twenty-first-century context of pluralism, working with other organisations for the well-being of the whole of society, rather than assuming control of such matters. The former archbishop of Canterbury Rowan Williams made this something of a commonplace for Anglicans in 2003 when he suggested to the General Synod that "mission is about finding out what God is doing and joining in."[30] He was speaking about newly emerging patterns of church attendance, but the comment also applies to public life, and indicates that in manifesting signs of the kingdom of God, the church contributes as one agent alongside others.

From a church perspective, therefore, a balance needs to be struck between the church claiming such motivators as "love," "compassion," "justice," and "freedom" as its own, and recognising that they might have the greatest opportunity to succeed beyond the life of the institutional church. Naming them as "kingdom values" and giving them explicitly Christian expression ties them to Scripture and derives them from God; while the church must also avoid looking as though it is attempting to take ownership of behaviour that others see as natural to the best of human endeavour. Indeed, in contemporary British society, there is evidence that secular liberals are now beginning to view the church as occupying the moral low ground,

---

28. Cf. Geoffrey Dearmer's freedom of expression as a layperson, as Peter Atkinson notes in his contribution to this volume.

29. Gill, *Society Shaped by Theology*, 55–70.

30. Archbishop's presidential address to General Synod, York, July 2003.

on account of its apparent exclusivity, and thus "kingdom values" are ironically being seen to be non-Christian, or non-church.[31]

This balance is often best found in practical expression, rather than in ideology. The experience of church groups involved in community projects is that, working with people of other faiths and no faith is an opportunity to put Christ's manifesto into practice, and to be explicit about their Christian motivation. Rather than simply claiming that kingdom values are exclusive to church-generated activity, such engaged Christians acknowledge the inclusive ministry of Jesus and work for the greater flourishing of all people. As Jesus noted, when his disciples found people beyond their small group who were teaching and healing, "whoever is not against us is for us."[32] If the common endeavour is compassion, hope, freedom, and justice for all, indiscriminately and without exception, then Christians must work alongside others who hold similar values—in whatever name or creed they hold them. A generous and Christ-like recognition that people who have no explicit religious faith are not only capable of living such values in the work that they do, but that they do this confidently and well and without recourse to religious language is a helpful start.

At the same time, Christians should be explicit in their belief that these are, indeed, "kingdom" values and that the motivation for church engagement is not simply humanitarianism, but gospel imperative. This is especially important for those operating in what is now not simply a pluralist culture, but an avowedly secular culture.[33] While these values might not be exclusive to Christian groups, they are precisely the motivation for Christians, and making that explicit both bears witness to the kingdom of God,[34] and reveals the gospel as inherently inclusive and transformational, perhaps undoing some of the negative perceptions of church-goers outlined above.

The church's role within pluralist society involves another balance and tension, that of making public comment in an environment in which every available media is taken up with commentary—some of it ill-considered and poorly argued. The increasingly widespread use of social media has given a public platform to anyone who has anything to say on any given subject. On the one hand, this has democratised public commentary, enabling people who, in previous generations, might have been overlooked or silenced, to be heard by a wider audience. On the other hand, it has given

31. Brown and Woodhead, *That Was the Church*, 215, and Woodhead, "Time to Get Serious," 24.

32. Mark 9:40, though cf. Matthew 12:30.

33. For the rise of "nones," that is to say, people who claim to be of no religion, see Brown and Woodhead, *That Was the Church*, 190.

34. Acts 1:8.

rise to "post-truth," which loudly and crudely expresses opinion, drowns out nuance, and stifles serious debate. In such a world, the loudest voice, the snappiest soundbite, might not win the day, but may elevate commentary or aspiration to the level of fact.

The church offers a "home" or space where thinking about the relationship between life and faith can be worked out, where anything and everything can be considered and discussed freely, a space where conversation and disagreement can take place in private. Church is a community of individuals, each committed to following Jesus Christ, meeting together to worship God and encourage one another. In small groups, in larger gatherings, where faith is discussed in the light of national and international events, or where daily life is thought through in the light of faith, individuals have opportunity to explore their own belief in the safe company of fellow disciples. The difficulty inherent in doing their thinking in private is that, by creating a safe space, they are in danger of lapsing into their own language, their own assumptions, that have no connection with secular culture. If the gospel is truly good news for the whole world, and not just for the church, then it must be heard, understood, and engaged with by all people. Sometimes, when national or international gatherings of Christians take place, this takes the form of a public display of disagreements, inconsistencies, and fallibilities. Yet Christians together are called upon to share deliberately the good news of Christ with the world beyond their own walls, and so it is also appropriate that they discover what faith means in an open dialogue that includes a variety of comments and views.

The final point about "balance" to which these essays testify is the importance of taking a long-term view. Georgina Byrne in this volume shows how the thought of Maude Royden, exhibiting the social witness that Studdert Kennedy lacked, changed over time, and also how far her views, "cranky" and unpopular to the church of her own day, represent wisdom for the church today. Prophets are not welcome in their own country,[35] neither, it seems, in their own time. In integrating theology and life experience, the Christian must beware of being swayed by the short-termism, fleetingness, and faddishness of contemporary culture. Some of the views expressed by thinkers of the early twentieth century now seem dated and wrong-headed, while others, with our gift of hindsight, seem much more perceptive. Being "mid-stream," we cannot know what will turn out to be prescient in the longer-term. Balance takes time to achieve.

35. Mark 6:4.

Fullness

What is it all for? "Integration" and "balance" are not explicit biblical imperatives, and are not ends in themselves. The *telos* or purpose of life, according to John's Gospel, is Life—life in all its fullness, joy that is complete.[36] It is to become like Christ, transfigured from one degree of glory to another.[37] This is, of course, a gift. All is grace. What these essays have hoped to show is that there are ways of co-operating with God's grace, ways in which life can emerge from tragedy, even the direst tragedy. This book has shown that life can come from homes in which negative experiences are constructively integrated with positive ones. It has shown that poetry and the arts can bring life out of tragedy, as they present us with new insights and horizons. It has uncovered models, images, and metaphors of God that integrate God's love within a full and serious acknowledgment of suffering. It has shown how the discernment of wisdom requires the balance of the long-term view. It has shown how the church needs to balance spiritual renewal with practical action for the flourishing of society in partnership with others. It has shown that openness to prophetic voices from the margins may help to reveal the church's own imbalance; and it has shown that life involves recognising our own shortcomings and deriving all grace from God. In this way, it is hoped that this book may play its own part in enabling all to "receive from his fullness, grace upon grace."[38]

---

36. John 10:10, 15:11, and 16:24; cf. John 17:13, 1 John 1:4, and 1 Corinthians 13:10.

37. 2 Corinthians 3:18.

38. John 16:16.

12

Afterword

Ilse Junkermann,
translated by Robert G. Jones

Like a tired child that has cried itself to sleep.[1]

I HAVE BEEN PARTICULARLY moved, in reading this book, by the account of
Geoffrey Studdert Kennedy, during his time as an army chaplain in the First
World War, coming across the body of a young dead soldier who looked
"like a tired child that has cried itself to sleep." What mother—or father—
would not be moved, picturing such a scene in their mind's eye? This dead
young man could be one of my relatives; or, if there were a war now, he
could be my child. The significance of this scene is that the dead young
man was a German, officially one of the enemy. It would have been understandable, given the context of war, if Studdert Kennedy's reaction had
been satisfaction, even malice or gratified revenge. But Studdert Kennedy
felt only sympathy. At that moment, it did not interest him that the dead
young man was German. Here was a human being, brutally torn from his
young life. Perhaps the young man indeed cried for his mother just before
he died—like a child, afraid of the dark, whose mother only can rock him
to sleep.

1. Cited above, 106.

The sight of the dead young "enemy" pierced Studdert Kennedy's soul, and, in that moment, he seems to have become aware of the senselessness of war. The incident symbolises his change from being an enthusiastic supporter of the war to being "an apostle of peace." It was a key "transformational" moment, such as lies at the heart of Christian faith: when one learns to see the world and everything that happens in it through the eyes of the other; when one learns that mercy comes first, because it could so easily be me, standing in the place of the other.

Such transformational moments are found in Scripture. Abraham, for example, found himself pleading with God to have mercy on Sodom and Gomorrah if just ten righteous persons were to be found in the cities.[2] Today, if a place is suspected to contain ten terrorists, it is bombed, despite all pleas. Only mercy makes for life. Or again, Joseph forgave his brothers who wanted to get rid of him and sold him into slavery: "Am I in the place of God?" he asked. "Even though you intended to do harm to me, God intended it for good."[3] Forgiveness, likewise, leads to life, for the desire for revenge drives only a spiral of violence, pain, and death. As he was arrested in Gethsemane, Jesus said to his disciples, "Put your sword back into its place, for all who take the sword will perish by the sword,"[4] showing the priority of non-violence, as he suffered the cross rather than achieve his goals through coercion. And, his non-violence having been vindicated by resurrection, the Risen One greeted his disciples with the words, "Peace be with you," not "Revenge be with you" or "Retribution be yours."[5] For two thousand years, we have read this in Scripture, and yet the major Christian churches throughout Europe have long considered war a perfectly acceptable way of doing politics, and each has strongly supported its own nation in waging it. Are we any further on today? Have we repented as Christian churches? Have we confessed that belief in military force and violence has played a large role within the churches?

From 1933 to 1945, the Nazi dictatorship in Germany brought unimaginable suffering upon Europe and the world. British forces, together with their Allies, made great sacrifices to bring the barbarism to an end. The memory of the First and Second World Wars is thus differently handled in Germany from the way in which it is dealt with in Great Britain. Germany, in both the East and the West, has had to work through guilt, unimaginable guilt, that such a war emanated from German soil: a conquering army

2. Genesis 18:16–33.
3. Genesis 50:19–20.
4. Matthew 26:52.
5. John 20:19, 21.

destroyed Europe and created millions of refugees, borne along by a racist ideology that justified the calculated mass-murder of Jews in Germany and other parts of Europe in extermination camps, and an ideology that justified the systematic hatred and murder of the disabled, homosexuals, and Sinti and Roma people, on the basis that they were "worthless," rather than "valuable." It was shocking, and still is shocking, that the majority of Germans went along with this ideology and that only a very few dared to offer any resistance.

The Christian churches, including my own, were also complicit, and in October 1945, in the Stuttgart Declaration of Guilt, the Council of the Evangelical Church in Germany (EKD) acknowledged that "we blame ourselves for not confessing the faith more courageously, not praying more faithfully, not believing more joyfully, nor loving more passionately."[6] It is an open secret that pressure from ecumenical partners was very important in producing this declaration, and that the declaration was still not fully accepted in Germany in the 1950s and 1960s. This is hardly surprising: self-justification and exclusive reference to the crimes of "others" are strategies for dealing with man-made catastrophes. Christian theology defines sin as life *incurvatus in se*, or "turned inward on itself"; sinners justify themselves, and point to the guilt of others. Christians have known this in theory, above all in Germany, because this description of sin came from none other than Martin Luther.[7] But how does such dogmatic truth reach daily living, self-awareness, and even social action? That is a long journey. And so we continue to work through our German guilt.

Some stages of that journey are only reached after the passage of time. On the fortieth anniversary of the outbreak of the Second World War, in 1979, the Protestant churches in East and West Germany produced a common statement on peace. It named the pain and scars of the war, deplored the cost, expressed bewilderment and guilt, and above all, stressed the task to work for peace.[8] For some years now, grandchildren have been freer than their parents to ask their family, "What did Grandpa do in the war? What happened in our family? Why was it never talked about? Was it too painful? Was it because we were bombed out of our homes and dispossessed? Or because it was too shameful to admit that our forebears were complicit in causing others to suffer?" As we work through our history in Germany today, we recognise a clear line leading from the First World War to the Second. On the centenary of the outbreak of the First World War, the Coun-

6. "Stuttgarter Schulderklärung."

7. Luther, *Lectures*, 260.

8. *Kirchliches Jahrbuch 106 (1979)*, 448–49.

cil of the EKD acknowledged the guilt of the church in 1914, the political consequences of which contributed to the Nazi seizure of power in 1933:

> The war clearly revealed how deeply damaged the church and theology were in Germany. They failed to contribute to peace and reconciliation, or even limit violence, or speak up for humanity and life, and thereby failed to follow the word of God. From the justification of national war aims in 1914 to the end of the war, faith in God's reconciling love did not keep the church and theology from enthusiasm for war and propaganda, neither did belonging with other churches to the one body of Christ, nor did the universality of faith.
>
> Thus, after the war, they could not become a force for reconciliation, and in 1933 could not escape the poison of re-emerging nationalism. Theology was captive to the nationalist Zeitgeist and ecumenical consciousness was too weak. This was particularly true of German Protestantism—at least the majority of it: the few warning voices were silenced. This failure and guilt fill us with deep shame today.[9]

One of the few people who, from the years before the First World War, consistently opposed it, was Pastor Friedrich Siegmund-Schultze. As early as 1910, he noted that "war is a sin against the conscience of a Christian nation."[10] In the summer of 1914, just as Germany was mobilising for war, he and others were organising a conference in Konstanz to which 153 Christians from thirteen countries around the world were invited, under the title "The Churches and Friendly Relations between Nations." In the confusion of the outbreak of war, only ninety-three turned up, including William Moore Ede, the dean of Worcester.[11] The conference was abandoned after two days, in order to allow participants a safe passage home. A long time in the planning, the conference for peace and friendship had come too late. Nevertheless, those present did not give up, and founded the World Alliance for Promoting International Friendship through the Churches. In December 1914, the English branch gave itself the name "Fellowship of Reconciliation." The foundation of a German branch, despite the efforts of Siegmund-Schultze, proceeded with far greater difficulty.

As modest as these first steps were, one of the participants, Frederick Lynch from the United States, clung to the vision of Konstanz that had so impressed him: "Outside Germans, French and English were going out

9. "Richte unsere Füße."

10. Steffensky, "'Gott mit uns,'" 5.

11. Bürger, *Befreit zum Widerstehen*, 5–6. See above, 26, n. 44.

to fight one another; here Germans, French and English were kneeling in prayer. Outside the people were calling for blood; here representatives of twelve peoples were praying for increased love for one another."[12] Siegmund-Schultze played a part in the peace movement in the church even after 1945. Fulbert Steffensky has emphasised the importance of remembering "those voices which are drowned out by the noise of war," because they have "a right to be heard and counted": "The Spirit should not be denied a voice, just because it did not prevail. The few signs of the Spirit in a dispirited time remind us that the course of history is not fatalistically determined nor bound for a blind destiny. They remind us *that things could have turned out differently and in similar circumstances can do so*. Hope needs witnesses, and it finds them in prophetic voices in every age, however little those voices are listened to."[13]

The Evangelical Church in Central Germany is a successor to the churches of the German Democratic Republic (GDR), or East Germany, which existed from 1949 to 1990. During that period, the Bund der Evangelischen Kirchen, or Federation of Evangelical Churches, needed to discover its place *in opposition to* the state, as the old alliance of church and state was dissolved. The wise settlement that had existed from the first democratic constitution of Germany of 1919 was no longer operating when the GDR came into being. The constitution of 1949 in West Germany maintained the settlement, declaring that there was no longer a state church, but that state and church were bound together in co-operation for the common good of all. In the East, on the other hand, a new ideology ruled the day: the communist aim was to force churches to the edge of society, because from a communist perspective, they were complicit in the war, and in oppressing and exploiting people. On such a view, religion, as the "opium" of the people, prevented people's problems from being genuinely addressed. The gap between this humanist claim and the reality on the ground became ever larger. Being actively marginalised by the state, there seemed little that the churches of the GDR could do.

Yet this problem was also an opportunity. Marginalisation from public life gave the church space, free from state influence, to consider for itself the questions of war and peace. The Christian churches in the GDR provided an important forum in which to work out ways of creating peace and trust between people and nations, beyond the cheap logic of military strength and demonisation of the other. The Protestant churches in East Germany became courageous in their witness for peace. So, for example, from 1965,

---

12. Lynch, *Through Europe*, 25.

13. Steffensky, "'Gott mit uns,'" 5 (my emphasis).

the stance of participating in national service without bearing arms was described in the guidelines for pastoral care of conscripts as a "clearer witness to the Lord's commandment for peace."[14] The statement led to heavy controversy between the Federation of Evangelical Churches in the GDR and the churches of West Germany. The more strongly the communist single-party government militarised the state—for example, making it compulsory to take part in military lessons in schools—the more deliberately the churches developed their peace mission. A framework of "education for peace" was drawn up. Its appendix read:

> The horrific experience of two world wars and a recognition of the complicity of Christians and churches in these wars have led the Protestant churches in Germany after 1945 to consider afresh the question of war and peace. The characteristic feature of this new consideration is a shift in interest, from the question of the justification of war to the question of the requirements for peace. During the growing nuclear armament of the 1950s, the traditional "just war" ethic, which had been held by Christian churches since Augustine, was overtaken by the need for a "just peace" ethic in a nuclear age. A peace ethic is not so much about the possibility of war as about the safeguarding of peace.[15]

The peace ethic of the EKD built on this focus in the wake of the peaceful revolution of 1989 in East Germany. The memorandum "To Live Out of God's Peace: To Care for a Just Peace," written in 2007, deliberately avoided the word "war." In the context of just peace, the teaching of *bellum iustum* no longer has a place.[16]

Currently this focus is being discussed again more widely. Those who want peace need to arrange political, social, and cultural life so as to be able to work through conflicts by non-violent means. How much money is invested worldwide in arms manufacture, compared with education, healthcare, and environmental sustainability? Are existing possibilities for mediation, diplomacy, and peaceful conflict resolution really exhausted? Or are we still fixated on the supposed security of ever larger arsenals of weapons? Our ecumenical partnerships have an important part to play in communicating the Christian witness to peace in society, especially at a time when polarisation and global confrontations seem to be increasing. In ecumenical partnerships, we meet one another face to face, look each other in the eye, listen to each other, and seek to understand each other,

14. "Friedensdienst," 8.
15. *Kirchliches Jahrbuch 107 (1980)*, 385.
16. *Aus Gottes Frieden leben*, 68.

coming from different contexts with different histories. And we share each other's grief, expressing sympathy and praying for one another, and thereby overcoming former enmities.[17]

The scene that so jolted Geoffrey Studdert Kennedy is thus a core theological image: the other, the enemy, is suddenly seen in such a way by the viewer that the other is just like them: the viewer could be the other; the viewer suddenly feels what the other felt; the viewer stands in the other's place—just as Christ did on the cross. Indeed, precisely after Studdert Kennedy saw the young soldier lying "like a tired child that has cried itself to sleep," he saw the battlefield only as a cross, a crucifix. "From that moment on I have never seen the world as anything but a Crucifix. I see the Cross set up in every slum, in every filthy over-crowded quarter, in every vulgar flaring street."[18]

The patience and laboriousness with which we, as a church, have had to wrestle with questions of war and peace are demonstrated not least by the First World War memorial in Magdeburg Cathedral by Ernst Barlach, discussed in chapter 9 of this book. Through his experiences of 1914–18, Barlach became a convinced opponent of war. He received a commission to make the memorial in 1927, and the group of figures that he carved, unlike the large majority of war memorials of this period, reveals the distress, death, and despair of war. The individuals within his artwork show the truth about war for soldiers, their wives, and their families. When the memorial was first shown at an exhibition in 1929, it led to considerable altercation. It was alleged to be un-German and un-Christian. The artist was accused of pacifism. Shortly after Hitler took power in 1933, the dean of Magdeburg, Ernst Martin, together with the cathedral congregation, proposed that the memorial be removed. It was taken out in 1934. From that time onwards in Nazi Germany, Ernst Barlach's art was classified as "degenerate." Ostracised, and without permission to work, the artist died in October 1938 in Rostock. Yet his memorial survived the Second World War and was returned silently to the cathedral in September 1955. Since then, it has become an icon for peace. It was here that Lothar Kreyssig developed his idea for "Action for Peace, Signs of Reconciliation." It was here that critical voices from East and West met in prayer for trust and reconciliation. Prayers for peace have been

17. For example, the letter that John Inge, bishop of Worcester, sent to me on 16 January 2015, the seventieth anniversary of the British bombing of Magdeburg, resonated deeply with the church in Magdeburg, and also in public life beyond the church. In the Second World War, Magdeburg had been one of the most important German cities for heavy industry and the war effort, and the bombing in 1945 destroyed 80 percent of it, with the loss of 16,000 lives.

18. See above, 90.

held at the Barlach memorial since 1983. Those prayers are still offered each week.

The apostle Paul, in his letter to the Ephesians, envisioned a community that joins together people of different nationalities, ethnicities, cultures, and worldviews: he urged his readers "to maintain the unity of the Spirit in the bond of peace."[19] Over many centuries, Christians have identified first and foremost with their own people; their own group and its presumed interests. This was evident in a sermon on Revelation 2:10 at the swearing-in of German soldiers for military service in the First World War:

> Write the word "discipline" large in your life as a soldier. German discipline, which our enemies cannot match, vouchsafes our successes, and these successes gloriously fulfil the promise, "I will give you the crown of life." . . . Isn't it part of true happiness when, as loyal defenders of the fatherland, you can dare to say of yourselves: I too have contributed to my dear German people becoming the bearer of the world's culture, the bearer of a right and truly Christian culture, after the wretched fiasco produced by the false pitiable pretend-Christianity that is England's fault!?
>
> But of course the promise will only be fulfilled when we, faithful to death, have overcome this last enemy and entered into the promised land of eternal peace . . . .
>
> Comrades, be faithful: faithful unto death! He will give you the crown of life. So now, swear on the flag your oath of allegiance as German Christian men. May the Lord God equip you with his gifts and power, so that you serve him aright and for eternity. Amen.[20]

As a Christian, I am ashamed to read these words. However common and self-evident this interpretation was in its day, it could hardly be further from the community of the Spirit and the bond of peace. Yet it is also necessary to ask if there are analogous sentiments in our own attitudes today that we do not recognise as un-Christian, but which are equally far from the community of the Spirit and the bond of peace.

In this regard, it is instructive to look at the theological development of Dietrich Bonhoeffer. Well known as a committed ecumenist and participant in the resistance to Hitler's dictatorship, he made, like most Germans in his generation, some very nationalistic comments in the years after the First World War, for example in his "Basic Questions of a Christian Ethic" of 1929: "God gave me my mother, my people. For what I have, I thank my

19. Ephesians 4:3.
20. Ruppelt, "Thron und Altar."

people; what I am, I am through my people, and so what I have should also belong to my people; that is in the divine order of things, for God created the peoples[;] . . . love for my people will sanctify murder, will sanctify war."[21]

These are indeed the words of Bonhoeffer, but that is not where he remained. His thinking was altered by his profound spiritual and theological work. Soon afterwards, and with very few others in Germany, he took decisive steps to witness to peace. In 1931, he became one of the international youth secretaries of the World Alliance for Promoting International Friendship through the Churches, and at a youth conference in Ciernohorské Kúpele, Czechoslovakia, in July 1932, he gave a lecture entitled "On the Theological Foundation of the Work of the World Alliance." He argued that, in the church of Jesus Christ, affiliation to one's own group or nation does not have first priority, but rather, the world community in which people are joined together in the Spirit through the bond of peace. This peaceable community should be visible and tangible in the universal church. At the same time, the promise of a peaceful, united world is for all people.

> The work of our World Alliance—consciously or unconsciously—is grounded in a very distinct conception of church. The church as the one church-community of the Lord Jesus Christ, who is the Lord of the world, has the task of speaking his word to the entire world. The range of the one church of Christ is the entire world. There are local boundaries for the proclamation of each individual church, but the *one* church has no boundaries around it. The churches of the World Alliance have joined together in order to express their claim, or rather the claim of our Lord, on the entire world. They understand the task of the church as that of making the claim of Christ audible to the entire world. This includes the rejection of the idea that there are God-willed characteristics of life that are removed from the lordship of Christ, that do not need to hear this word. It is not a holy, sacred district of the world that belongs to Christ but rather the entire world.[22]

In his famous peace speech at the conference of the World Alliance in Fanø in August 1934, Bonhoeffer clarified his thinking, because the situation in Germany had come to a head through the National Socialists' seizure of power, criminal politics, and preparations for another war. His speech laid the theological foundation for the ecumenical movement up to the present day, for it developed the thought of Paul as expressed in his letter

---

21. Bonhoeffer, *Works*, 10:371–72.

22. Ibid., 11:358–59 (original emphasis).

to the Ephesians. Bonhoeffer asked what Christians and the church could do in the face of the threat of another war, which would bring even greater suffering to millions of people. His theology led him to conclude that the churches must decisively be engaged against war and for peace. To this end, Bonhoeffer went as far as suggesting that an ecumenical council should be summoned: "Only the one great Ecumenical Council of the Holy Church of Christ over all the world can speak out so that the world, though it gnash its teeth, will have to hear, so that the peoples will rejoice because the church of Christ in the name of Christ has taken the weapons from the hands of their sons, forbidden war, and proclaimed the peace of Christ against the raging world."[23]

These words still have contemporary relevance. When I visit ecumenical partners, such as the diocese of Worcester, what continues to move me is how, despite the differences and difficulties, we continue to worship together, pray together, and work together for peace, justice, and the integrity of creation; how in Christ we have been bound together in a unique worldwide network, long before the internet; and how this network continues to be built as an alternative to the other networks and complexities of the world. It is my great longing and prayer that through our unequivocal and clear Christian witness, the Christian commitment to peace might be strengthened and proclaimed.

23. Ibid., 13:309.

Bibliography

Angier, Carole. *The Double Bond: Primo Levi: A Biography.* London: Penguin, 2003.

Ardrey, Robert. *The Territorial Imperative: A Personal Inquiry into the Animal Origins of Property and Nations.* New York: Atheneum, 1966.

Athanasius. *Contra Gentes and De Incarnatione.* Edited and translated by Robert W. Thomson. Oxford: Clarendon, 1971.

————. *The Life of Antony and the Letter to Marcellinus.* Edited and translated by Robert C. Gregg. London: SPCK, 1980.

————. *Orationes Contra Arianos.* In *A Select Library of Nicene and Post-Nicene Fathers of the Christian Church: Second Series,* edited by Philip Schaff and Henry Wace, vol. 4, 306–447. Grand Rapids: Eerdmans, 1971.

Atkinson, Peter G. *Friendship and the Body of Christ.* London: SPCK, 2004.

Aus Gottes Frieden leben: für gerechten Frieden sorgen: Eine Denkschrift des Rates der Evangelischen Kirche in Deutschland. Gütersloh: Gütersloher Verlagshaus, 2007.

Austin, Michael R. *"Like a Swift Hurricane": People, Clergy and Class in a Midlands Diocese, 1914–1919.* Chesterfield, UK: Merton Priory, 2014.

Bailey, Charles E. "The British Protestant Theologians in the First World War: Germanophobia Unleashed." *Harvard Theological Review* 77 (1984) 195–221.

————. "Gott mit uns: Germany's Protestant Theologians in the First World War." PhD diss., University of Virginia, 1978.

Baillie, Albert V. *My First Eighty Years.* London: Murray, 1951.

Bainton, Roland H. Letter to the Editor. *Theology* 74 (1971) 32–33.

Baker, John Austin. *The Foolishness of God.* London: Darton, Longman and Todd, 1970.

Barbeau, Aimee E. "Christian Empire and National Crusade: The Rhetoric of Anglican Clergy in the First World War." *Anglican and Episcopal History* 85 (2016) 24–62.

Barnard, Leslie W. "The Date of S. Athanasius' *Vita Antonii.*" *Vigiliae Christianae* 28 (1974) 169–75.

Barnard, Sylvia M. *To Prove I'm Not Forgot: Living and Dying in a Victorian City.* 2nd ed. Stroud, UK: History, 2009.

Barrett, Clive. *Subversive Peacemakers: War Resistance 1914–1918: An Anglican Perspective.* Cambridge: Lutterworth, 2014.

Barry, F. Russell. *Period of My Life.* London: Hodder and Stoughton, 1970.

Barth, Karl. *Dogmatics in Outline.* Translated by G. T. Thomson. London: SCM, 1949.

————. *The Epistle to the Romans.* Translated by Edwyn C. Hoskyns. London: Oxford University Press, 1933.

Bauckham, Richard J. "'Only the Suffering God Can Help': Divine Passibility in Modern Theology." *Themelios* 9 (1984) 6–12.

Beaken, Robert W. F. *The Church of England and the Home Front 1914–1918: Civilians, Soldiers and Religion in Wartime Colchester.* Woodbridge, UK: Boydell, 2015.

Becker, Matthew L. *Fundamental Theology: A Protestant Perspective.* London: Bloomsbury T. & T. Clark, 2015.

Beeson, Trevor R. *The Canons: Cathedral Close Encounters.* London: SCM, 2006.

Bell, George K. A. *Randall Davidson: Archbishop of Canterbury.* 3rd ed. London: Oxford University Press, 1952.

Bell, George K. A., and G. Adolf Deissmann, eds. *Mysterium Christi: Christological Studies by British and German Theologians.* London: Longmans, 1930.

Bell, Stuart A. "The Church and the First World War." In *God and War: The Church of England and Armed Conflict in the Twentieth Century,* edited by Stephen G. Parker and Tom Lawson, 33–59. Farnham, UK: Ashgate, 2012.

——. "Faith in Conflict: A Study of British Experiences in the First World War with Particular Reference to the English Midlands." PhD thesis, University of Birmingham, 2016.

——. "From Collusion to Condemnation: The Evolving Voice of 'Woodbine Willie.'" In *Landscapes and Voices of the Great War,* edited by Angela K. Smith and Krista Cowman, 151–72. Abingdon, UK: Routledge, 2017.

——. "Malign or Maligned? Arthur Winnington-Ingram, Bishop of London, in the First World War." *Journal for the History of Modern Theology* 20 (2013) 117–33.

——. "'Patriotism and Sacrifice': The Preaching of Geoffrey Studdert Kennedy ('Woodbine Willie'), 1914–1918." In *Delivering the Word: Preaching and Exegesis in the Western Christian Tradition,* edited by W. John Lyons and Isabella Sandwell, 190–208. Sheffield, UK: Equinox, 2012.

——. "'Soldiers of Christ Arise': Religious Nationalism in the East Midlands during World War I." *Midland History* 39 (2014) 219–35.

——. "The Theology of 'Woodbine Willie' in Context." In *The Clergy in Khaki: New Perspectives on British Army Chaplaincy in the First World War,* edited by Michael F. Snape and Edward T. M. Madigan, 95–110. Farnham, UK: Ashgate, 2013.

Beresford, Charles J. *The Christian Soldier: The Life of Lieutenant Colonel the Rev Bernard William Vann VC, MC and Bar, Croix de Guerre avec palme.* Solihull, UK: Helion, 2017.

Berger, Peter L., et al. *The Homeless Mind: Modernization and Consciousness.* Harmondsworth, UK: Pelican, 1974.

Bernhardi, Friedrich A. J. von. *Germany and the Next War.* Translated by Allen H. Powles. London: Arnold, 1912.

Bickersteth, John M., ed. *The Bickersteth Diaries: 1914–1918.* Barnsley, UK: Cooper, 1995.

Blagden, Claude M. *Well Remembered.* London: Hodder and Stoughton, 1953.

Bonhoeffer, Dietrich. *Dietrich Bonhoeffer Works.* Vol. 10, *Barcelona, Berlin, New York: 1928–1931.* Edited by Clifford J. Green et al. Minneapolis, MN: Fortress, 2008.

——. *Dietrich Bonhoeffer Works.* Vol. 11, *Ecumenical, Academic, and Pastoral Work: 1931–1932.* Edited by Victoria J. Barnett et al. Minneapolis, MN: Fortress, 2012.

——. *Dietrich Bonhoeffer Works.* Vol. 13, *London: 1933–1935.* Edited by Keith W. Clements et al. Minneapolis, MN: Fortress, 2007.

————. *Letters and Papers from Prison*. Edited by Eberhard Bethge. Enlarged ed. London: SCM, 1971.

Bontrager, Shannon Ty. "The Imagined Crusade: The Church of England and the Mythology of Nationalism and Christianity during the Great War." *Church History* 71 (2002) 774–98.

Bourke, Joanna. *Dismembering the Male: Men's Bodies, Britain and the Great War*. London: Reaktion, 1996.

Brant, Jonathan D. *Running into No Man's Land: The Wisdom of Woodbine Willie*. Farnham, UK: CWR, 2014.

Brennan, Brian R. "Dating Athanasius' *Vita Antonii*." *Vigiliae Christianae* 30 (1976) 52–54.

Brierley, Michael W. "'Ambassadors in Bonds' and Other Ironies of Ripon Hall." *Modern Believing* 45/4 (2004) 4–12.

————. "Introducing the Early British Passibilists." *Journal for the History of Modern Theology* 8 (2001) 218–33.

————. "Panentheism." In *The Encyclopedia of Christianity*, edited by Erwin Fahlbusch et al., vol. 4, 21–25. Grand Rapids: Eerdmans, 2005.

————. "Panentheism: The Abiding Significance of *Honest to God*." *Modern Believing* 54 (2013) 112–24.

————. "The Panentheist Revolution: Aspects of Change in the Doctrine of God in Twentieth-Century British Theology." PhD thesis, University of Birmingham, 2007.

————. Review of *Shellshocked Prophets* and *A Fool for Thy Feast*, by Linda M. Parker. *Modern Believing* 57 (2016) 457–59.

————. Review of *Woodbine Willie*, by Bob Holman, *Muddling Through*, by Peter J. Howson, *Faith under Fire*, by Edward T. M. Madigan, and *The Clergy in Khaki*, edited by Michael F. Snape and Edward T. M. Madigan. *Modern Believing* 55 (2014) 305–11.

————. "Ripon Hall, Henry Major and the Shaping of English Liberal Theology." In *Ambassadors of Christ: Commemorating 150 Years of Theological Education in Cuddesdon 1854–2004*, edited by Mark D. Chapman, 89–155. Aldershot, UK: Ashgate, 2004.

Brittain, Vera M. *Testament of Youth: An Autobiographical Study of the Years 1900–1925*. London: Fontana, 1979.

Brown, Andrew, and Linda Woodhead. *That Was the Church, That Was: How the Church of England Lost the English People*. London: Bloomsbury Continuum, 2016.

Brown, Callum G. *The Death of Christian Britain: Understanding Secularisation 1800–2000*. London: Routledge, 2001.

————. "Piety, Gender and War in Scotland in the 1910s." In *Scotland and the Great War*, edited by Catriona M. M. Macdonald and Elaine W. McFarland, 173–91. East Linton, UK: Tuckwell, 1998.

————. *Religion and Society in Twentieth-Century Britain*. Harlow, UK: Pearson, 2006.

Brown, David W. *God and Enchantment of Place: Reclaiming Human Experience*. Oxford: Oxford University Press, 2004.

Brown, Stewart J. "'A Solemn Purification by Fire': Responses to the Great War in the Scottish Presbyterian Churches, 1914–19." *Journal of Ecclesiastical History* 45 (1994) 82–104.

Brueggemann, Walter. *The Land: Place as Gift, Promise and Challenge in Biblical Faith*. London: SPCK, 1978.

Buelens, Geert. *Everything to Nothing: The Poetry of the Great War, Revolution and the Transformation of Europe*. Translated by David A. McKay. London: Verso, 2015.

Bürger, Eberhard. *Befreit zum Widerstehen: Friedens-Bewegungen in der Ökumene um die Zeit des Ersten Weltkrieges*. Minden, Germany: Internationaler Versöhnungsbund, 2015.

Byrne, Georgina A. *Modern Spiritualism and the Church of England, 1850–1939*. Woodbridge, UK: Boydell, 2010.

Cabanes, Bruno. *The Great War and the Origins of Humanitarianism, 1918–1924*. Cambridge: Cambridge University Press, 2014.

Câmara, Hélder P. *Essential Writings*. Edited by Francis McDonagh. Maryknoll, NY: Orbis, 2009.

Campbell, Alastair V. *Rediscovering Pastoral Care*. London: Darton, Longman and Todd, 1981.

Cannadine, David. "War and Death, Grief and Mourning in Modern Britain." In *Mirrors of Mortality: Studies in the Social History of Death*, edited by Joachim Whaley, 187–242. London: Europa, 1981.

Carey, Douglas F. "Studdert Kennedy: War Padre." In *G. A. Studdert Kennedy: By His Friends*, 115–61. London: Hodder and Stoughton, 1929.

Carpenter, Humphrey W. B. *Robert Runcie: The Reluctant Archbishop*. London: Hodder and Stoughton, 1996.

Carpenter, Spencer C. *Winnington-Ingram: The Biography of Arthur Foley Winnington-Ingram, Bishop of London, 1901–1939*. London: Hodder and Stoughton, 1949.

Chadwick, W. Owen. Review of *The Last Crusade*, by Albert Marrin. *American Historical Review* 80 (1975) 648.

Champneys, Arthur C. *"Criticism" as Made in Germany and Common Sense*. London: Skeffington, 1915.

Chandler, Andrew M., ed. *The Church and Humanity: The Life and Work of George Bell, 1883–1958*. Farnham, UK: Ashgate, 2012.

———. *George Bell, Bishop of Chichester: Church, State, and Resistance in the Age of Dictatorship*. Grand Rapids: Eerdmans, 2016.

———. Introduction to *Brethren in Adversity: Bishop George Bell, the Church of England and the Crisis of German Protestantism 1933–1939*, edited by Andrew M. Chandler, 1–32. Woodbridge, UK: Boydell, 1997.

Chapman, Mark D. *Bishops, Saints and Politics: Anglican Studies*. London: T. & T. Clark, 2007.

———. *The Coming Crisis: The Impact of Eschatology on Theology in Edwardian England*. Journal for the Study of the New Testament Supplement Series 208. Sheffield, UK: Sheffield Academic, 2001.

———. *"Essays and Reviews:* 150 Years On." *Modern Believing* 52/2 (2011) 14–22, reprinted in *A Point of Balance: The Weight and Measure of Anglicanism*, edited by Robert B. Slocum and Martyn W. Percy, 67–74. London: Canterbury Press Norwich, 2013.

———. "Kikuyu, Anglo-Catholics and the Church of England." In *Costly Catholicity: Sacramental Strife in the Anglican Communion, 1913–2013*, edited by Jeremy Bonner and Mark D. Chapman. Leiden: Brill, forthcoming.

————. Review of *Woodbine Willie*, by Bob Holman. *Journal of Anglican Studies* 12 (2014) 237–38.

————. *Theology at War and Peace: English Theology and Germany in the First World War*. Abingdon, UK: Routledge, 2017.

Chesterton, G. K. *Collected Works*. Vol. 30, *The Illustrated London News 1914–1916*. San Francisco: Ignatius, 1988.

Christie, Agatha M. C. *An Autobiography*. London: Collins, 1977.

Clark, Christopher M. *The Sleepwalkers: How Europe Went to War in 1914*. London: Allen Lane, 2012.

Clayton, Philip D. "Panentheism." In *The Cambridge Dictionary of Christian Theology*, edited by Ian A. McFarland et al., 365–67. New York: Cambridge University Press, 2011.

Clements, Keith W. *Lovers of Discord: Twentieth-Century Theological Controversies in England*. London: SPCK, 1988.

————. *A Patriotism for Today: Love of Country in Dialogue with the Witness of Dietrich Bonhoeffer*. London: Collins, 1986.

Collini, Stefan A. *Common Writing: Essays on Literary Culture and Public Debate*. Oxford: Oxford University Press, 2016.

Common Worship: Ordination Services: Study Edition. London: Church House, 2007.

Common Worship: Services and Prayers for the Church of England. London: Church House, 2000.

Coughlan, Sean. "Graphic Eyewitness Somme Accounts Revealed." Online: http://www.bbc.co.uk/news/education-37975358.

Cowling, Maurice J. *Religion and Public Doctrine in Modern England*. Vol. 2, *Assaults*. Cambridge: Cambridge University Press, 1985.

David, Albert A. "A Loving God?" *Modern Churchman* 1 (1911) 514–23.

Davidson, Randall T. *Kikuyu*. London: Macmillan, 1915.

Davies, Horton M. *Varieties of English Preaching 1900–1960*. London: SCM, 1963.

————. *Worship and Theology in England*. Vol. 5, *The Ecumenical Century, 1900–1965*. Vol. 6, *Crisis and Creativity, 1965–Present*. Grand Rapids: Eerdmans, 1996.

Davies, John G. *A High Ideal: Leeds Grammar School and the Great War*. Leeds, UK: Old Leodiensian Association, 2015.

Davies, John H. "Divine Kenosis and the Power of the Church." PhD thesis, University of Lancaster, 1999.

Dearmer, Geoffrey. *A Pilgrim's Song: Selected Poems to Mark the Poet's 100th Birthday*. Edited by Laurence E. S. Cotterell. London: Murray, 1993.

Dell, Edmund E. *A Strange Eventful History: Democratic Socialism in Britain*. London: HarperCollins, 2000.

Donne, John. *Complete Poetry and Selected Prose*. Edited by John D. Hayward. London: Nonesuch, 1972.

Dowding, A. T. Woodman. Review of *G. A. Studdert Kennedy: By His Friends*. *Modern Churchman* 19 (1930) 667–68.

Doyle, Arthur I. Conan. *Sherlock Holmes: The Complete Short Stories*. London: Murray, 1928.

Dunant, Henry. *A Memory of Solferino*. Geneva: International Committee of the Red Cross, 1986.

Edwards, David L. *Leaders of the Church of England 1828–1944*. London: Oxford University Press, 1971.

————. "'Woodbine Willie' Was a True Prophet: Centenary Assessment of Geoffrey Studdert Kennedy." *Church Times*, 24 June 1983, 11 and 5.

Eliade, Mircea. *The Sacred and the Profane: The Nature of Religion*. Translated by Willard R. Trask. London: Harcourt, 1987.

Eliot, T. S. *Selected Essays 1917–1932*. London: Faber and Faber, 1932.

Ellis, Robert A. "Geoffrey Studdert Kennedy: The Pastor and the Suffering God." *Transformation* 22 (2005) 166–75.

Evans, Gillian R. *Edward Lee Hicks: Pacifist Bishop at War*. Oxford: Lion, 2014.

Farrer, Austin M. "The Christian Apologist." In *Light on C. S. Lewis*, edited by Jocelyn E. Gibb, 23–43. London: Bles, 1965.

Ferguson, John, and Francis Clark. *War, Peace and Religion*. Milton Keynes, UK: Open University Press, 1973.

Ferguson, Niall C. *The Pity of War*. London: Penguin, 1999.

Field, Clive D. "Gradualist or Revolutionary Secularization? A Case Study of Religious Belonging in Inter-War Britain, 1918–1939." *Church History and Religious Culture* 93 (2013) 57–93.

————. "Keeping the Spiritual Home Fires Burning: Religious Belonging in Britain during the First World War." *War and Society* 33 (2014) 244–68.

Fletcher, Sheila M. *Maude Royden: A Life*. Oxford: Blackwell, 1989.

Ford, David F. "Tragedy, Theology and the Discernment of Cries." In *Christian Theology and Tragedy: Theologians, Tragic Literature and Tragic Theory*, edited by T. Kevin Taylor and Giles E. Waller, 233–40. Farnham, UK: Ashgate, 2011.

Francis, Leslie J., ed. *Anglican Cathedrals in Modern Life: The Science of Cathedral Studies*. New York: Palgrave Macmillan, 2015.

"Zum Friedensdienst der Kirche: Eine Handreichung für Seelsorge an Wehrpflichtigen." Online: http://www.ekmd.de/attachment/aa234c91bdabf36adbf227d333e5305b/2f100511036e3f121cbb9c43d27928cf/Zeitdokument+-+Friedensdienst+Handreichung_6.11.1965.pdf.

Fuller, Roy B. *Owls and Artificers: Oxford Lectures on Poetry*. London: Deutsch, 1971.

Fussell, Paul. *The Great War and Modern Memory*. 2nd ed. New York: Oxford University Press, 2000.

Gardiner, Alfred G. *Certain People of Importance*. London: Cape, 1926.

Gill, Robin M. *Society Shaped by Theology*. Vol. 3 of *Sociological Theology*. Farnham, UK: Ashgate, 2013.

Goddard, Andrew J. *Rowan Williams: His Legacy*. Oxford: Lion, 2013.

Goldman, Lawrence N. *The Life of R. H. Tawney: Socialism and History*. London: Bloomsbury Academic, 2014.

Goldsborough, C. Neal. *Where Is God Amidst the Bombs? A Priest's Reflections from the Combat Zone*. Cincinnati, OH: Forward Movement, 2008.

Gore, Charles. *The Basis of Anglican Fellowship in Faith and Organisation*. London: Mowbray, 1914.

Gorringe, Timothy J. *Karl Barth: Against Hegemony*. Oxford: Oxford University Press, 1999.

————. *A Theology of the Built Environment: Justice, Empowerment, Redemption*. Cambridge: Cambridge University Press, 2002.

Gray, Donald C. *Percy Dearmer: A Parson's Pilgrimage*. Norwich, UK: Canterbury Press, 2000.

Green, Simon J. D. *The Passing of Protestant England: Secularisation and Social Change c.1920–1960*. Cambridge: Cambridge University Press, 2011.

Gregory, Adrian M. *The Last Great War: British Society and the First World War*. Cambridge: Cambridge University Press, 2008.

Gregory, Adrian M., and Annette Becker. "Religious Sites and Practices." In *Capital Cities at War: Paris, London, Berlin 1914–1919*. Vol. 2, *A Cultural History*, edited by Jay M. Winter and Jean-Louis Robert, 383–427. Cambridge: Cambridge University Press, 2007.

Gregson, Adrian S. "The 1/7th Battalion King's Liverpool Regiment and the Great War: The Experience of a Territorial Battalion and Its Home Towns." PhD thesis, Coventry University, 2004.

Grierson, Herbert J. C. *Metaphysical Lyrics and Poems of the Seventeenth Century: Donne to Butler*. Oxford: Clarendon, 1921.

Grimley, Matthew. *Citizenship, Community, and the Church of England: Liberal Anglican Theories of the State between the Wars*. Oxford: Oxford University Press, 2004.

Grundy, E. Michael. *A Fiery Glow in the Darkness: Woodbine Willie—Padré and Poet*. Worcester, UK: Osborne, 1997.

Gurling, Jonathan A. "Padre Who Offered a Light to Servicemen." *Church Times*, 6 March 2009, 20–21.

Hammond, John A. "British Great War Remembrance: The Influence of Christian Text, Teaching and Iconography." PhD thesis, University of Wales, 2014.

Hardy, Mary S. *Hardy VC: An Appreciation*. London: Skeffington, 1920.

Hauerwas, Stanley M. *Against the Nations: War and Survival in a Liberal Society*. Minneapolis, MN: Winston, 1985.

Healey, Denis W. *The Time of My Life*. London: Penguin, 1990.

Hedley, Douglas. "Sacrifice and the Tragic Imagination." In *Christian Theology and Tragedy: Theologians, Tragic Literature and Tragic Theory*, edited by T. Kevin Taylor and Giles E. Waller, 199–211. Farnham, UK: Ashgate, 2011.

Hendry, Samuel D. "Scottish Baptists and the First World War." *Baptist Quarterly* 31 (1985) 52–65.

Henson, H. Hensley. *Retrospect of an Unimportant Life*. 2 vols. London: Oxford University Press, 1942.

Herbert, George. *The Works of George Herbert*. Edited by Francis E. Hutchinson. Oxford: Clarendon, 1941.

Hertling, Ludwig von. *Antonius der Einsiedler*. Innsbruck: Felizian Rauch, 1929.

Holman, Bob. *Woodbine Willie: An Unsung Hero of World War One*. Oxford: Lion, 2013.

Hoover, Arlie J. *God, Germany, and Britain in the Great War: A Study in Clerical Nationalism*. New York: Praeger, 1989.

Horton, Walter M. *Contemporary English Theology: An American Interpretation*. London: SCM, 1936.

Hoskyns, Edwyn C. *Cambridge Sermons*. London: SPCK, 1938.

House, Francis H. "The Barrier of Impassibility." *Theology* 83 (1980) 409–15.

Housman, A. E. *Collected Poems*. London: Cape, 1939.

Howson, Peter J. *Muddling Through: The Organisation of British Army Chaplaincy in World War One*. Helion Studies in Military History 25. Solihull, UK: Helion, 2013.

Hughes, John M. D. *Graced Life: The Writings of John Hughes*. Edited by Matthew J. Bullimore. London: SCM, 2016.

Bibliography

Hypher, Paul A. "The Compassionate Hero: Theodore Bayley Hardy VC, DSO, MC." *Pastoral Review* 11/6 (2015) 22–27.

Inge, John G. *A Christian Theology of Place.* Aldershot, UK: Ashgate, 2003.

Inman, Daniel D. *The Making of Modern English Theology: God and the Academy at Oxford, 1833–1945.* Minneapolis, MN: Fortress, 2014.

Iremonger, Frederic A. *William Temple, Archbishop of Canterbury: His Life and Letters.* London: Oxford University Press, 1948.

Jackson Groves, Naomi, ed. *Ernst Barlach: Life in Work: Sculpture, Drawings and Graphics, Drama, Prose Works and Letters in Translation.* 2nd ed. Königstein im Taunus, Germany: Langewiesche-Köster, 2009.

Jeffs, Ernest H. *Princes of the Modern Pulpit: Religious Leaders of a Generation.* London: Sampson Low, Marston and Co., 1931.

Jenkins, J. Philip. *The Great and Holy War: How World War I Became a Religious Crusade.* Oxford: Lion, 2014.

Jowett, Benjamin. "On the Interpretation of Scripture." In *Essays and Reviews,* edited by John William Parker, 330–443. London: Parker, 1860.

Keegan, John D. P. *The First World War.* London: Pimlico, 1999.

Kew, W. Richard. "The Great War's Damage to the English Soul and Church." Online: http://livingchurch.org/covenant/2016/11/16/the-great-wars-damage-to-the-english-soul-and-church/.

Kingsolver, Barbara. *Small Wonder.* New York: HarperCollins, 2002.

Kirchliches Jahrbuch für die Evangelische Kirche in Deutschland 106 (1979). Edited by W.-D. Hauschild et al. Gütersloh: Gütersloher Verlagshaus Gerd Mohn, 1983.

Kirchliches Jahrbuch für die Evangelische Kirche in Deutschland 107 (1980). Edited by W.-D. Hauschild et al. Gütersloh: Gütersloher Verlagshaus Gerd Mohn, 1984.

Kirk, P. T. R. "Studdert Kennedy: I. C. F. Crusader." In *G. A. Studdert Kennedy: By His Friends,* 165–91. London: Hodder and Stoughton, 1929.

Klemperer, Klemens W. von. *The Passion of a German Artist: Käthe Kollwitz.* Bloomington, IN: Xlibris, 2011.

Kollwitz, Hans, ed. *The Diary and Letters of Kaethe Kollwitz.* Translated by Richard and Clara Winston. Evanston, IL: Northwestern University Press, 1988.

Koss, Stephen E. *Nonconformity in Modern British Politics.* London: Batsford, 1975.

Kristeva, Julia. *Strangers to Ourselves.* Translated by Leon S. Roudiez. New York: Columbia University Press, 1991.

Langford, Thomas A. *In Search of Foundations: English Theology, 1900–1920.* Nashville, TN: Abingdon, 1969.

Laudan, Ilona. *Ernst Barlach: Das Denkmal des Krieges im Dom zu Magdeburg.* Wettin-Löbejün: Stekovics, 2016.

Lewis, C. S. *An Experiment in Criticism.* Cambridge: Cambridge University Press, 1961.

———. *A Grief Observed.* London: Faber and Faber, 1961.

Lieber, Francis, ed. *Instructions for the Government of Armies of the United States, in the Field.* New York: Van Nostrand, 1863.

Lloyd, Roger B. *The Church of England 1900–1965.* London: SCM, 1966.

Louden, Stephen H. *Chaplains in Conflict: The Role of Army Chaplains since 1914.* London: Avon, 1996.

Luther, Martin. *Lectures on Romans.* Edited by Hilton C. Oswald, translated by Jacob A. O. Preus. Luther's Works 25. Saint Louis, MO: Concordia, 1972.

Lynch, Frederick H. *Through Europe on the Eve of War: A Record of Personal Experiences; Including an Account of the First World Conference of the Churches for International Peace*. New York: Church Peace Union, 1914.

MacDonald, Lyn, ed. *Anthem for Doomed Youth: Poets of the Great War*. London: Folio Society, 2000.

MacGregor, R. Neil. *Germany: Memories of a Nation*. London: Allen Lane, 2014.

Machin, G. Ian T. *Politics and the Churches in Great Britain 1869 to 1921*. Oxford: Clarendon, 1987.

MacIntyre, Alasdair C. "A Partial Response to My Critics." In *After MacIntyre: Critical Perspectives on the Work of Alasdair MacIntyre*, edited by John P. Horton and Susan L. Mendus, 283–304. Notre Dame, IN: University of Notre Dame Press, 1994.

MacKenzie, Iain M., ed. *Cathedrals Now: Their Use and Place in Society*. Norwich, UK: Canterbury Press, 1996.

MacLeod, James Lachlan. "'Its Own Little Share of Service to the National Cause': The Free Presbyterian Church of Scotland's Chaplains in the First World War." *Northern Scotland* 21 (2001) 79–97.

———. "'The Mighty Hand of God': The Free Presbyterian Church of Scotland and the Great War." *Bridges* 12 (2007) 19–41.

Macquarrie, John. *The Humility of God: Christian Meditations*. London: SCM, 1978.

Madigan, Edward T. M. *Faith under Fire: Anglican Army Chaplains and the Great War*. Basingstoke, UK: Palgrave Macmillan, 2011.

———. "'Their Cross to Bear': The Church of England and Military Service during the First World War." *Annali di Scienze Religiose* 8 (2015) 165–200.

Mantle, Jonathan. *Archbishop: The Life and Times of Robert Runcie*. London: Sinclair-Stevenson, 1991.

Marrin, Albert. *The Last Crusade: The Church of England in the First World War*. Durham, NC: Duke University Press, 1974.

Matheson, Peter C. "Scottish War Sermons 1914–1919." *Records of the Scottish Church History Society* 17 (1972) 203–13.

Matthews, Charles H. S. *Dick Sheppard: Man of Peace*. London: Clarke [1948].

———. "Studdert Kennedy: 1883–1929." In *Great Christians*, edited by Richard S. Forman, 299–317. London: Nicholson and Watson, 1933.

McLeod, D. Hugh. *Religion and the People of Western Europe 1789–1989*. 2nd ed. Oxford: Oxford University Press, 1997.

———. *Religion and Society in England, 1850–1914*. London: Longman, 1996.

———. *The Religious Crisis of the 1960s*. Oxford: Oxford University Press, 2010.

Mews, Stuart P. "Religion and English Society in the First World War." PhD thesis, University of Cambridge, 1974.

———. "Religious Life between the Wars, 1920–1940." In *A History of Religion in Britain: Practice and Belief from Pre-Roman Times to the Present*, edited by Sheridan Gilley and William J. Sheils, 449–66. Oxford: Blackwell, 1994.

Middlebrook, Martin. *The First Day on the Somme*. London: Penguin, 1984.

———. *Your Country Needs You*. Barnsley, UK: Cooper, 2000.

Moltmann, Jürgen. *The Crucified God: The Cross of Christ as the Foundation and Criticism of Christian Theology*. Translated by R. A. Wilson and John S. Bowden. London: SCM, 1974.

———. *The Trinity and the Kingdom of God: The Doctrine of God*. Translated by Margaret Kohl. London: SCM, 1981.

Moore, Charles H. *Margaret Thatcher: The Authorized Biography.* Vol. 1, *Not for Turning.* London: Allen Lane, 2013.

Moore Ede, William. "His Life in Worcester." In *G. A. Studdert Kennedy: By His Friends,* 87–111. London: Hodder and Stoughton, 1929.

Moorehead, Caroline M. *Dunant's Dream: War, Switzerland and the History of the Red Cross.* London: HarperCollins, 1998.

Morgan, D. Densil. *Barth Reception in Britain.* London: T. & T. Clark, 2010.

———. *The Span of the Cross: Christian Religion and Society in Wales 1914–2000.* Cardiff: University of Wales Press, 1999.

Morgan, Susan E. "A 'Feminist Conspiracy': Maude Royden, Women's Ministry and the British Press, 1916–1921." *Women's History Review* 22 (2013) 777–800.

Mozley, J. Kenneth. "Epilogue: Prophet, Pastor and Teacher." In *G. A. Studdert Kennedy: By His Friends,* 241–51. London: Hodder and Stoughton, 1929.

———. "Home Life and Early Years of His Ministry." In *G. A. Studdert Kennedy: By His Friends,* 13–83. London: Hodder and Stoughton, 1929.

———. *The Impassibility of God: A Survey of Christian Thought.* Cambridge: Cambridge University Press, 1926.

———. *Some Tendencies in British Theology: From the Publication of* Lux Mundi *to the Present Day.* London: SPCK, 1951.

Mulley, Clare M. *The Woman Who Saved the Children: A Biography of Eglantyne Jebb, Founder of Save the Children.* Oxford: Oneworld, 2009.

Murdoch, J. Iris. *The Sovereignty of Good.* London: Routledge and Kegan Paul, 1970.

Mursell, A. Gordon. *Out of the Deep: Prayer as Protest.* London: Darton, Longman and Todd, 1989.

Neville, Graham. *Radical Churchman: Edward Lee Hicks and the New Liberalism.* Oxford: Clarendon, 1998.

———. "William Moore Ede: Dean of Worcester 1908–1934." Worcester, UK: Booklet printed by the Friends of Worcester Cathedral, 2008.

Nicholls, David G. *Deity and Domination: Images of God and the State in the Nineteenth and Twentieth Centuries.* London: Routledge, 1989.

Norman, Edward R. *Church and Society in England 1770–1970: A Historical Study.* Oxford: Oxford University Press, 1976.

Oakeley, Hilda D. "German Thought: The Real Conflict." *Church Quarterly Review* 79 (1914) 95–119.

Orwell, George. *Decline of the English Murder and Other Essays.* Harmondsworth, UK: Penguin, 1980.

Owen, Wilfred E. S. *Poems.* London: Chatto and Windus, 1920.

———. *The Poems of Wilfred Owen.* Edited by Jon H. Stallworthy. London: Hogarth, 1985.

Palgrave, Francis T., ed. *The Golden Treasury of the Best Songs and Lyrical Poems in the English Language.* London: Oxford University Press, 1907.

Paret, Peter. *An Artist Against the Third Reich: Ernst Barlach, 1933–1938.* Cambridge: Cambridge University Press, 2003.

Parker, Linda M. *A Fool for Thy Feast: The Life and Times of Tubby Clayton, 1885–1972.* Solihull, UK: Helion, 2015.

———. "'Shell-shocked Prophets': Anglican Army Chaplains and Post-war Reform in the Church of England." In *The Clergy in Khaki: New Perspectives on British Army*

Chaplaincy in the First World War, edited by Michael F. Snape and Edward T. M. Madigan, 183–97. Farnham, UK: Ashgate, 2013.

———. *Shellshocked Prophets: Former Anglican Army Chaplains in Interwar Britain.* Wolverhampton Military Studies 6. Solihull, UK: Helion, 2015.

———. *The Whole Armour of God: Anglican Army Chaplains in the Great War.* Solihull, UK: Helion, 2009.

Patch, Harry [Henry J.], with Richard van Emden. *The Last Fighting Tommy: The Life of Harry Patch, the Oldest Surviving Veteran of the Trenches.* 2nd ed. London: Bloomsbury, 2008.

Paul, Marcus K. *The Evil That Men Do: Faith, Injustice and the Church.* Durham, UK: Sacristy, 2016.

Pearson, Clive R. "Henry Major and the Foundation of *The Modern Churchman.*" *Modern Believing* 52/2 (2011) 6–14.

———, et al. *Scholarship and Fierce Sincerity: Henry D. A. Major: The Face of Anglican Modernism.* West Harbour, Auckland: Polygraphia, 2006.

Pinker, Steven A. *The Better Angels of Our Nature: A History of Violence and Humanity.* London: Penguin, 2012.

Pitre, Brant J. *Jesus and the Jewish Roots of the Eucharist: Unlocking the Secrets of the Last Supper.* New York: Doubleday, 2011.

Platten, Stephen G., ed. *Holy Ground: Cathedrals in the Twenty-First Century.* Durham, UK: Sacristy, forthcoming.

Platten, Stephen G., and Christopher A. Lewis, eds. *Dreaming Spires? Cathedrals in a New Age.* London: SPCK, 2006.

———, eds. *Flagships of the Spirit: Cathedrals in Society.* London: Darton, Longman and Todd, 1998.

Pope, Robert P. "Christ and Caesar? Welsh Nonconformists and the State, 1914–1918." In *Wales and War: Society, Politics and Religion in the Nineteenth and Twentieth Centuries*, edited by Matthew F. Cragoe and Christopher M. Williams, 165–83. Cardiff: University of Wales Press, 2007.

Prestige, G. Leonard. *The Life of Charles Gore: A Great Englishman.* London: Heinemann, 1935.

Pugh, Martin D. *"We Danced All Night": A Social History of Britain between the Wars.* London: Vintage, 2009.

Pullan, Leighton. *Missionary Principles and the Primate on Kikuyu: Three Addresses with Some Observations on the Present German Movement in the Church of England.* Oxford: Mowbray, 1915.

———. *New Testament Criticism during the Past Century.* London: Longmans, 1907.

Purcell, William E. *Woodbine Willie: An Anglican Incident: Being Some Account of the Life and Times of Geoffrey Anketell Studdert Kennedy, Poet, Prophet, Seeker after Truth, 1883–1929.* 2nd ed. Oxford: Mowbray, 1983.

Quash, J. Ben. "Four Biblical Characters: In Search of a Tragedy." In *Christian Theology and Tragedy: Theologians, Tragic Literature and Tragic Theory*, edited by T. Kevin Taylor and Giles E. Waller, 15–33. Farnham, UK: Ashgate, 2011.

Quasten, Johannes. *Patrology.* Vol. 3, *The Golden Age of Greek Patristic Literature: From the Council of Nicaea to the Council of Chalcedon.* Utrecht: Spectrum, 1960.

Quiller-Couch, Arthur T., ed. *The Oxford Book of English Verse 1250–1900.* Oxford: Clarendon, 1900.

Ramsey, A. Michael. *From Gore to Temple: The Development of Anglican Theology between* Lux Mundi *and the Second World War 1889–1939: The Hale Memorial Lectures of Seabury-Western Theological Seminary, 1959.* London: Longmans, Green and Co., 1960.

———. *God, Christ and the World: A Study in Contemporary Theology.* London: SCM, 1969.

Raw, J. David. *"It's Only Me": A Life of the Reverend Theodore Bayley Hardy VC, DSO, MC 1863–1918: Vicar of Hutton Roof, Westmorland.* Gatebeck, UK: Peters, 1988.

Rawls, John B. *A Theory of Justice.* Cambridge, MA: Belknap, 1971.

Reckitt, Maurice B. *Maurice to Temple: A Century of the Social Movement in the Church of England: Scott Holland Memorial Lectures, 1946.* London: Faber and Faber, 1947.

Religion in Life: A Book for Lent. London: Longmans, Green and Co., 1936.

Richards, Ivor A. *Practical Criticism: A Study of Literary Judgment.* London: Kegan Paul, Trench, Trubner and Co., 1929.

"Richte unsere Füße auf den Weg des Friedens: Wort des Rates der EKD zum 100. Jahrestag des Beginns des Ersten Weltkrieges." Online: http://www.ekd.de/EKD-Texte/wort_des_rates_zum_ersten_weltkrieg.html.

Robbins, Keith G. "The British Experience of Conscientious Objection." In *Facing Armageddon: The First World War Experienced,* edited by Hugh P. Cecil and Peter H. Liddle, 691–706. London: Cooper, 1996.

———. *England, Ireland, Scotland, Wales: The Christian Church 1900–2000.* Oxford: Oxford University Press, 2008.

Roberts, R. Ellis. *H. R. L. Sheppard: Life and Letters.* London: Murray, 1942.

Roberts, Richard H. *A Theology on Its Way? Essays on Karl Barth.* Edinburgh: T. & T. Clark, 1991.

Robertson, Edwin H. *Unshakeable Friend: Bishop Bell and the German Churches.* London: CCBI, 1995.

Robinson, John A. T. *Honest to God.* London: SCM, 1963.

Robinson, Marilynne S. *Home.* London: Virago, 2008.

Rolt, Clarence E. *The World's Redemption.* London: Longmans, Green and Co., 1913.

Rose, Gillian R. *Mourning Becomes the Law: Philosophy and Representation.* Cambridge: Cambridge University Press, 1996.

Rowell, D. Geoffrey, et al., eds. *Love's Redeeming Work: The Anglican Quest for Holiness.* Oxford: Oxford University Press, 2001.

Royden, A. Maude. *Christ Triumphant.* London: Putnam's Sons, 1924.

———. *The Great Adventure: The Way to Peace.* London: Headley Brothers, 1915.

———. *Political Christianity.* London: Putnam's Sons, 1922.

Ruppelt, Georg. "Thron und Altar." *Politik und Kultur* (May–June 2010), 28.

Ruston, Alan R. "Protestant Nonconformist Attitudes towards the First World War." In *Protestant Nonconformity in the Twentieth Century,* edited by Alan P. F. Sell and Anthony R. Cross, 240–63. Carlisle, UK: Paternoster, 2003.

Sacks, Jonathan H. *The Home We Build Together: Recreating Society.* London: Continuum, 2007.

Sanday, William. "The Apocalyptic Element in the Gospels." *Hibbert Journal* 10 (1911) 83–109.

———. *Bishop Gore's Challenge to Criticism: A Reply to the Bishop of Oxford's Open Letter on the Basis of Anglican Fellowship.* London: Longmans, 1914.

————. "On Continuity of Thought and Relativity of Expression." *Modern Churchman* 5 (1915) 125–42.

————. *The Deeper Causes of War.* Oxford: Oxford University Press, 1914.

————. *The Life of Christ in Recent Research.* Oxford: Clarendon, 1907.

————. *The Meaning of the War for Germany and Great Britain: An Attempt at Synthesis.* Oxford: Oxford University Press, 1915.

————. *Outlines of the Life of Christ.* 2nd ed. Edinburgh: T. & T. Clark, 1906.

————. *In View of the End: A Retrospect and a Prospect.* Oxford: Oxford University Press, 1916.

————. *When Should the War End?* London: Evangelical Information Committee, 1917.

Sanday, William, and N. P. Williams. *Form and Content in the Christian Tradition: A Friendly Discussion between W. Sanday, DD and N. P. Williams, MA.* London: Longmans, 1916.

Schweitzer, Richard. *The Cross and the Trenches: Religious Faith and Doubt among British and American Great War Soldiers.* Westport, CT: Praeger, 2003.

————. "The Cross and the Trenches: Religious Faith and Doubt among Some British Soldiers on the Western Front." *War and Society* 16 (1998) 33–57.

Schymura, Yvonne. *Käthe Kollwitz: Die Liebe, der Krieg und die Kunst: Eine Biographie.* München: Beck, 2016.

Scott, Carolyn. *Dick Sheppard: A Biography.* London: Hodder and Stoughton, 1977.

Selbie, William B. *The War and Theology.* London: Oxford University Press, 1915.

Selby, Peter S. M. *BeLonging: Challenge to a Tribal Church.* London: SPCK, 1991.

————. *An Idol Unmasked: A Faith Perspective on Money.* London: Darton, Longman and Todd, 2014.

Self, William W. *Psychogeography.* London: Bloomsbury, 2007.

Selwyn, E. Gordon. "Preface." In J. Kenneth Mozley, *Some Tendencies in British Theology: From the Publication of Lux Mundi to the Present Day,* 7–9. London: SPCK, 1951.

Sheffield, Gary D. *Forgotten Victory: The First World War: Myths and Realities.* London: Headline, 2001.

Sheppard, H. R. L. "Studdert Kennedy: A Friend." In *G. A. Studdert Kennedy: By His Friends,* 195–202. London: Hodder and Stoughton, 1929.

Shortt, Rupert. *Rowan's Rule: The Biography of the Archbishop.* London: Hodder and Stoughton, 2008.

Sinclair, Ronald S. B. *When We Pray: A Method of Prayer Taught by G. A. Studdert Kennedy.* 2nd ed. Oxford: Mowbray, 1951.

Slocum, Robert B. "Geoffrey Studdert Kennedy ('Woodbine Willie'): The Crucified God." *Modern Believing* 58 (2017).

Smoot, Jonathan F. "Does God Suffer? Divine Passibility in Anglican Theology from *Lux Mundi* to the Second World War: With Particular Reference to the Thought of William Temple and John Kenneth Mozley." PhD thesis, University of Aberdeen, 1996.

Snape, Michael F., ed. *The Back Parts of War: The YMCA Memoirs and Letters of Barclay Baron, 1915–1919.* Church of England Record Society 16. Woodbridge, UK: Boydell, 2009.

————. "The Bible, the British and the First World War." *Bible in Transmission* (Summer 2014) 17–20.

———. "British Catholicism and the British Army in the First World War." *Recusant History* 26 (2002) 314–58.

———. "Church of England Army Chaplains in the First World War: Goodbye to 'Goodbye to All That." *Journal of Ecclesiastical History* 62 (2011) 318–45.

———. "Civilians, Soldiers and Perceptions of the Afterlife in Britain during the First World War." In *The Church, the Afterlife and the Fate of the Soul: Papers Read at the 2007 Summer Meeting and the 2008 Winter Meeting of the Ecclesiastical History Society*, edited by Peter D. Clarke and Anthony M. Claydon, 371–403. Studies in Church History 45. Woodbridge, UK: Boydell, 2009.

———. *God and the British Soldier: Religion and the British Army in the First and Second World Wars*. Abingdon, UK: Routledge, 2005.

———. *Revisiting Religion and the British Soldier in the First World War*. London: Dr. Williams's Trust, 2015.

———. *The Royal Army Chaplains' Department 1796–1953: Clergy under Fire*. Woodbridge, UK: Boydell, 2008.

Snape, Michael F., and Edward T. M. Madigan, eds. *The Clergy in Khaki: New Perspectives on British Army Chaplaincy in the First World War*. Farnham, UK: Ashgate, 2013.

Spinks, G. Stephen. *Religion in Britain since 1900*. London: Dakers, 1952.

Squire, John C., ed. *Second Selections from Modern Poets*. London: Secker, 1924.

Stallworthy, Jon H., ed. *The New Oxford Book of War Poetry*. 2nd ed. Oxford: Oxford University Press, 2014.

Stark, Freya M. *Traveller's Prelude: Autobiography 1893–1927*. London: Century, 1983.

Steffensky, Fulbert. "'Gott mit uns' haben alle gesagt: Was blendet die Augen und rüstet für Kriege?" Online: http://www.denk-mal-gegen-krieg.de/assets/Texte/4-Theologie/Steffensky-zu-Krieg-im-NDR.pdf.

Stephenson, Alan M. G. *The Rise and Decline of English Modernism: The Hulsean Lectures 1979–80*. London: SPCK, 1984.

———. "Theology in the Theological College." *Modern Churchman* 9 (1965) 88–101.

Storr, Katherine. *Excluded from the Record: Women, Refugees and Relief 1914–1929*. Bern: Lang, 2010.

Strachan, Kenneth A. G. "Studdert Kennedy on Evangelism." *Theology* 96 (1993) 260–69.

Strachey, G. Lytton. *Queen Victoria*. London: Penguin, 2000.

Streeter, Burnett H., ed. *Foundations: A Statement of Christian Belief in Terms of Modern Thought: By Seven Oxford Men*. London: Macmillan, 1912.

———. *War, This War and the Sermon on the Mount*. Papers for War Time 20. London: Oxford University Press, 1915.

Studdert-Kennedy, Andrew G. "How the Somme Changed People's Perceptions of God." *Times*, 12 November 2016, 90.

Studdert Kennedy, Geoffrey A. *Democracy and the Dog-Collar*. London: Hodder and Stoughton, 1921.

———. *Food for the Fed-up*. London: Hodder and Stoughton, 1921.

———. *The Hardest Part*. London: Hodder and Stoughton, 1918.

———. *Lies!* London: Hodder and Stoughton, 1919.

———. *Lighten Our Darkness: Some Less Rough Rhymes of a Padre*. London: Hodder and Stoughton [1925].

———. *More Rough Rhymes of a Padre*. London: Hodder and Stoughton, 1919.

―――. *The New Man in Christ*. Edited by William Moore Ede. London: Hodder and Stoughton, 1932.

―――. *Peace Rhymes of a Padre*. London: Hodder and Stoughton, 1920.

―――. "The Religious Difficulties of the Private Soldier." In *The Church in the Furnace: Essays by Seventeen Temporary Church of England Chaplains on Active Service in France and Flanders*, edited by Frederick B. Macnutt, 375–405. London: Macmillan, 1917.

―――. *Rough Rhymes of a Padre*. London: Hodder and Stoughton, 1918.

―――. *Rough Talks by a Padre: Delivered to Officers and Men of the B. E. F.* London: Hodder and Stoughton, 1918.

―――. *Songs of Faith and Doubt*. London: Hodder and Stoughton, 1922.

―――. *The Sorrows of God and Other Poems*. London: Hodder and Stoughton, 1921.

―――. *The Unutterable Beauty*. London: Hodder and Stoughton, 1927.

―――. *The Warrior, the Woman and the Christ: A Study of the Leadership of Christ*. London: Hodder and Stoughton, 1928.

―――. *The Wicket Gate, or Plain Bread*. London: Hodder and Stoughton, 1923.

―――. *The Word and the Work*. London: Longmans, Green and Co., 1925.

Studdert Kennedy, Hugh A. *Arise Shine: Being a Remaintenance of an Old Truth in a New Way*. London: Putnam, 1938.

Studdert-Kennedy, W. Gerald. *Dog-Collar Democracy: The Industrial Christian Fellowship, 1919–1929*. London: Macmillan, 1982.

―――. "'Woodbine Willie': Religion and Politics after the Great War." *History Today* 36 (December 1986) 40–45.

"Die Stuttgarter Schulderklärung." Online: https://www.ekd.de/glauben/grundlagen/stuttgarter_schulderklaerung.html.

Tawney, R. H. *Religion and the Rise of Capitalism*. London: Murray, 1926.

Taylor, A. J. P. *English History 1914–1945*. Oxford: Clarendon, 1965.

Taylor, John V. *The Christlike God*. London: SCM, 1992.

Taylor, T. Kevin, and Giles E. Waller. "Introduction." In *Christian Theology and Tragedy: Theologians, Tragic Literature and Tragic Theory*, edited by T. Kevin Taylor and Giles E. Waller, 1–11. Farnham, UK: Ashgate, 2011.

Temple, William. *Christianity and War*. Papers for War Time 1. London: Oxford University Press, 1914.

―――. "The Man and His Message." In *G. A. Studdert Kennedy: By His Friends*, 205–37. London: Hodder and Stoughton, 1929.

Thatcher, Margaret H. *The Downing Street Years*. London: HarperCollins, 1993.

Thompson, David M. "War, the Nation, and the Kingdom of God: The Origins of the National Mission of Repentance and Hope, 1915–16." In *The Church and War*, edited by William J. Sheils, 337–50. Studies in Church History 20. Oxford: Blackwell, 1983.

To the Christian Scholars of Europe and America: A Reply from Oxford to the German Address to Evangelical Christians. Oxford: Oxford University Press, 1914.

Todman, Daniel W. *The Great War: Myth and Memory*. London: Hambledon Continuum, 2007.

Vanstone, William H. *Love's Endeavour, Love's Expense: The Response of Being to the Love of God*. London: Darton, Longman and Todd, 1977.

Vines, Maxwell L. "The Theological Struggle of Woodbine Willie." *Foundations* 22 (1979) 261–72.

Wakefield, Gordon S. "Biographical Introduction." In Edwyn C. Hoskyns and F. Noel Davey, *Crucifixion–Resurrection: The Pattern of the Theology and Ethics of the New Testament*, edited by Gordon S. Wakefield, 1–81. London: SPCK, 1981.

Walker, David A. "Pastoral Theology and the Suffering God." In *Studies in Pastoral Theology and Social Anthropology*, edited by Douglas J. Davies. 2nd ed., 92–103. Birmingham: University of Birmingham, 1990.

Waller, Giles E. "Freedom, Fate and Sin in Donald MacKinnon's Use of Tragedy." In *Christian Theology and Tragedy: Theologians, Tragic Literature and Tragic Theory*, edited by T. Kevin Taylor and Giles E. Waller, 101–18. Farnham, UK: Ashgate, 2011.

Walters, Kerry S. "Introduction: Woodbine Willie: The Man and His Message." In Geoffrey A. Studdert Kennedy, *After War, Is Faith Possible? An Anthology*, edited by Kerry S. Walters, 1–31. Eugene, OR: Cascade, 2008.

War Office. *Statistics of the Military Effort of the British Empire during the Great War, 1914–1920*. London: HMSO, 1922.

Weil, Simone. *The Need for Roots: Prelude to a Declaration of Duties towards Mankind*. Translated by Arthur Wills. London: Routledge and Kegan Paul, 1952.

Wells, H. G. *Mr. Britling Sees It Through*. London: Cassell, 1916.

Wells, Samuel M. B. *How Then Shall We Live? Christian Engagement with Contemporary Issues*. London: Canterbury Press Norwich, 2016.

———. *A Nazareth Manifesto: Being with God*. Chichester, UK: Wiley-Blackwell, 2015.

West, Frank H. *"FRB": A Portrait of Bishop Russell Barry*. Bramcote, UK: Grove, 1980.

Weston, Frank. *The Case Against Kikuyu: A Study in Vital Principles*. London: Longmans, 1914.

———. *Ecclesia Anglicana: For What Does She Stand? An Open Letter to the Right Reverend Father in God, Edgar, Lord Bishop of St Albans*. London: Longmans, 1913.

Wickham, Edward R. *Church and People in an Industrial City*. London: Lutterworth, 1957.

Wilkinson, Alan B. "Changing English Attitudes to Death in the Two World Wars." In *The Changing Face of Death: Historical Accounts of Death and Disposal*, edited by Peter C. Jupp and Glennys Howarth, 149–63. Basingstoke, UK: Macmillan, 1997.

———. *The Church of England and the First World War*. 3rd ed. Cambridge: Lutterworth, 2014.

———. *Dissent or Conform? War, Peace and the English Churches 1900–1945*. London: SCM, 1986.

———. "Searching for Meaning in Time of War: Theological Themes in First World War Literature." *Modern Churchman* 27/2 (1985) 13–21.

Williams, Rowan D. *The Lion's World: A Journey into the Heart of Narnia*. London: SPCK, 2012.

———. "A Sermon at a Service to Mark the Passing of the World War One Generation." Online: http://rowanwilliams.archbishopofcanterbury.org/articles.php/857/a-sermon-at-a-service-to-mark-the-passing-of-the-world-war-one-generation.

———. *The Tragic Imagination*. Oxford: Oxford University Press, 2016.

———. *The Wound of Knowledge: Christian Spirituality from the New Testament to St John of the Cross*. London: Darton, Longman and Todd, 1979.

Wilson, A. N. *C. S. Lewis: A Biography*. London: Collins, 1990.

Wilson, James M. *An Autobiography 1836–1931*. London: Sidgwick and Jackson, 1932.

Winnington-Ingram, Arthur F. *The Church in Time of War*. London: Wells Gardner, Darton and Co., 1916.

————. *A Day of God*. London: Wells Gardner, Darton and Co., 1915.

————. *Rays of Dawn*. London: Wells Gardner, Darton and Co., 1918.

————. *Victory and After*. London: Wells Gardner, Darton and Co., 1919.

Woodhead, Linda. "Time to Get Serious." *Church Times*, 31 January 2014, 23–24.

Woollcombe, Kenneth J. "'A Fiery Glow in the Darkness': The Influence of Studdert Kennedy (Woodbine Willie) on the Thinking of the Church." Printed booklet, 1999, in Worcester Cathedral Library, Muniments Add. Mss. 480.

————. "The Pain of God." *Scottish Journal of Theology* 20 (1967) 129–48.

Yeats, W. B. *The Collected Poems*. 2nd ed. London: Macmillan, 1950.

Young, Frances M. "A Reconsideration of Alexandrian Christology." *Journal of Ecclesiastical History* 22 (1971) 103–14.

Scripture Index

General Index

Bold text indicates a brief biographical précis and/or bibliography.

Lightning Source UK Ltd.
Milton Keynes UK
UKOW04f1121130717

305235UK00002B/89/P